THE WESTERN FRONTIERS OF IMPERIAL ROME

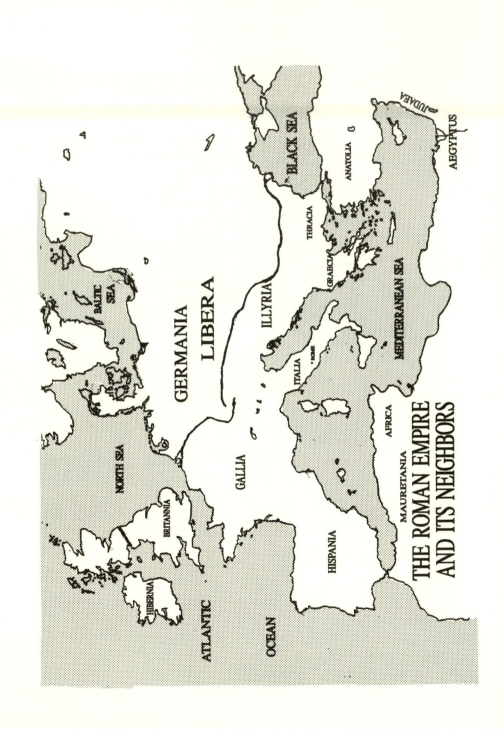

THE ROMAN EMPIRE
AND ITS NEIGHBORS

THE WESTERN FRONTIERS OF IMPERIAL ROME

STEVEN K. DRUMMOND
LYNN H. NELSON

M. E. Sharpe
ARMONK, NEW YORK
LONDON, ENGLAND

Copyright © 1994 by M. E. Sharpe, Inc.
80 Business Park Drive, Armonk, New York 10504

Library of Congress Cataloging-in-Publication Data

Drummond, Steven K., 1949–
The western frontiers of imperial Rome / Steven K. Drummond,
Lynn H. Nelson.
p. cm.
Includes bibliographical references and index.
ISBN 1-56324-150-1. — ISBN 1-56324-151-X
1. Frontier and pioneer life—Rome.
2. Rome—History—Empire, 30 B.C.–284 A.D.
3. Rome—Army. 4. Frontier thesis.
I. Nelson, Lynn H. (Lynn Harry), 1931– . II. Title.
DG271.D78 1993
937'.06—dc20
93-3650
CIP

Printed in the United States of America
The paper used in this publication meets the minimum
requirements of American National Standard for
Information Sciences—Permanence of Paper for
Printed Library Materials, ANSI Z 39.48-1984.

BM (c) 10 9 8 7 6 5 4 3 2 1

BM (p) 10 9 8 7 6 5 4 3 2 1

CONTENTS

List of Maps

PREFACE

We have directed this work not only to students of ancient history but also to those interested in frontier studies who may lack an extensive background in Roman history. For this reason, we have attempted to supply the reader with some amenities not usually provided in monographs in ancient history. We have tried to define all Latin expressions in the course of discussion and generally to use English equivalents if it is possible to do so without distorting the precise meaning of the terms involved. (We have provided a glossary at the back of the book, as well.) Where it is helpful to do so, we have provided the modern names, as well as the contemporary Latin names, of places.

There are several subjects, such as the army, the villa, and agriculture, that are particularly important to our discussion, and we have introduced each with a description of its general nature. The first chapter, for instance, begins with a portrayal of the organization and conditions of service of the Roman army in early imperial times; the third chapter, on farming, includes discussions of Roman agricultural technology and the organization of the villa system. The reader will appreciate that these characterizations are necessarily general and brief. The reader who is interested in greater detail and fuller treatments of the complexities of a subject will find that the bibliography offers both general introductions and specific studies in the areas discussed.

Although Roman history has a long tradition of intellectually rigorous scholarship, opinions still differ on many matters. Syntheses and generalizations frequently require extensive citations and justifications for the authors' accepting one point of view over another. It is also often necessary to acknowledge apparent exceptions to the general points being made. When it has been reasonable to do so, we have relegated such discussions to the endnotes in order to avoid overburdening our account. Chapter I discusses the general orientation of our approach and provides an overview of the processes we consider in greater detail in the body of the work. The succeeding chapters are topical in treatment, and the reader may find the chronology of major events in the history of the Roman frontier furnished as an appendix a useful aid. We have attempted throughout to present with precision an approach to early imperial Roman history that we believe to be important to an understanding of the times, but to do so in a manner that will enable the reader who is not a specialist in the field to follow the discussion with ease and, we sincerely hope, with interest.

THE WESTERN
FRONTIERS OF
IMPERIAL
ROME

I THE EDGE OF EMPIRE

The Roman Frontier from an American Perspective

For generations, Roman historians tended to concentrate their energies on constitutional and political history, and to focus their interest on the Mediterranean heartland of the empire. This situation has changed dramatically in recent times. The increased sophistication of archaeological techniques and the rapid accumulation of archaeological data are providing scholars with a far clearer picture of the economic, social, and technological aspects of Roman life. Such archaeological research is most advanced in northwestern Europe and, although to a lesser degree, in southeastern Europe. As a consequence, an increasing amount is being learned about Roman life in Britain, the Netherlands, Germany, and the other countries and regions that once formed the western frontiers of the empire. Much of that information is not being applied effectively, however. Many historians are unwilling to admit the validity of any data not supported by a textual source, and many archaeologists regard literary evidence as unreliable when compared with the tangible "facts" they have uncovered. Such differences have impeded attempts to provide those interested in the subject with an integrated and comprehensible account of the Roman frontier.

Given the fact that both authors of the present work have long shared an interest in Roman history as well as American westward expansion, it was perhaps inevitable that our attention should be drawn to the study of the Roman frontier and that we should approach the subject with some of the perspectives provided by the American frontier. American students are close to their own frontier experience and often find accounts of the Roman frontier curiously lacking. There is little attention paid to the fundamental questions of clearing the land, developing its resources, and the special character developed by societies who settle the frontier. Moreover, there is a neglect of the hostilities between peoples and the prejudices that divide them, as well as of the resentment felt by frontier societies toward the metropolis that impedes, regulates, and often exploits them. The Roman frontier cannot have been as different from others as it is so often pictured.

We must also note that we are both products of a post-imperial age and cannot view Roman expansion, Roman government, Roman religion, or the processes of Romanization generally with the same undisguised admiration that was possible for previous generations of scholars. Americans are familiar with a not too distant past in which their nation was nothing more than a group of resentful colonies within a worldwide empire. This experience makes them sensitive to imperial rhetoric such as "White Man's Burden," and aware that empires are not usually founded and administered for the benefit of subject peoples. Here, too, it is difficult to believe that the Roman Empire was so different from the others of which we know.

At the same time, however, the American national experience has shown us that, in spite of the desires of imperial administrators to the contrary, new societies and dynamic economies can arise along the frontier. New powers have so often arisen in the frontier provinces of the old that here, too, we cannot believe that the Roman Empire was so different. This study will focus upon the European frontiers of the Roman Empire. We will try to view these districts and their residents as forming disparate parts of a unified whole, sharing common challenges, impeded by common difficulties, and responding—in somewhat different ways—to the same stimuli.

There are two aspects to the study of the Roman frontier in the West—imperial policy and frontier development—and it is important to keep the two separate. We view imperial policy on the frontier as the means by which the Roman government controlled and used the residents of the frontier, and it was not always a pretty sight. Some readers may find our treatment iconoclastic for this reason. On the other hand, we consider that many of the developments on the frontier occurred independently of the wishes of imperial administrators, who often seemed unwilling or unable to control the processes that they had set in motion. The western frontier developed largely in accordance with its own internal principles of logic.

Many people are best acquainted with the American frontier process as it was conceived by Frederick Jackson Turner and his followers, and this conception offers a convenient base for comparison of the American and Roman frontiers. At the risk of oversimplifying a complex and often-debated formulation, we would summarize Turner's view of the American frontier in the following terms. The essential characteristics of the frontier were the economic opportunities offered by free land and the constant recession of that free land with the advance of settlement. The frontier process was one in which settlers, moving into an unfamiliar and often hostile environment, were forced to adapt their traditions and attitudes to the needs of assuring their personal survival and success. By mastering one method of exploiting their environment, settlers often opened the way for another. Thus, a given frontier district could pass through one or more of a series of stages of economic development, from mining, to ranching, to farming, to commerce, and to manufacturing.

Expressed in such basic terms, there are a number of similarities between the American and Roman frontier experiences, but it might be well to begin by pointing out some of the major differences. In America, the frontier was settled, for the most part, by individuals and nuclear families; the frontier was defined in terms of population density. The Roman frontier, by contrast, was defined by the roads and fortifications of the imperial army, and units of the Roman army of the frontier led the way in settlement and development. In America, the frontier was a moving phenomenon, an expression of the increasing population of the heartland coupled with the decline of effective native resistance to exploitation and occupation. Once it was established, the Roman frontier was stationary, with the population of its heartland slowly declining, and its army facing Germanic tribes constantly growing in numbers, political and economic sophistication, and power. On the American frontier, the indigenous population was clearly inferior to the settlers in technology in general and armaments in particular. No such disparity existed on the Roman frontier; the advantages enjoyed by the Romans over the Germans consisted largely of the superior discipline and organization of their military. The dynamism of the American frontier was provided by the desire of the settlers to exploit the natural resources of the land. The official function of the Roman frontier was to control passage, whether peaceful or hostile, across the borders established by the empire; the economic and social development of the frontier regions was considered by the imperial government as purely subsidiary to this main purpose. Finally, the rate of change was relatively rapid on the American frontier. Given the limited industrial and technological base of the Romans, frontier development for them was a slow process, but it did occur. The process began with the formation of an elite, but disgruntled and disoriented, Roman army of the frontier.

The End of Expansion and the Search for Borders

Throughout most of the first century B.C., Rome had been racked by civil wars caused by growing disparities of wealth in the population and an inability to solve imperial problems with a cumbersome republican form of government. These wars reached their climax in the struggle between Marc Antony and Augustus Caesar. The conflict was finally over by 27 B.C. The Roman Republic had been overthrown, and Augustus (27 B.C.–A.D. 14) began to lay the foundations of an imperial government. One of his tasks was the reorganization of the military. By the close of the civil war, some seventy legions with over 400,000 men were in the field, together with another 400,000 men in various special and support units. The Roman economy could not sustain such a burden, and the new emperor could not tolerate so many organized troops who had only recently been fighting for his enemies. As a consequence, he eventually broke up this massive force and demobilized over half of the legions.

Many of these men were reintroduced into civilian life by providing them with bonuses and settling them in veterans' colonies. Such *coloniae* were scattered throughout the empire, and many, such as Zaragoza and Mérida in Spain, survive as major cities today. The role of these settlements in pacifying the internal provinces of the empire and in spreading Roman traditions and values there is worth a detailed discussion in itself, but lies beyond our present scope.

Augustus's new army was an elite fighting force. Many of the troops who were retained in the new twenty-eight–legion imperial army were veterans who had proven themselves on the field of battle and who had achieved honors and rank. Some of their units had fought throughout the empire, from France to Egypt and from Tunisia to Turkey. They were accustomed to winning at least part of their pay through plunder, fighting in great battles, and gaining decisive victories or suffering disastrous defeats. They had been the source of political power and had made and unmade the rulers of Rome. They had been trained to march and maneuver, and to seek out the enemy for a conclusive encounter. Most of all, they had been trained to seek the offensive. Such had been the Roman military tradition for a matter of centuries, but all of that was to change.

It is safe to assume that many of the men in the new army had been forced to accept demotion in order to remain in service, and former heroes found that awards and honors were commonplace in their new units. The new army in its first years must have been not unlike the professional peacetime army established in the wake of the American Civil War, in which many individuals served in ranks and positions far below their capacities and in which veterans of Gettysburg and Antietam chafed at the boredom of peacetime service and garrison duty. The American army had, at least, the consolation that they were serving the needs of an expanding people, and some individuals may have been comforted by this thought.

The Augustan army did not enjoy a similar confidence that they were serving to expand the empire. If they did, that sentiment did not last for long. After centuries in which the Romans had attempted to attack potential enemies before they were attacked themselves, Augustus was forced to abandon that policy and to establish a fixed and fortified defensive frontier in the West. The legions were moved out to, and even beyond, the fringes of the empire, to find firm geographical features on which to fix their lines. At first, it would appear, this advance was merely a preparation for the invasion and conquest of Germany, but a stubborn rebellion in Illyria (modern Croatia) delayed this massive action. Augustus's offensive inclinations came to a sudden end in A.D. 9, when a force of three legions advanced into Germany to determine whether the Elbe River might not make a better frontier than the Rhine. Attacked by the Germans in a dense forest, they were annihilated. Augustus was shaken by a loss of military manpower that he could not easily replace and enlightened as to how many more men and how much wealth would be required to guarantee the success of his plans. His conclusion was that Rome no longer had the available resources to mount such an effort and that it could no longer seek its security through pre-emptive wars. He realized that the time had come for the empire to adopt a defensive policy and he resolved that Rome should no longer seek far frontiers. By the time of Augustus's death in A.D. 14, some legions had already taken up station along the Rhine River and others were advancing deliberately toward the Danube.

By this time, of course, Augustus's veterans had long since passed out of the service, but the slow evolution of the emperor's thoughts on the matter had not allowed him or his successor to formulate a new statement of the mission of the military or to institute new organization, equipment, or training to meet the role that the legions were to play in the future. The Roman army of the frontier thus found itself in an unfamiliar situation with few military traditions to guide it. Its positions were so far forward in many areas that the troops not only faced hostile German tribes beyond the frontier, but also had to guard themselves against unpacified Celtic tribes to their rear, constantly threatening their lines of communications and supply. There were still other problems to tax the spirit of the troops. Their commanders were imperial appointees who normally remained with their units only two or three years. These commanders received their general orders from emperors who were sometimes more interested in satisfying their own vanity than in formulating legitimate military policies. The soldiers' pay was low, amenities few and expensive, living conditions hard, and prospects of profitable plunder nil. Through their common experience in adjusting to their new role and to the life of the frontier stations, however, the troops gained a sense of unity that the Roman legions had not experienced for some time.

This unity gave them political power. Occasional mutinies had occurred before, but the revolt of the troops of Spain in A.D. 68 was more than a mutiny; it was a political rejection by the military of the tyranny and incompetence of the emperor Nero (A.D. 54–68). The legions elected their own commander as emperor, and the Roman Senate helplessly ratified this action. In the aftermath of the civil war that ensued, it became clear that, even in peacetime and stationed on distant frontiers, the new professional Roman army would be a decisive political force in imperial affairs.

Once this was generally understood, imperial authorities accepted the fact that they would put their positions, and even their lives, at risk by ignoring the needs and opinions of the army. With this improved relationship between the military and civil authorities, the processes of occupying and developing a defensible frontier began to accelerate.

The pioneering legions began to transform the countryside, building roads and bridges, docks and harbors. Moreover, each unit established around itself an extensive zone of relative security. Their very presence was a catalyst for change among the native peoples of the frontier districts in which they were stationed.

The Frontier Process

The steady appetite of the Roman units for food and materials was the fundamental factor that led to the economic development of the frontier districts. We shall talk a good deal about markets, but it should be remembered that free enterprise was not a Roman institution. Wherever the army was, there also were the imperial tax collectors. Local populations were required to pay taxes, in money if possible, in kind if necessary, and the army was prepared to use force to ensure that these taxes were collected. In order to meet these demands, the inhabitants of the frontier districts were forced to produce a surplus, and most of this surplus went directly toward supplying the army. Army agents, however, would also buy needed materials from local producers, and the soldiers, enjoying a cash salary, would purchase from local merchants. The markets of which we shall speak were thus complex entities, but the need to supply this local demand was the driving force behind the economic development of the Roman frontier districts. Ranching supplied the endless need of the legions for leather and meat, and the Roman camps, particularly those with cavalry units, required an increased local production of wheat and barley. Army units also needed large supplies of tile, bricks, lead pipes and pellets, iron nails, heavy timbers, cut stone, woolen cloth, and the like. Many of these items could be produced by the legions themselves, but, as time passed, the people of the frontier regions learned how to supply an increasing proportion of these requirements.

The Roman frontier process was not solely an economic phenomenon. If the American frontier saw the erosion of traditional values and attitudes among the pioneers, the Roman frontier saw the transformation of the traditional patterns of life of the native inhabitants. The survival of the frontier army depended on its organization and discipline, and these were maintained by fostering and preserving traditional Roman values and attitudes within the legions. Even though many of its troops lived and died without ever seeing the imperial capital, the army of the frontier became in many ways more Roman than the residents of Rome itself. The inhabitants of the frontier, on both sides of the border, envied the power of the legions and deduced that that power derived from the Roman way of life. Peoples in many of the frontier regions began to emulate the Roman soldier in speech, dress, building, and religion. As time passed, however, an increasing number of military recruits were drawn from the local populations of the frontier, and the army tended to adapt in some areas to local traditions. The result was the emergence of an amalgamation of cultures and traditions.

Traders from the heartland of the empire visited the frontier regularly to sell luxuries and delicacies to the troops and their dependents, and were more than ready to return to the interior carrying local products of value. Thus the frontier districts were introduced, at least to a degree, into the imperial economy. As on the American frontier, settlements of sutlers, wives and children, pawn shops, and places to drink sprang up near the legionary posts, and the local population was introduced through these to a form of urban life.

Finally, the Roman troops were not without refinement. Although posted to a distant frontier, they brought their culture with them. When the immediate necessity of building defenses was over, they constructed horse tracks, theaters, and temples near their camps. Moreover, they occasionally encouraged local economic development and adoption of Roman ways by building trading posts (*ventae*) for friendly tribes, and some of these evolved into urban settlements of their own. After their twenty-five years of service, veterans often retired in the neighborhood of their camp; their sons, often by local wives, entered the legion to repeat the process. In the course of time, the army of the frontier came to be composed almost entirely of Celtic troops recruited from the native population of the frontier.

Over the years, the Roman frontier experienced still other changes. With the security and the market assured by a permanent military post, some manufacturers from the heartland began to move their operations to the frontiers. Given the dense population and large numbers of slaves in the interior, Roman agriculture and industry were generally labor-intensive, and businesses normally invested in more slaves rather than more durable and efficient equipment. The situation on the frontier was quite different. Population was relatively sparse here, and military recruiters competed with employers for the available manpower. Slaves were difficult to keep with a nearby border across which to escape, and they were, in any case, more profitable when sold in the interior. Under such conditions, a form of proto-capitalist economy began to emerge as manufacturers began increasingly to rely on salaried workers and to invest in the development of improved equipment.

This tendency coincided with some basic changes that occurred in Roman technology as a result of the wars of conquest. As the supply of cheap slaves began to diminish, the manufacturers of the interior of the empire also began to turn to the development of labor-saving machines. Contrary to common opinion, the period saw significant advances in Roman technology, primarily based on the harnessing of water-power. Geography and climate provided the frontier a great advantage in this respect, however. The Mediterranean summer is dry, and many streams simply dry up until the rains of autumn. The perennial rivers of the region, such as the Po, Ebro, and Nile, are slow-moving and provide little power to any but the largest and most expensive installations. Water-power is neither plentiful nor constant in the Mediterranean basin. The situation is quite different in the areas that formed the empire's western frontiers. Rainfall is comparatively heavy, there are numerous snow- and spring-fed rivers and streams, and water-power is relatively plentiful and constant. The more mechanized an economy becomes, the greater its tendency to shift production to areas of cheap and plentiful power becomes. The water-power of the frontiers exerted a constant attraction on the manufacturers, artisans, and entrepreneurs of the interior. By the end of the Roman Empire in the West, if some anecdotal literary evidence and scattered archaeological finds are to be believed, the most advanced industry of the Western Empire may have been concentrated along its frontier periphery.

Meanwhile, the Germanic tribes on the other side of the Roman defensive line were undergoing their own frontier experience. Initially pressed forward by population pressure, these peoples had been driven up against the barrier of the Roman frontier defenses and had settled there. Politically and economically unsophisticated, they remained in close contact with the Roman frontier over a considerable period of time. Roman traders introduced them to manufactured products and encouraged them to obtain trading goods by gathering amber, mining silver and gold, bringing in pelts and horn, honey and hawks, and whatever else of worth their region could produce. Since slaves were always a marketable commodity, even the most primitive of the Germans could participate in an increasingly active trade across the frontier. Their frontiers with Rome became a land of opportunity for the Germans, and they were attracted there in bands and as individuals. Under Roman influence, these disparate settlers began to consolidate into political units. Some of the German tribes were thus creations of the frontier itself. The name "Marcomanni" was simply a Germanic form of "Frontiersmen," while the tribe of the Allemanni was open to "all men."

The traders of the frontier thus stimulated both the German economy and German society by developing the German appetite for Roman goods and introducing them to Roman ideas and values. Although it would not have seemed so at the time, these energetic traders were arranging not only for the end of the frontier but of the Western Empire itself. The Germans were also learning Roman ways of governing and fighting, and were becoming ever more formidable adversaries. The time would come in the early fifth century when the Germans would no longer be content with enjoying Roman life piecemeal and secondhand, and would cross the frontier to take by force those things they had come to appreciate over the centuries.

The Roman frontier was a complex phenomenon, composed of several regions with widely differing characteristics. This fact, combined with our varying levels of knowledge concerning each of these regions, makes it almost impossible to generalize about the frontier as a whole. For various reasons, we have limited our attention to the frontier in Europe, which was basically undeveloped and sparsely inhabited land, and the disparity in cultural and organizational sophistication between the Romans and the local populations was far greater than in the East. This meant that the frontier processes in the West were clearer and their effect more dramatic. In addition, an almost continuous water route composed of the North Sea and the Rhine and Danube rivers acted to unify the European frontier to such a degree that it can be treated as a single social and economic region. We shall attempt to demonstrate how the complex interaction between the Roman army of the frontier and the local populations, coupled with the human geography of the region itself, led to the formation of a frontier society, similar in some basic ways to American frontier society, that played an important role in the history of the empire as a whole.

II THE FRONTIER TAKES SHAPE

The Army of the Frontier

The study of the Roman army, its history, organization, and development, has a long and illustrious past. Machiavelli's *Discourses on Livy* is one of the more famous works of this tradition, but it was neither the earliest nor the most influential. From the beginning of the early modern period, professional soldiers, military planners, and would-be generals have turned to the works of Vegetius, Caesar, Livy, Sallust, Tacitus, Josephus, and other ancient authors for inspiration and guidance in military affairs. Shakespeare pokes fun at this tradition in *King Henry V*, when the Welshman Fluellen heatedly urges his companion to speak more softly in camp:

> It is the greatest admiration in the universal world, when the true and ancient prerogatives and laws of the wars is not kept. If you would take the pains but to examine the wars of Pompey the Great, you shall find, I warrant you, that there is no tiddle taddle nor pibble pabble in Pompey's camp. I warrant you, you shall find the ceremonies of the wars, and the cares of it, and the forms of it, and the sobriety of it, and the modesty of it, to be otherwise.[1]

Given all of the commentary and debate that has accumulated over the centuries on the subject of the Roman army, it is inevitable that there should be many disputed areas. It is also true that the army changed over time and there are exceptions to almost any general statement one may make. It is nevertheless useful to present at least the

13

broad outlines of the organization and activities of the institution that transformed the frontiers of the empire.

The Roman imperial army was composed of various specialized units, each with its unique character and functions. The core of Rome's military power, however, and the most highly regarded of Roman troops, were the large infantry formations called legions, composed exclusively of Roman citizens. Each legion was organized, equipped, and trained to fight as an independent force, although they were often employed in groups and in conjunction with auxiliary units. Each legion was distinguished by a number, but the system of nomenclature was so irregular that different legions could bear the same number. Each legion therefore had a nickname; for example, the unit stationed for many years at León in Spain was called Legio VII Gemina, the Seventh "Twin" Legion.[2]

The basic component of the legion was the century, which, despite its name, at full strength generally consisted of eighty men. The century shared quarters and rations, and was commanded by a centurion, an officer who had worked his way up through the ranks. Each century had a staff of other officers: the second in command, a record keeper, a commander of the guard, and a quartermaster.[3]

Six centuries, or 480 men, made up a cohort, commanded by the senior centurion of the unit, and ten cohorts constituted a legion. At some time in the first century A.D., the First Cohort of each legion was doubled in size to provide a particularly heavy force on the right of the legion's line. At full strength, then, the typical legion consisted of 5,280 infantry. Each legion also had a unit of 120 cavalry and a number of headquarters staff, medical personnel, and the like, so the full strength of a legion would have been in the neighborhood of 6,000 men. The legion commander was a legate (*legatus legionis*), appointed by the emperor and holding command of a given legion for only a few years. The legate was accompanied by a staff of officers called tribunes. The tribunes were usually inexperienced young Romans qualifying themselves for appointment as legate, or provincials hoping to advance a career in the imperial civil service. Although such military service was an essential step in a career in government, the tribunes had few command responsibilities. These were in the hands of the sixty to seventy centurions of the legion, and the senior centurion was in many ways the true commander of the unit.

Each legion had within its ranks a number of specialists and craftsmen such as surveyors, weapons-makers, engineers, miners, carpenters, stonecutters, and the like, who served within the centuries as infantrymen, but were excused from heavy duties. There are records of over a hundred different types of specialists who served at one time or another with the legions. With such expertise at its disposal, the typical legion could, and did, perform a remarkably wide variety of tasks, such as building roads and bridges, mining and smelting ores, setting up and operating brick and tile factories, making shoes, and planning and building cities and massive forts. The Roman imperial system of roads and bridges, which was not equaled in Europe until the nineteenth century, was planned and constructed almost entirely by Roman military forces. The discipline and flexibility of the legion was in large measure a result of its reliance on the veteran centurions for leadership and its ability to tap the technical expertise of its special personnel. A final factor contributing to the effectiveness of the legionary forces was the length of enlistment. Legionary troops were usually Roman citizens who joined the army at about age eighteen and served a single enlistment of twenty-five years. It was this length of service that allowed some troops to learn a profession in addition to mastering their military duties, and provided the legions with such a large number of seasoned veterans from which to draw their centurions. At the same time, the average soldier, committed to the legion for his active life, came to regard his unit as his home and family.[4] This created within the legions an esprit de corps that did much to make them probably the most formidable fighting units of the time. All told, in the time of Augustus (27 B.C.–A.D. 14), the Roman military establishment consisted of about twenty-eight such units, with a total of almost 170,000 men.[5]

The number of auxiliary troops (*auxilia*) was approximately the same.[6] The auxiliaries were usually recruited from the provinces and so were not Roman citizens. By the middle of the first century of the empire, however, auxiliary troops were granted citizenship upon retirement as a reward for faithful service.[7] Auxiliary units performed many useful functions, such as garrisoning the smaller forts and signal stations on the frontiers, as well as providing mobile forces to complement the more heavily armed and slower moving legions. Others were special weapons and supply troops. The most prestigious auxiliary detachments, in terms of both status and pay, were the cavalry wings (*alae*). Auxiliary infantry units, organized at the cohort level (*cohortes peditatae*) were also highly regarded. Units composed of mixed infantry and cavalry (*cohortes equitatae*) performed well, although the cavalry wings enjoyed greater prestige and higher pay than the mixed units.[8] Still other auxiliary units were composed of provincial forces possessing particular skill with a particular weapon, such as the slingers of the Balearics and Cretan archers.

The *auxilia* had originally been local levies of Roman allies raised to assist Roman forces, hence the name *auxilia*, which means "helpers." By the 70s, however, they had evolved into regular units, with uniform equipment and commanders promoted from their own ranks or assigned to them from the legions. The total number of auxilia within the Roman army in the time of Augustus was certainly as great as that of the legions, and probably greater.[9] Like the legionaries, these provincial troops served for twenty-five years. The initial policy of posting auxiliary units on a more or less permanent basis to frontier districts far from their home provinces was eventually altered. By the early second century, recruits for the frontier auxiliaries were being drawn primarily from among the local populations in the districts in which they were stationed. Moreover, the imperial policy of extending Roman citizenship to the inhabitants of the provinces ensured that many of the auxiliaries in service were already citizens.

Thus, by the second century, the distinction between the legions and the auxiliaries was slowly disappearing.[10] At the same time, however, the auxiliaries offered the inhabitants of the frontier regions a convenient means of entering Roman society and culture. Young men of fighting spirit who might otherwise have been led to resist the Roman presence entered the auxiliary units instead. Here they learned Latin, even if imperfectly, wore Roman dress, ate Roman food, worshiped Roman gods, and absorbed Roman values and attitudes. Upon retirement, they received Roman citizenship and a land grant. Retiring among their own people, those veterans who had survived their tour of duty served to spread Roman ways still further and at an even deeper social and cultural level.

The Roman Fleets

The Romans were primarily land-minded, and so it is not surprising that they considered the navy as a distinctly inferior branch of the army. The navy was divided into fleets (*classes*), with its fighting ships concentrated in the Mediterranean where there was always work to do in putting down pirates. There were various fleets along the frontier, where they were employed for patrols, transport, supply, communications, and amphibious assaults. Fleet needs and functions should never be forgotten when assessing the effect of the Roman military upon frontier districts. Units such as the British Fleet (*Classis Britannica*), stationed at Boulogne, not only provided ready communication between Britain and the continent, but also constituted a ready market for the wide variety of materials necessary to build ships, keep them in trim, and provide for the sustenance and equipment of their crews. Cloth, leather, ropes, metal, timber, caulking, and pitch and tar were only a few of the items the fleet required. Moreover, given the rate at which the equipment of wood and sail navies wore out under the conditions of active service, the supply of such goods had to be steady and assured. Within each fleet's area of operations were a number of smaller bases and depots of ship's stores, each of which drew supplies and raw materials from its immediate district, transshipping some surplus goods to other stations less plentifully supplied.

The fleets that plied the rivers and lakes were of even greater importance to the overall defensive system and to the economic and social development of the frontier districts. There was a fleet on the Seine, based in Paris; on the lower Rhine near Cologne; two on the Danube, one on the Rhone, and probably yet others. These river fleets materially improved shipping conditions by establishing river ports, marking channels, and providing the experience for the development of expert pilots. In addition to serving as scouts and messengers, and providing rapid transport for troops along the fortified frontier, the fleets supplemented the legion-built road system by shipping supplies. In a sense, the fleets helped to integrate the defensive system and to connect it with the interior of the empire by furnishing secure heavy transport. The various units along the fortified frontier could exchange with each other the materials and supplies in abundance in their own districts for scarce or unobtainable commodities, and, in case of need, necessary goods could be brought up quickly from the interior.[11] Despite the value of their services, the fleets were regarded as inferior to the land services, and treated as such. Fleet commanders, called prefects, were restricted to naval service and were not permitted to transfer to other branches of the army. The sailors themselves received lower pay and poorer quarters, and were expected to serve for twenty-six years, rather than the twenty-five years required in the land forces.

One generally thinks of the Roman legions as bringing Roman ways to the frontier and forging links between the frontier peoples and the imperial heartland. Although this was undoubtedly true, the frontier fleets were also an important element in this complex process. By the time the frontier was fixed, the fleets provided virtually uninterrupted transport from Britain in the West, along the Rhine and Danube to the Black Sea in the East.[12] The produce and manufactures of the native peoples of the frontier soon moved along this water route and along tributary waters. Although the administrators of the frontier might look to Rome as the heart of the empire, the ease and speed of river transport and communication ensured that the natives would think of themselves as inhabitants of a complex and varied, but interconnected, series of districts that formed the Roman frontier in the West.[13]

Civil Administration of Border Peoples

It would be a mistake to regard the evolution of the imperial Roman frontier as resulting only from the character of the military forces stationed there and from the natural progress of frontier processes. The location of that frontier, the number and nature of the troops stationed there, the training and activities of the troops, the status of the resident population, relations with the peoples beyond the frontier, and most other significant factors were either the intended or the accidental result of policies of the imperial administration. We shall refer to "imperial administration" often, but the imperial administration is not simple to define.

Frontier administration and the governing of subject peoples was not a new experience for the Roman government. Since the Samnite and Latin wars of the mid fourth century B.C., Roman power and influence had been steadily expanding, and the Romans had developed a more or less permanent policy for dealing with newly conquered lands and peoples. There were a limited number of Roman citizens, so the settlement of conquered lands was rarely attempted, and maintaining a standing army was both an expensive and unpopular measure, so the Romans tended to befriend and work with native populations rather than dominating them by force. These attitudes were strengthened by the fact that the Romans were generally moving into areas of relatively dense population, well-developed local cultures, and some measure of economic wealth.

Roman administrators therefore attempted to ally themselves with local leaders in maintaining the peace and cementing firm and friendly relations with Rome. Where it seemed possible to do so, the Roman administration attempted to convert the local elites to a Roman way of life. The traditional administrative goal seemed to be to surround Rome with semi-autonomous client-states ruled by friendly and Romanized local elites who could be depended upon to promote Roman interests generally.[14] Over the course of centuries, the Romans had developed a sophisticated policy of ethnic and cultural diplomacy based upon a respect for the integrity of their subject peoples.

The peculiar circumstances attending the fixing of the frontier fundamentally altered this approach. The establishment of a fortified line and the supply of its garrisons required great levies of labor and materiel, and the security of the army's lines of communication demanded a pacified local population. The civilian administration may have preferred to win the natives over by accommodation and acculturation, but that could be a long and fitful process. The military leaders, for their part, needed the full cooperation and complete submission of the residents of the frontier, and they needed it immediately. Augustus and his successors were constantly faced with the necessity of balancing the conflicting demands of their local administrators and integrating them into a consistent frontier policy. Although the nature of this balance and the aims of imperial policy varied from time to time and place to place, military concerns generally predominated in the frontier districts, and local social and economic development conformed to the needs of the army rather than to the ideal of "capturing the hearts and minds" of the inhabitants through the inculcation of Roman ways of life and thought.

Imperial Policy and the Fixing of the Frontier

We have already seen that the last century of the Roman republic had been a period of great civil wars. Augustus's victory opened an era of relative peace, and the emperor faced the task of reorganizing the various armies scattered throughout the empire into a permanent military establishment for peacetime service. This meant that the army would henceforth have to be less expensive, be able to maintain its effectiveness without the bloody training grounds of full-scale combat, and perform useful functions in addition to that of fighting at the orders of the state. There was also, from the emperor's point of view, the need to limit the ability of the military to influence or control the civil government.

Augustus's first step was to reduce the armed forces from some sixty to eighty legions to a permanent establishment of twenty-eight.[15] In the process more than 100,000 men were demobilized, many of them being settled in veterans' colonies throughout the empire.[16] Not only did such establishments contribute to the Romanization of the provinces, which in time would provide Rome with poets, philosophers, and even emperors, but the young men of the *coloniae* became an important source of legionary recruits.[17]

The auxiliaries presented a somewhat different problem. Although superfluous units were easily demobilized, the remainder resisted posting to stations very far from the lands in which they had been recruited. In the early stages of the frontier's establishment, the auxiliary units were therefore generally drawn from nearby regions.[18] Since many of the occupying troops were actually from neighboring tribes, this had the accidental but significant effect of reducing the shock of Roman occupation among the inhabitants of the frontier districts. With time, as we have noted, recruitment for auxiliary units was no longer restricted to the region from which the units had originally been drawn. They were opened to the inhabitants of frontier districts as well as others, and their personnel became ethnically more diverse. With this, their disinclination to accept distant postings lessened. The relatively small sizes of auxiliary units, 500 or 1,000 men, made them a particularly flexible source of manpower since they could be moved to points needing temporary reinforcement with far greater ease than the larger and more heavily equipped legions. The heterogeneous personnel and frequent movement of the auxiliary units made them another of the important factors helping to unite the Roman frontier and its inhabitants.

Perhaps the most significant innovation introduced by Augustus came from his realization that if the army was no longer to support itself through plunder, it was the responsibility of the state to provide it with regular pay.[19] While this was an essential first step in the professionalization of the armed forces, it also brought home to the emperor that, given the limited resources of the state, the size of its military establishment had to be restricted.[20] This meant that the empire could no longer afford to maintain a full-time offensive army and that the expansion of the empire, with the constant acquisition of new territories to be pacified and new frontiers to defend, had to be ended.[21] Augustus was so determined in this matter that he repeated his injunction against expansion in his testament, which his successor, Tiberius

(A.D. 14–37), was required to read before the Roman Senate.[22]

Augustus had not reached this conclusion easily. Early in his reign, in 29 B.C., he had closed the gates of the temple of Janus in Rome. The closing of these gates was a symbolic act signifying that Rome was now at peace with the entire world.[23] This peace lasted less than a decade, however. The defeat of a Roman contingent by the Germans called for retaliation, and Augustus led a war of conquest that annexed territories in what is now Switzerland and Austria, and established the frontier on the upper Danube. Almost immediately following, the inhabitants of Pannonia (modern Croatia and Serbia) began a dogged rebellion that took the Romans over twenty years to quell and led to the establishment of the frontier on the middle Danube.

Throughout this long conflict, Augustus continued to press the German war. It is not known whether he contemplated a frontier fixed on the Elbe or even the Vistula, or even if he had any clear idea himself. It is clear, however, that he intended that Roman power should reach beyond the Rhine. This ambition came to an end in A.D. 9, when a Roman force of three legions that had ventured into Germany was surrounded and annihilated.[24] Although several punitive expeditions were launched against the Germans in following years, Augustus had realized that the economic and human resources of the empire were not sufficient to wage a successful war of conquest against the Germans. Troops were moved up to the supply bases that had been established along the Rhine to support the invasion of Germany, and they quickly began converting them into permanent defensive posts. In this almost accidental way, the Roman frontier in the West was established, a fortified line that was to endure for almost 400 years.

Augustus's abandonment of the great Roman tradition of conquest was neither universally admired nor uniformly accepted. There was a constant temptation for emperors to attempt territorial conquest, since a victorious military campaign was the surest way to gain them popular acclaim and the favor of the army. There were, consequently, frequent fluctuations of the frontier, particularly in the East. In the West, however, military operations were generally directed at making relatively minor adjustments in the defensive line. There were only three major territorial acquisitions during the four centuries in which Roman western defenses were fixed upon their frontier line: Britain in A.D. 43, the German lands between the Rhine and Danube in c. A.D. 75–c. 135, and Dacia in A.D. 101–107.[25] (See the maps on pages 22 and 23.)

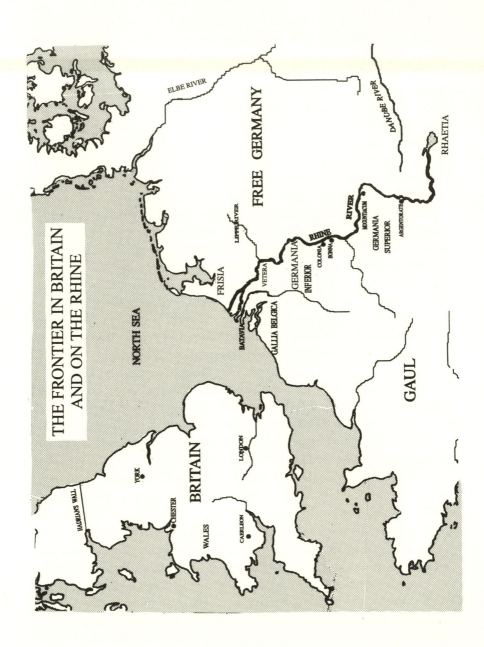

THE FRONTIER IN BRITAIN
AND ON THE RHINE

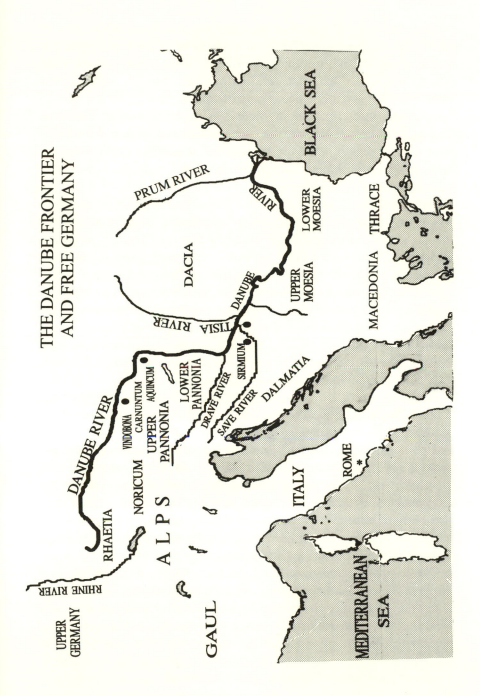

THE DANUBE FRONTIER AND FREE GERMANY

BLACK SEA

PRUM RIVER

RIVER

DACIA

LOWER MOESIA

UPPER MOESIA

MACEDONIA

THRACE

DANUBE

TISIA RIVER

DANUBE RIVER

VINDOBONA

CARNUNTUM

AQUINCUM

UPPER PANNONIA

LOWER PANNONIA

DRAVE RIVER

SAVE RIVER

SIRMIUM

DALMATIA

NORICUM

RHAETIA

A L P S

RHINE RIVER

UPPER GERMANY

GAUL

ITALY

ROME

MEDITERRANEAN SEA

Augustus had stationed five legions along the Rhine River, five in Illyria, four in Greece, four in Syria, three in Egypt, two in Africa, and five in Spain.[26] The loss of Varus's three Rhine legions took some time to repair. By the reign of Tiberius (A.D. 14–37), eight legions were stationed on the Rhine, three in Spain, two in Africa, two in Egypt, four in Syria, two in Moesia (Bulgaria), two in Pannonia (Hungary), and two in Dalmatia (the eastern coast of the Adriatic).[27] Although the total number of legions was still three short of Augustus's establishment, the remaining legions were gradually being concentrated on the frontier.

The emperor Claudius (A.D. 41–54) remains something of an enigma to historians. Handicapped in speech and walk, he was also a scholar and an astute politician who had survived a series of palace intrigues and conspiracies to reach power. Although generally inclined to peace, he ordered the first major departure from Augustus's policy against further conquest. Various reasons have been given for his decision to conquer Britain: the British were supporting rebels among the population of Gaul (France); Claudius was attempting to curry public favor through military success; the Romans were attempting to gain the sources of British gold and pearls.[28] Whatever his real goal, in A.D. 43, Claudius ordered the conquest of Britain.

The invasion of Britain was conducted by three legions from the Rhine and one from the Danube and resulted in the rapid conquest of southern and central England. The Romans failed to subdue Scotland and portions of the North of England,[29] but southeastern Britain became the western anchor of the imperial frontier. Moreover, due to intensive work by British archaeologists, more is known about the army and the economic and social development of this region than about any other sector of the frontier.[30] The studies conducted on the fortifications along the northern frontier of Britain provide an excellent example of the depth and extent of archaeological activity in the area.

The tribes of Scotland had not been conquered and, although the northern legions had attempted to restrain their small-scale incursions with units of frontier scouts (*exploratores*) and regular patrols, it was clear that the northern districts would never be secure without a more heavily fortified frontier. Under the emperor Hadrian (A.D. 117–138), great attention was paid to constructing an unbroken line of fortifications along the entire western frontier, and Britain was no exception to this general flurry of activity. A permanent defensive system was built, featuring a continuous stone wall reaching from the Tyne to the Solway. This massive work, known as Hadrian's Wall, was constructed by Roman legionaries and formed a barrier measuring over seventy-three miles in length stretching across the island from the North Sea to the Irish Sea.[31]

The wall was built of cut stone, eight feet thick and at least fifteen feet high to the rampart walk, with a parapet adding an additional six feet.[32] The deep ditches cut both in front of and behind the wall were impressive projects in themselves.[33] Signal turrets were built every one-third of a mile and turreted gates every mile. Auxiliary forts were constructed on the wall itself. At the western terminus of the wall, a series of forts continued the defense line along the coast. Three more forts were built north of the wall as scout bases.[34] The legionary fortresses at York (Eburacum) and Chester (Deva) were located approximately a hundred miles south of the wall itself, but a special road system facilitated the rapid forward deployment of troops.

It is fortunate that the remains of Hadrian's Wall are sufficient for the archaeologist to derive such an accurate picture of the scope of the works, since it provides the historian with a dramatic example of the magnitude of the projects that could be accomplished with the expertise, manpower, and discipline of legionary troops. It also provides a good indication of how far the army could go in accomplishing its mission of defending the frontier. The erection of this complex and massive system of fortifications served its purpose. The raids of the northern Picts and Scots were contained, and, until the decline of the empire itself, the northern frontier district of Britain was confined to the area lying between the legionary forts at Chester and York, and Hadrian's Wall.[35]

Despite its restricted extent, the northern frontier of Britain was perhaps the most heavily defended district of the empire. Approximately 30,000 troops were stationed there during the second century. The two legions at Chester and York totaled about 12,000 men, while the rest of the troops were auxiliary units concentrated near the wall. The Romans posted auxiliaries to garrison the three outpost forts and sixteen wall forts. Some 5,500 cavalry and 10,000 infantry were always ready in the vicinity, although the number of guards and lookouts on the wall itself totaled less than 3,000 at any given time. In addition to these forces, the northern frontier could call for reinforcements from an additional 10,000 or more troops stationed on the Welsh frontier.[36]

The Rhine frontier had been the first in the West to be established, and the Rhine legions had led the way in adapting to their new environment and mission. This adaptation had not been an easy one, and for some time the Roman army of the Rhine was as great a danger to imperial authority as the possible German invasions against which they were on guard. A series of minor mutinies and disputes culminated in the great legionary revolt of 69. All eight legions united in refusing further support to the emperor Galba (68–69), who had been put in power by the Roman troops in Spain. They instead acclaimed their own commander, Vitellius (69), as emperor. The troops then marched upon Rome. At first successful, they were eventually defeated by Vespasian (69–79), a legate to Judaea who had secured the support of the Danubian legions. A sporadic series of mutinies by Rhine troops and by a combination of Gallic auxiliaries and their fellow countrymen continued to trouble the new emperor, who took drastic action to eliminate these threats. Four of the mutinous legions were disbanded, and a policy was instituted that auxiliary troops could no longer serve in the districts of their recruitment. Finally, Vespasian distracted the Rhine units by setting them the task of occupying and fortifying the region between the upper Rhine and the upper Danube, an area that had long constituted a weak point in the continental frontier system. With the legions reasonably pacified, the Rhine and Danube lines better integrated, and Britain protected, the imperial frontier in Europe was essentially complete. It is now possible to attempt an overview of the frontier system.

We have already discussed the establishment and location of the British frontier districts, and will have much more to say about them in later chapters. There is more known about the frontier process in Britain than elsewhere and, for that reason, British examples and developments will loom rather large in our discussions. It is well to remember, however, that Britain formed only a small part of the western frontier. Moreover, the swift decay of Roman Britain after the withdrawal of Roman civil and military government in the late fourth and early fifth centuries suggests that neither the cultural nor the economic development of the area under the Romans had really penetrated very deeply among the native inhabitants of the region.

By contrast, the Rhine frontier had a substantial and lasting effect on its region. The areas occupied by the Roman army of the frontier still constitute the line between the Germanic and Romance languages of western Europe. The Rhine frontier consisted of northeastern Gaul, (including Luxembourg, and parts of France, Belgium, and the Netherlands) and Lower and Upper Germany (centered respectively on the lower and upper Rhine). These regions were flourishing by the second century and developing a unique cultural tradition founded on the merging of the native Celtic-Germanic population with Roman immigrants. The towns and industries that arose in these regions clearly illustrated the area's successful development. The number of cities and towns that have survived from frontier times indicates the success of urbanization and economic development in the region.[37]

The prosperity of the Rhine frontier resulted in large measure from extensive commercial traffic and the existence of substantial numbers of military personnel. The large cities on the left bank of the river were almost all of a military origin. Colonia Agrippina (Cologne), Moguntiacum (Mainz), Bonna (Bonn), Castra Vetera (Xanten), and Novaesium (Neuss) all developed from settlements that had sprung up around military establishments, while Aachen, with its hot springs, was originally a rest and rehabilitation center. Five legions were stationed on the middle and lower Rhine by about A.D. 6. These legions were accompanied by numerous auxiliary units, and the total force must have numbered some 60,000 men. By the year 20, the number of Rhine legions had risen to eight, with auxiliary troops bringing the total number of troops to about 100,000. The emperor Trajan (98–117) was able to reduce this number to about 45,000, 24,000 thousand of which were legionaries. This number remained fairly constant thereafter, except for the stationing of larger forces of auxiliary troops in the frontier forts.[38]

The line of the river marked the frontier on the lower Rhine throughout the imperial period.[39] The original garrison of four legions accompanied by auxiliaries, stationed in forts along the lower portion of the river, was reduced to three under Domitian (81–96) and to two under Trajan. Permanent legionary forts were established at Bonn and Xanten in the second century.[40]

The boundary of Upper Germany, by contrast, experienced progressive and frequent alterations during the first and second centuries. The region between the headwaters of the Rhine and Danube presented a significant problem for the Romans. This area formed a substantial wedge between the two rivers, providing the Germans with a large salient from which they could attack weak sections of either frontier.

Moreover, the Rhine and Danube were no more than streams near their headwaters and constituted no real barriers to attack. If the Romans had left this region unoccupied, rapid communication between the Rhine and Danube armies would have been imperiled, and an attractive route for the possible invasion of Italy through the Black Forest would have been left open.

The solution reached by Vespasian was the construction of a fortified frontier that left the Rhine north of Cologne, circled the Taunus Mountains, continued south-southeasterly to Lorch, and then ran parallel to and north of the Danube until it joined the river at Ingolstadt. This frontier remained secure for more than a century, and the lands behind it experienced substantial development.[41] This advance into German territory was not so much a departure from Augustus's frontier policy as an attempt to improve the frontier line. Under Vespasian, forts were established beyond the upper Rhine, and a road was constructed from Strassburg to the upper Danube. Domitian extended the frontier boundary in this region by constructing a line of watchtowers and stone forts in the area of the Taunus Mountains and the Main River.[42] The next fifty years saw the establishment of auxiliary forts forward of both the upper Rhine and the Danube.[43]

As had been the case in Britain, it was Hadrian who provided a definitive solution to this weak point in Rome's frontier defenses, and he accomplished this with the same policy of massive construction that he had employed in Britain. He ordered all auxiliary units transferred to the frontier line and there had them build a massive wooden palisade forming a continuous barrier and line of demarcation from Cologne to Ingolstadt.[44] In addition, the emperor began the construction of a completely new series of cut-stone fortresses across the territory. The construction of such stone forts reflects a profound change in the attitude of the Roman army. By this point, they had come to accept their permanent posting to the frontier regions and were ready to take great pains in consolidating the frontier and in improving its defensive works.

By the second century, then, the Upper German frontier had been moved east into Germany. It now followed a relatively straight course from Cologne on the Rhine to Ingolstadt on the Danube. Behind this line lay a new frontier district, composed of parts of southern Germany and northern Switzerland. The Roman army of the frontier now occupied a frontier in Upper Germany composed of both Celtic and Germanic districts, with the Rhine serving as a unifying path for commerce and communication. The pacification and Romanization of the Germanic frontier districts provided the Romans with commercial access to the resources of the interior of Germany. Wax, furs, timber, resins, amber, gold, cattle, slaves, honey, and a number of other valuable goods flowed into the Rhine frontier districts, and Roman manufactured goods, such as glassware, mirrors, boxes, swords, and tools, flowed out into Germany.[45] The commercial opportunities of the German trade, coupled with the profits to be gained from supplying the army, stimulated the development of the area and attracted merchants and manufacturers from the interior of the empire to the Rhine *limes.*[46]

From the military point of view, the Danube line was probably the most important of the three frontier regions in Europe. Its length was almost twice that of Britain and the Rhine combined, it faced the powerful and potentially hostile kingdom of Dacia, and it was vulnerable to the nomadic tribes who roamed the plains of southern Russia. Most of the Danube frontier lay in the four provinces of the two Pannonias and the two Moesias. The frontier districts of Upper and Lower Pannonia (eastern Austria, western Hungary, and Serbia) extended along the Danube from Vienna to near present-day Belgrade. The frontier districts of Upper and Lower Moesia (portions of Yugoslavia, Bulgaria, and Romania) reached from Belgrade to the mouth of the Danube and the Black Sea.[47]

The army of the frontier took some time to reach the middle Danube, and left behind them a series of abandoned camps.[48] The potential of a Roman army base to stimulate local economies is powerfully illustrated by the urban centers left behind in the army's wake. Like archaeological strata, the successive lines of towns on the Save River (Siscia and Sirmium), on the Drave (Poetovio and Mursa), and the Danube (Vindobona [Vienna], Carnuntum [Deutsch-Altenburg], Brigetio [Szny], Aquincum [Budapest], Singidunum [Belgrade], and Ratiaria [Arcer]) indicate the successive advances of the legions to their positions on the middle Danube. Each of these cities, and a number of others in the region, marks the site of a former legionary base.

Despite the importance of the Danube, the Rhine frontier was the area of primary military concern and effort for the Romans during most of the first century. This situation changed in the year 85, however, when the various tribes of Dacia (Romania) united under an able king, Decebalus. The Dacians adopted a hostile attitude toward the

Romans, and a series of wars kept the Danubian frontier in turmoil until the early second century. The emperor Trajan (98–117) undertook to end this threat with drastic action. Frontier fortifications were ungraded with stone fortresses, and new legions were raised. By the year 101, there were thirteen legions ready on the Danube, and Trajan invaded Dacia. By 107, the kingdom had fallen in hard fighting and had been absorbed into the Roman Empire as a new province. A legion and some twenty-three auxiliary units were stationed in the area. There they built a permanent fortification system linked by an extensive road network. The countryside had been devastated and depopulated due to the long wars, and the Romans began to move settlers in to develop the resources of the region and help to supply the troops there. It was this part of the Roman frontier that most resembled the classical formulation of the American frontier. Although Roman troops were withdrawn in the course of the third century, the Romanization of the area was virtually complete; the name of the territory today is Romania, from Roma, and its inhabitants speak what can only be described as a dialect of Latin.

The Danubian army was left permanently strengthened. As part of Hadrian's general consolidation and rationalization of the frontier system, three legions were stationed in Britain, four on the Rhine—two each in Lower and Upper Germany—and ten on the Danubian frontier—three in Upper Pannonia, one in Lower Pannonia, two in Upper Moesia, three in Lower Moesia, and one in Dacia.[49] The Danubian legions, with the exception of the one in Dacia, along with the great majority of auxiliaries, were located on the Danube frontier itself.

The results of Trajan's occupation of Dacia were not unlike those of Hadrian's pacification of the lands between the upper Rhine and upper Danube a few years later. Dacia itself constituted a great market for Roman goods and a source of valuable materials.[50] Moreover, the Romans of Dacia could trade with central and southern Russia. The result of the opening of these vast new markets—the influx of new goods from the North and East—and the security provided by the pacification of the frontier provided the bases of an economic boom along the lower Danube, in Thrace (Bulgaria), and along the Roman-held portions of the Black Sea shore. This was reflected in new wealth, greater commercial and manufacturing activity, and an increase in the number and size of urban centers in the region.

The reign of Hadrian (117–137) saw the final consolidation and rationalization of the Roman frontier. Hadrian realized that the Roman economy could not support the conquests of Trajan,[51] and withdrew to more defensible lines. As we have noted, he established a continuous series of strong barriers and attempted to improve the fitness of the army to defend these lines.[52] Aware that trade with the peoples beyond the imperial frontiers had become an economic asset for both the frontier and the heartland of the empire, he established regular gates and trading stations along the frontier barrier. Although Hadrian's main purpose was to regulate movement across the border, these regular and secure markets and the roads leading to them from both sides of the frontier probably increased trade across the border considerably.

Unity in Diversity: Integrating Forces

By the early second century, the Roman frontier in the West had become relatively clearly defined. The regions that composed it were varied in nature and circumstances, but were integrated by a number of factors. The northern frontier in Britain was a relatively small area confined between the legionary camps of Chester and York to the south and Hadrian's Wall to the north. Nevertheless, the permanent stationing of a large number of troops in the district created a steady demand for supplies and materials that stimulated the economy of the entire Southeast of the island.

The frontier along the lower Rhine below Cologne was also a relatively small district since much of the area on both sides of the river consisted of swamps and marshes. Nevertheless, the British Fleet, stationed at Boulogne, and the Rhine fleet united this area with the rest of the frontier. The relatively small population of the lower Rhine utilized the substantial resources of their environment to supply the Roman units in their midst, and used the river and sea traffic between Britain and the upper Rhine frontier for trade. The district was a good source of military recruits for much of the period under consideration.[53]

The upper Rhine, from Cologne to Ingolstadt, was a rich and well-developed area. Hadrian's pacification of the lands between the Rhine and Danube had provided a region of exchange between Germany and the areas of northeastern Gaul that lay west of the Rhine and supplied the large forces established there. The Upper Danube frontier, by contrast, lay along the Danube itself, and its development was restricted by the powerful and potentially hostile tribes of the Quadi and

Marcomanni.[54] The gradual advance of the legions through the districts of the Save and Drave rivers to their positions on the upper Danube had stimulated economic development. Like the districts of the lower Rhine, these areas benefited from the markets provided by military posts and supported a substantial increase in agricultural production. Characterized by small family farms, the area of the Save and Drave became excellent recruiting grounds, and Pannonian troops gained an outstanding reputation.

Dacia and the lower Danube underwent perhaps the most successful frontier experience. Dacia offered free land and abundant natural resources for local exploitation, as well as an excellent location for long-distance trade. The growth of the Dacian economy, which was first stimulated by the need to provision the garrisons and miners of the region, had effects far beyond the borders of the new province. The entire eastern portion of the frontier shared in a new prosperity.

The disparity between these various frontier districts is evident, but it is important also to recognize the factors that united them. The North Sea, Rhine, Danube, and Black Sea formed an almost continuous waterway upon which every frontier district touched. The British, Rhine, Danube, and Black Sea fleets, together with lesser units on lakes and tributary waters, maintained ports, harbors, shipyards, stores depots, channel markers, local security, and other amenities throughout the vast extent of this water route. Until modern times, water transport was always faster and immeasurably cheaper than overland hauling. The ease of communication and heavy transport along the frontier water route would have induced the bulk of local production to move along the frontier, rather than overland toward the interior of the empire. Although there is little direct evidence on the matter, there was no doubt a complex web of business and personal relations uniting the native peoples who used the rivers.[55] The existence of this water route served to unite the peoples who lived along it into a single community, similar to the way the Mississippi–Missouri river system, as depicted by Mark Twain, united the different and various peoples who lived along its shores.

A second unifying factor lay in the fact that the residents of the frontier, most of whom were non-Roman in any event, were in constant contact with the "barbarians" beyond the frontier. The population of the tribes beyond the frontier was great and their lands vast, while the demands of the army and a growing civilian population initially left little of the production of the frontier districts available for trade. This meant that the success of the traders with free Germany was not limited by competition, but by the amount of export commodities they could procure and by their own sense of adventure. The residents of the frontier were in regular contact with the "barbarian" peoples beyond the border. This gave them a ready basis of comparison by which to judge Roman ways and Roman actions. This capacity for critical thought could lead to rebellion and mutiny, but it could also give rise to an independence of spirit that was rare in the ancient world and was a product of the frontier experience.[56]

The last and perhaps most important factor unifying the inhabitants of the Roman frontier lay in the presence throughout the frontier districts of large numbers of Roman military units. Except for Dacia and southern Germany, the Roman settlers of the frontier were neither farmers nor traders; they were soldiers. In contrast to settlers during the American frontier process, the Roman troops did not seek to displace the native peoples of the regions into which they moved; they needed their manpower too much. Finally, and also in contrast to the American experience, these army units were not segregated from the local population or excluded from civil processes. The Roman army of the frontier was a new and evolving military force with a mission for which it had no traditional doctrine. It adapted itself to its frontier environment and its new functions with an empirical attitude, developing new concepts of the proper function of the military, drawing upon the native inhabitants for necessary assistance, and devoting the full resources of its expertise to the accomplishment of the formidable tasks at hand.

In order to succeed in its mission, the army had to accept responsibilities far beyond that of merely garrisoning the frontier. It had to secure law and order within its jurisdiction; many of the administrative and judicial responsibilities of provincial government along the frontier came to rest with army staff officers. It was also to the advantage of the army to promote the economic prosperity of its district. Legionary engineers, architects, surveyors, craftsmen, accountants, and other specialists doubtless provided the civilian population of the frontier with advice and technical aid. The troops busied themselves with the construction of roads, bridges, wharfs, and ports, as well as fortifications. By doing so, they created the infrastructure for the economic development of their districts. The provision of these essentially civilian services by resident military units, together with recruitment of noncitizens into the auxiliaries and their discharge as citizens, greatly enhanced the process of the integration of native civil populations and Roman military forces along the frontier. At the same time, these building projects fostered the growth of towns around the military establishments and promoted urbanization.

The development of the frontier districts, however, depended in great measure on other necessary factors. Successful military occupation depended upon the ability of the units involved to find the means of filling their continuing needs for supplies and materials from local resources. The supplying of such materials in the relatively large quantities needed required substantial local resources in the form of fertile land, mineral deposits, pasturelands, or an effective means of communication and transport to draw the necessary goods from farther afield. Levies in kind forced the residents to extend and amplify their economies, but assured opportunities for profit that then encouraged the local population to continue the process of economic growth. The permanent presence of the army provided the local population with an unaccustomed freedom from internal disorder and external threats, and allowed them to devote a greater part of their energies to economic pursuits. The availability of abundant and relatively unexploited resources on the frontier, coupled with assured military markets, served to draw individuals engaged in various economic pursuits, such as agriculture, ranching, mining, or manufacturing, to the frontier to profit from these opportunities. At the same time, the native population, often accustomed to small-scale production for restricted local markets, began to learn the requisite techniques for expanding their operations. Various peoples with disparate levels of competence were drawn to the profits available in supplying the army of the frontier. The efforts of these groups, and the relative ease or difficulty in exploiting the natural resources of a district, often produced an unequal rate of development among the various fields involved in military supply. The typical frontier district, therefore, underwent various stages of economic development. Like the American frontier, the Roman frontier can be viewed in various economic aspects: commerce, ranching, agriculture, and industry.

The presence of the army in the frontier regions provided the impetus and inspiration for development in each of these economic fields. The army, in the course of providing security for the heartland of the empire, established the markets and built the transportation and communications networks necessary for effective economic development.

The intensified exploitation of local resources gave rise to trading, pastoral, and agricultural economies that satisfied military, civilian, and external markets alike. The profits generated by this relatively rapid expansion not only promoted native development along the frontier, but attracted immigrants interested in similar gains from other areas of economic endeavor. The subsequent development of new ventures in manufacturing and mining, combined with the expansion of existing areas of production, eventually created a series of economically developed districts along the frontier. Each of these districts possessed a complex economy. The basic function of production was to fill the needs of the local military units. Beyond this was the possibility of the development of a particularly abundant local resource for shipment along the great water route that united both the units comprising the army of the frontier and the local economies of the districts in which they were stationed. Even beyond this was the possibility of developing local trade goods to use in tapping the rich resources beyond the frontier. The establishment of the frontier and the arrival of great numbers of foreign troops taking up permanent stations in their midst suddenly placed incredible burdens on the frontier populations, but also opened great opportunities to them. In time, the opportunities came to outweigh the burdens, and a dynamic and distinctive frontier society began to emerge.

Notes

1. William Shakespeare, *King Henry V*, Act 4, Scene 1.
2. Legions with the cognomen of Gemina were those formed by consolidating the troops of two previous legions. Among other nicknames were "Devourers," "Lightning Hurlers," and "Iron Clads." It is interesting to note that León is a short and corrupted from of *civitas legionis*, "city of the legion," just as Caerleon in Wales is derived from *castrum legionis*, "camp of the legion." The names of other cities and towns of Europe also recall their military origins.
3. The Latin terms for these officers were *optio, signifer, tesserarius,* and *custos armorum*, respectively.
4. See Ramsay MacMullen, "The Legion as a Society," *Historia* 33 (1984): 440–456.
5. H. M. D. Parker, *The Roman Legions*, p. 90, claims that the early imperial army comprised a rather small fighting force. Twenty-five legions remained of the twenty-eight retained by Augustus after the annihilation of Varus and the three legions under his command in Germany in A.D. 9. Tiberius maintained the number at twenty-five, but eight new legions were formed between A.D. 37 and 70. The emperor Vespasian (69–79) discharged four after quelling the revolt of

69, leaving a total of twenty-nine. Graham Webster, in *The Roman Imperial Army of the First and Second Centuries* A.D., pp. 107–109, 113, states that the recruiting areas of legionaries during the first two centuries A.D. changed markedly. Italy supplied 65 percent of the recruits in the period from Augustus to Caligula (37–41), but by the second century, fewer than 1 percent of the legionaries were natives of Italy.

6. For the *auxilia*, see G. R. Watson, *The Roman Soldier*, pp. 24–25: Webster, *The Roman Imperial Army*, p. 113.

7. Parker, *The Roman Legions*, p. 243–244, mentions that auxiliaries, upon completion of their term of service, received certificates of citizenship or *diplomata*, made of two inscribed bronze plates fastened together. These granted the recipient citizenship for himself and for his children and the right of a recognized Roman marriage with his wife—the latter not obtaining citizenship. One of the reasons for extending the grant to the veteran's children was that his sons would thus be able to enlist in the legions, for which Roman citizenship was a requisite. This custom continued until A.D. 140, when only children born subsequent to their father's grant were themselves granted citizenship. See also A. N. Sherwin-White, *The Roman Citizenship* (Oxford: Clarendon Press, 1939), p. 215.

8. Anne Johnson, *Roman Forts of the First and Second Centuries* A.D. *in Britain and the German Provinces*, p. 9.

9. Paul Petit, *Pax Romana*, p. 18; Edward Luttwak, *The Grand Strategy of the Roman Empire from the First Century* A.D. *to the Third*, p. 16; Webster, *The Roman Imperial Army*, pp. 142–154, states that the total number of Roman troops—auxiliary and legionary—before A.D. 70 did not exceed 350,000. For the number of auxiliary troops in Britain, see S. S. Frere, *Britannia: A History of Roman Britain*, p. 207.

10. Parker, *The Roman Legions*, pp. 171–172; Michael Grant, *The Climax of Rome* (New York: New American Library, 1968), p. 36.

11. See, for example, D. P. S. Peacock, "Roman Shipping and Trade: Britain and the Rhine Provinces" in *The Council for British Archaeology Research Report 24* (1978): 49.

12. There was a break in this route between the upper Rhine and the upper Danube. Although the distance between navigable stretches of each is not great, cargo would have had to be broken. In any event, there is no indication of a substantial long-distance trade along this route. Materials were apparently shipped between Britain and Lower Germany, and between Lower Germany and Upper Germany, for instance. To travel far, goods would have had to pass through a series of middlemen and transshippers.

13. The standard study of the Roman navy is that of Chester G. Starr, *The Roman Imperial Navy, 31 B.C.–A.D. 324.*

14. The origins and development of Roman frontier administration during the republican period is admirably handled by Stephen L. Dyson, *The Creation of the Roman Frontier*. The essential characteristics of the process known as "Romanization" are delineated by D. B. Saddington, "The Parameters of Romanization," in *Roman Frontier Studies 1989*, ed. V. A. Maxfield and M. J. Dobson, pp. 413–418. The traditional goal of the Roman administration was most closely met by the client kingships, more common in the East than in the less developed West. David Braund, *Rome and the Friendly King: The Character of the Client*

Kingship, provides an excellent modern analysis of the system, while his *Administration of the Roman Empire: 241 B.C.–A.D. 193* is well worth reading for its portrayal of the evolution of the administrative system in general.

15. This point had been debated for some time, but the present consensus allows Augustus's peacetime army to have included twenty-eight legions.

16. For an example of a provincial *colonia*, see H. Hurst, "Gloucester (Glevum): A Colonia in the West Country," in *The Roman West Country*, ed. Keith Branigan and P. J. Fowler.

17. See J. C. Mann, *Legionary Recruitment and Veteran Settlement during the Principate*.

18. Webster, *The Roman Imperial Army*, p. 26.

19. See Suetonius, "Augustus," chapter 9.

20. Keith Hopkins, "Taxes and Trade in the Roman Empire (200 B.C.–A.D. 400)," *Journal of Roman Studies* (hereafter cited as *JRS*) 70 (1980): 101–102, concentrates on the army's role as a recipient of tax money and the subsequent effect of army pay on the monetization of the frontier economy.

21. C. M. Wells, in *The German Policy of Augustus*, pp. 5–10, 13, states that Augustus, following the loss of three legions under Varus in Germany in A.D. 9, decided to abandon the area between the Rhine and Elbe rivers and to fix the northern boundaries of the empire along the Rhine and Danube. See also R. Syme, "The Northern Frontier under Augustus," in *Cambridge Ancient History*, ed. J. B. Bury et al.

22. Tacitus, *Annales* 1: 11. Wells, *The German Policy under Augustus*, pp. 5, 15, claims that the idea that there existed a controllable limit to the size of the empire first occurred with Augustus. The emphasis upon protection of the frontier regions from barbarian incursions became an important part of official concern during the entire imperial period.

23. They had last been closed in 235 B.C. during an interlude in the wars with Carthage.

24. This was the famous battle of the Teutoberg Forest, the first serious defeat of a substantial Roman force since the stunning victories of Hannibal in the course of the Second Punic War (218–212 B.C.). Although the site of the battle has been long disputed, and numerous German towns and villages have claimed the honor, recent excavations are almost conclusive in fixing the site about ten miles north of Osnabrück. It would seem that Arminius (Herman), the German leader, had trapped the Roman forces extended along a narrow road that led between a swamp and his own fortified lines extending along the hill that lay on the other side of the road.

The German victory was complete, and Varus, the Roman commander, and the other officers committed suicide rather than be captured. Arminius hacked off Varus's head and sent it to Rome as a grisly report to Augustus that his forces had been destroyed. The loss caused a great shock among the Romans. The biographer Suetonius portrays Augustus as being obsessed by the defeat and beating his head against the wall while crying, "Quinctilius Varus! Give me back my legions!"

For a short, but well-illustrated account of the Osnabrück excavations, see John Dornberg, "Battle of the Teutoberg Forest," *Archaeology* 45(5) (September/October 1992): 26–32.

25. Luttwak, *The Grand Strategy of the Roman Empire*, p. 104, points out that

in the East, Trajan's conquests of Armenia and Mesopotamia down to the Persian Gulf in the war of A.D. 113–117 were abandoned by Hadrian immediately after Trajan's death. The Parthian Wars of Marcus Aurelius's co-emperor, Lucius Verus, in A.D. 162–166 and of Septimius Severus in A.D. 194–198 led to the creation of a new province of Mesopotamia and the extension of Roman domination to the Tigris River. For the conquest of Britain, see Frere, *Britannia*, pp. 61–62.

26. This distribution is open to some dispute, but the relative proportions are accurate. Grant, *The Climax of Rome*, p. 35, estimates a total of about 160,000 legionary troops before the German disaster in the year A.D. 9. These losses were not made up for some time, and there were about 150,000 legionary troops until the reign of Vespasian (69–79). Even after the military expansion of Trajan (98–117), there were probably no more than 174,000 men in the legions. See also Luttwak, *The Grand Strategy of the Roman Empire*, p. 16. It is important to remember, however, that the army counted at least an equal number of auxiliary and naval troops. The empire kept the remarkably large number, at least for the ancient world, of some 300,000 or more men continually under arms for almost 200 years.

27. Tacitus, *Annales* 4:5.

28. There was not much British gold and much of what there was came from Irish mines. Colchester oysters were superb to eat, but they produced few and almost worthless pearls.

29. The peninsula of Wales also avoided Romanization. The Roman army established legionary camps at Chester and Caerleon and a system of auxiliary and naval bases throughout the region, linked by an elaborate road network. This frontier system was partially designed to protect the west coast of Britain from Irish and Scottish sea raids, and partially to keep the native population under control. In contrast with virtually every other part of the frontier, the Roman army in Wales seems to have made very little effort to maintain cooperative relations with the Welsh population.

30. This is partially due to the long tradition of local antiquarianism in England. Most Church of England personnel were trained in the classics, and many devoted their spare time to investigating the antiquities of their parishes. Since the Second World War, a rational and generous plan of government sponsorship of archaeological work and preservation of ancient sites has made British archaeology perhaps the best in the world. Excellent work has been done in both Germany and France, but the area to be covered there is greater and Roman sites denser. Roman archaeology in Eastern Europe has tended to be underfunded, but a number of important sites are currently being investigated.

31. The construction of the wall probably began at Hadrian's direct order in the year 122.

32. See R. G. Collingwood and Ian A. Richmond, *The Archaeology of Roman Britain*, pp. 16–20, 76–79. Also Frere, *Britannia*, pp. 127, 129–133; Eric Birley, *Research on Hadrian's Wall*, p. 125; and Ian Richmond, *Roman Britain* (London: Jonathan Cape, 1963), p. 18.

33. G. M. Durant, *Britain, Rome's Most Northerly Province*, p. 49. Webster, *The Roman Imperial Army*, p. 57, states that the wall was fronted by a twenty-foot berm and a ditch with an average width of about twenty-seven feet and a depth of approximately nine feet. The vallum, situated on the south side of the wall, was a

flat-bottomed ditch eight feet wide at the bottom, twenty feet at the top, and ten feet deep. The Romans placed the dirt taken from the ditch in two berms, on each side of and equidistant from the ditch. Each of the berms was twenty feet wide and six feet high, with turf revetments placed so that the distance from crest to crest was a hundred feet. See also Frere, *Britannia*, pp. 132–133. It is striking to note that over five million cubic yards of earth would have been excavated to form the ditches.

34. Ian A. Richmond, "Hadrian's Wall, 1939–1949," *JRS* 40 (1950): 43–56. Collingwood and Richmond, *Archaeology of Roman Britain*, pp. 76–79. Frere, *Britannia*, pp. 132–133, mentions that the milecastles, situated every Roman mile, were miniature forts, varying in inside dimensions from fifty to sixty feet in width and sixty-five to seventy-five feet in length. They contained one or two gateways, one into the milecastle and one through the wall itself. A stairway led up to the patrol track on the wall. The turrets, so distributed as to form three intervals between the milecastles, were recessed into the wall and measured fourteen feet internally. An essential feature of the wall system was the Military Way, a road located behind the wall and linking the forts, milecastles, and turrets.

35. During the reign of Antoninus Pius (A.D. 138–161), the frontier was temporarily transferred north to the Forth–Clyde line, where a turf wall was constructed on a stone base, with a ditch in front and forts at intervals. This new border was probably abandoned about 186–187, and, under Septimius Severus, Hadrian's Wall again became the primary frontier line. See Fergus Millar, *The Roman Empire and its Neighbours*, p. 111; Collingwood and Richmond, *Archaeology of Roman Britain*, p. 88; Frere, *Britannia*, pp. 141–147.

36. See Collingwood and Richmond, *Archaeology of Roman Britain*, pp. 16–20, 25: Frere, *Britannia*, pp. 61–62; Luttwak, *The Grand Strategy of the Roman Empire*, p. 73.

37. H. Schonberger, "The Roman Frontier in Germany: An Archaeological Survey," *JRS* 49 (1969): 149–153; Millar, *The Roman Empire and Its Neighbours*, pp. 111–112.

38. Theodor Mommsen, *The Provinces of the Roman Empire*, p. 123. See also Schonberger, "The Roman Frontier in Germany," pp. 149–153; Colin M. Wells, *The German Policy of Augustus*, pp. 101–147; Petit, *Pax Romana*, p. 27.

39. The Romans had earlier been able to occupy the territory of the modern Netherlands, but excessively harsh taxation policies had sparked a native revolt through which the Romans lost the region. This incident is discussed in detail in chapter 4.

40. U. Kahrstadt, "The Roman Frontier on the lower Rhine in the Early Imperial Period," in *Congress of Roman Frontier Studies. 1949*, pp. 96–98. See also Millar, *The Roman Empire and Its Neighbours*, pp. 111–112; and Schonberger, "The Roman Frontier in Germany," pp. 141–154.

41. Millar, *The Roman Empire and Its Neighbours*, p. 112. See also Petit, *Pax Romana*, pp. 33–37; and Schonberger, "The Roman Frontier in Germany," p. 166.

42. Webster, *The Roman Imperial Army*, p. 69, credits Domitian with strengthening the defenses of the middle Rhine by subduing the Chatti and building a new frontier in the Taunus and Wetterau between the Lahn and the Main, some thirty miles east of the Rhine. The result was a broad salient pushed into Germany, fortified with a line of timber watchtowers and signal stations, and in

communication with the forts by then established in the plain of the Main. See also Schonberger, "The Roman Frontier in Germany," pp. 166–173.

43. See Millar, *The Roman Empire and Its Neighbours*, p. 112; also Schonberger, "The Roman Frontier in Germany," p. 170; and Johnson, *Roman Forts of the First and Second Centuries* A.D., p. 67. Johnson suggests that by the second century, in the reigns of Trajan and Hadrian, the earth-and-timber forts constructed during the Flavian pacification of Wales and northern Britain and those built along the frontier of Upper Germany had begun to decay and required substantial repairs and refurbishment.

44. Webster, *The Roman Imperial Army*, p. 87, describes this barrier as consisting of a wooden palisade set in a steep-sided trench three to four feet deep. The tree trunks were generally one foot in diameter and set at approximately one foot intervals. This timber fence stood about nine feet high above the ground. Unmortared wall was occasionally used in rocky areas. See also Schonberger, "The Roman Frontier in Germany," p. 171. This palisade is generally considered a less impressive accomplishment than the British wall, but one should note that if the palisade were only 500 miles in length, and it was more, over two-and-a-half million trees were felled, hauled, and set in place to construct it. See also Johnson, "Roman Forts," p. 9.

45. See G. Behrens, *Römisch Gläser aus den Rheinlanden*; Olwen Brogan, "Trade between the Roman Empire and the Free Germans," *JRS* 26 (1936): 196–223; Jurgen Kunow, *Der römische Import in der Germania libera bis zu den Markomannenkriegen: Studien zu Bronze- und Glasgefassen*; Hans Norling-Christensen, "Danish Imports of Roman and Roman Provincial Objects in Bronze and Glass," in *Congress of Roman Frontier Studies. 1949*, p. 76.

46. It would be well to consider what the Romans meant when they used the word *limes*. It was neither border nor fortifications. Benjamin Issac, "The Meaning of the Terms Limes and Limitanei," *JRS* 78 (1988): 125, 146, notes that modern scholars generally refer to the *limes* as an organized system of permanent fortifications linked by roads following a set boundary. Latin literary sources, however, never described a *limes* as a series of forts. Several literary sources refer to Germanic campaigns in the first century and employ the term in describing the building of military roads. From the end of the first until the third century, *limes* is used to describe a demarcated land border of the empire, but not military structures or frontier organization.

47. Andrès Mócsy, *Pannonia and Upper Moesia: A History of the Middle Danube Provinces of the Roman Empire*, pp. 39, 80–81; Geza Alföldy, *Noricum*, pp. 52–62. See also Grant, *The Climax of Rome*, p. 16.

48. Mócsy, *Pannonia and Upper Moesia*, pp. 80–120, places three Pannonian legions in the southwest of the province, not far from the border with Italy, in the year A.D. 14. Auxiliary detachments were stationed in forts at Aquincum (Budapest) and Arrabona on the Danube. The first legionary base on the Danube itself was established at Carnuntum in A.D. 15. The legions in Moesia were originally stationed south of the Danube, but the legionary base at Carnuntum was joined by three more in the middle of the century. See also Millar, *The Roman Empire and Its Neighbours*, pp. 112–113.

49. Webster, *The Roman Imperial Army*, p. 113; Luttwak, *The Grand Strategy of the Roman Army*, p. 85.

50. See Ioan Glodariu, *Dacian Trade with the Hellenistic and Roman World*; and Mócsy, *Pannonia and Upper Moesia*.

51. In addition to the conquest of Dacia, Trajan had extended Rome's eastern frontier to Basra on the Persian Gulf. This latter conquest was particularly expensive since it encroached on the territory of a powerful Persian empire. Hadrian was restrained from abandoning Dacia only because of the large numbers of Roman colonists already resident there.

52. Hadrian spent most of his reign traveling throughout the empire, directing local works and inspecting army units. This personal supervision had much to do with the success of his policies.

53. Tacitus, *Germania* 29, states that the Batavians, a tribe of this area, provided men for fighting service in lieu of taxes.

54. In fact, the Marcomanni and their allies broke through the upper Danube defenses in 166. Their attack was contained only by allowing large numbers of them to settle depopulated regions of the empire.

55. Part of the reason for the absence of substantial evidence of a massive trade along the frontier water route is that much of the material moved in this fashion—grain, cloth, meats and fish, timber, pitch and tar, for example—would have been consumable or perishable.

56. The historian Tacitus had extensive experience with the British and upper Rhine frontiers. He certainly had enough knowledge to write the description of the German tribes contained in the *Germania*. The reader of this work cannot help but be struck by the degree to which his description of the German "barbarians" also serves as a criticism of the lack of simple virtues in the Roman way of life.

III FEEDING THE ARMY: THE AGRARIAN SETTLEMENT

Demand and Supply

The imperial administrators had no intention of supplying indefinitely the tens of thousands of troops they were moving to the new frontier. Nor would they have been able to do so if they had wanted to. They intended from the start that the army would be supplied as fully and quickly as possible from local resources and with a minimal financial burden on the imperial treasury. Levies in kind in lieu of taxes began almost as soon as the first troops arrived on station. The huge military requirements for foodstuffs provided a critical demand that necessitated a rapid increase in local production.[1]

Moreover, the military attracted civilians to the frontier. These immigrants fell into two general groups. The first consisted of a nonagricultural population of administrators, craftsmen, merchants, and their families, who provided an additional market for foodstuffs and raw materials. Since both Germans and Celts had traditionally been pastoralists, particularly stockmen, there were extensive tracts of essentially free, agriculturally underutilized lands in the frontier regions, at least in the early days of frontier settlement. Free lands and the prospect of immediate profits from the sale of agricultural products attracted a second group of Roman and Romanized newcomers composed of agricultural laborers and developers; this group led the way in the agricultural development of the frontier districts.[2]

Military procurement policies were of primary importance in the location and success of agricultural centers, but civil settlements also played a role. The civilian population tended to concentrate near sources of raw materials or fertile land, and where there were convenient roads or water routes leading to military depots and procurement centers.[3] The typical civil settlement that emerged at such locations consisted of an urban center, in which governmental activities, trading, processing, and manufacturing were centered, surrounded by farms and estates producing a surplus of farm products as well as supporting some processing and light manufacture. Farm goods were hauled to the urban center, where merchants either arranged for local retail sale or shipment for the military markets.[4] This integrated rural-urban settlement pattern was not only well adapted to the Romans' immediate frontier needs, but it allowed them to reproduce on the frontier the pattern of local government and economy typical of the heartland of the empire.[5] These frontier settlements were atypical, however, in the abundant natural resources they normally commanded and in the degree to which their activities were conditioned, or even controlled, by military needs. Although the hinterlands of the frontier regions were frequently under civil administration, the frontier districts themselves were generally under direct military government. In either case, the army provided a generally secure environment in which economic development could be pursued, and it offered a normally steady and predictable market for surplus agricultural produce.[6] One might add to these factors the army's assumption of responsibility for providing efficient means of transportation and communication, and the military's general disinclination to engage in economic planning for a civilian population.[7] The combination of these factors allowed purely economic considerations to work with unaccustomed freedom on the Roman frontier. The result was the eventual production of a substantial surplus of agricultural commodities along the frontier, coupled with the growth of new markets to absorb that surplus.[8]

The methods by which surplus agricultural production was achieved varied according to local conditions, but the introduction of Roman managerial techniques was a common aspect of the process throughout the frontier regions. The sophisticated Roman approach to agrarian development and exploitation was, paradoxically enough, at least partly the result of the limitations of Roman agricultural technology.

Roman Agriculture

The basic tool of Roman agriculture,[9] other than the spade, was the simple scratch plow, without share or coulter. The limitations of agriculture dependent upon such a plow were many. Only light upland soils could be tilled; more fertile bottom lands required a plow that would cut through the earth. Plowing was necessarily shallow, and the fertility of arable land was quickly depleted. Moreover, since the earth was not turned in the process of plowing, each plot had to be tilled twice, in a crisscross pattern, before seeding and harrowing. Roman fields therefore tended to be rectangular, and required a large number of time-consuming turnings of the plow in addition to their need to be tilled twice.[10] The advantages of the overall system were that it required little capital investment in the way of draft animals, harness, and plows.[11] The disadvantages were that it was labor-intensive and relatively low in productivity per unit of both land and labor. Nevertheless, it was a system that was sufficiently well adapted to the lands of the Mediterranean littoral, where Roman society had originated and where the bulk of its population was still concentrated. Much of the land there consisted of light, rocky soils in which the use of expensive heavy plows would have provided only a small increase in productivity at best.

The Roman diet was consonant with the limited agricultural resources of the region. While the Germans and Celts consumed beef, butter, and beer, the Romans preferred bread, oil, and wine. Moreover, caloric intake in the colder northern climates was considerably higher than along the Mediterranean, and the sea supplemented the Roman diet with a plentiful supply of fish. Finally, their appetite for fruits and vegetables provided the Romans with variety and vitamins. In short, Roman dietary habits compensated in large measure for the shortcomings of Roman agricultural technology.

This balance between production and consumption could be maintained, however, only when a proper balance was maintained between the agricultural and nonagricultural populations, and when the population of a given region did not exceed the capacity of the land to support it. As Rome expanded, however, and as an increasing proportion of its population was absorbed into the processing and service sectors of its economy, agriculture had to be improved both in terms of production and productivity. The Romans possessed a constant source of agricultural laborers in the form of war prisoners and conquered peoples. During the late republic, slaves began to compensate for the diversion of so many Romans from agriculture into administrative and military pursuits.

The Roman Villa as a Frontier Institution

The development of an effective slave system is dependent upon organization and management, and the Roman upper classes provided that management and enjoyed the profits of increased agricultural production. The Roman upper classes had possessed country estates from time immemorial, and generally divided their time between their official, urban lives, and their private lives in the country. It was the ambition of every owner of such an estate, called a villa, to make his main house as elegant as possible, to acquire as many amenities as possible, and to make the entire establishment as self-sufficient and profitable as possible. As a result, a typical villa was more like a village than a farm.[12] It employed a number of workers, both free and slave, and consisted of several buildings, some reserved for specialized functions such as the processing of animal and agricultural products, as well as light manufacture. The villa was similar in many ways to some of the better-managed plantation estates of the antebellum American South.

The estates of the American South expanded quickly with the development of staple crops such as cotton and tobacco, coupled with an increased supply of slave labor. The Roman estates expanded in much the same manner, and under much the same circumstances. In the early stages of this expansion, villa owners bought up abandoned farms in their vicinity and brought them back into cultivation. Soon, however, the productive capacities of such large, well-managed establishments began to drive small independent farmers off the land, which was then bought up to increase the size and number of villas even further. The strengths of the villa system were in some ways similar to those of the Roman legions. The villa owner controlled the disciplined labor of large slave gangs, often run by senior slaves, as well as being able to rely on specially trained slaves for expertise in a number of areas such as accounting, wine-making, pottery, stewardship, carpentry, architecture, and the like.

The productive capacities of the villa system were so great, and its flexibility so superior, that it was the preferred means by which the Romans exploited their agricultural frontiers of underutilized or newly seized lands. The villa slave gangs and expert managers and craftsmen could quickly bring land under cultivation and construct, if needed, a walled and fortified main house. With time and pacification, a villa could become like a small Roman town, featuring a library, bath and swimming facilities, appointments for refined entertaining, well-planned gardens, carefully selected or commissioned works of art, and a professionally conceived architectural plan.[13] The villa was not intended merely as a tourist sight, however. The artisans and craftsmen of the villa produced objects for sale, and it is probable that these villas served their neighborhoods as trading centers. Finally, a villa owner was usually wealthy and cultured, a man his native neighbors could admire and emulate.[14]

From the scholar's point of view, the flexibility of the villas provides an unusual opportunity to gain insights into some of the social and economic processes at work on the Roman frontier. The organization and functions of the villa were not abstract qualities, but were directly reflected in the architecture of the villa's buildings, the layout of its fields, the number and activities of its labor force, and its relationship to its neighbors. All of these features have left their mark on the archaeological remains of the villas. Since the villas were so flexible, much can be deduced from their floor plans, successive rebuilding, and relationship to local transportation networks, and from the general debris left behind from centuries of occupation.

The first demand placed upon a frontier district was that it should develop the agricultural capacity to feed the local units of Roman troops. This was not an aspiration, but a requirement. Anyone who failed to respond to this challenge would eventually find himself without his land, and perhaps even without his freedom.[15] The immediacy of this challenge was mitigated by two factors, however. First, the military units were usually prepared to have supplies shipped in from other districts for a period of time, and, second, villas quickly appeared in new lands to take advantage of the free land and military markets in the vicinity. Such villas were often imitated by the upper classes of the native population, and the future development of the agricultural potential of the district then depended on the evolution of a productive and stable mixture of Roman-style villas, and the surviving native farms and villages.[16]

The Roman villa was not only flexible, but adaptable. Estate owners had successfully managed to integrate the villa system into the varied social and economic systems of the Roman world, and were quite capable of adapting it to the peculiar conditions of the frontier. This ability of the villa system to integrate with its surrounding environment served as an essential element in the development of the agricultural frontier. A Roman villa was not an isolated entity but a part of a much more extensive social and economic structure. This was reflected in part by the type of labor employed on the frontier villas. The use of slave gangs had been a fundamental aspect of the early growth of the great villas of the empire, but the imperial decision to end expansion slowly closed off the major source of slaves. A steady flow of prisoners and enslaved tribes had previously compensated for the short life span and low reproduction rate of gang slaves,[17] but this flow had now ended and the price of slaves in the heartland of the empire had begun to rise.

There were more ample supplies of slave labor on the frontier, since frontier tribes were always able to secure human beings as trade goods. Nevertheless, the difficulty of keeping slaves so close to a frontier, coupled with the fact that such slaves would yield more profit if sold in the interior than if employed in farming the frontier, led the villa owners to seek other sources of labor. This fact is evident in the physical remains of many of the frontier villas, in which there are no barracks for slave gangs. In this sense, the Roman frontier was a land of relative freedom. It would appear that the villa owners of the frontier, although there were many variations and exceptions, had come generally to rely on tenant farmers, and salaried workers and artisans, for their labor force.[18]

In the process of becoming centers of free labor, the frontier villas began to perform a number of incidental, but significant functions. With a large number of sharecropping tenants, they became agricultural administrative centers. Seed was stored there, and decisions were made as to what crops were to be planted, by whom, and where. Individual tenants were loaned equipment and draft animals, and could expect supplementary labor from the villa if it were needed. The villa artisans made and repaired agricultural equipment, and stewards and accountants forced the tenant to rationalize his farming methods. A portion of the crop went to the villa owner, and, if the tenant could increase his total production, he would retain his share of that increase. Throughout the frontier, Roman-style villas are found in proximity to native farms and villages. Although it cannot be determined to what degree native farmers may have worked in conjunction with the villas as tenants, it is probable that the managers of the villas directed much native agricultural production. Moreover, the villas offered a source of salaried employment for the local population, in the course of which the employees would have received a good education in agricultural, processing, and managerial techniques. In abandoning their dependence on slave labor, the villa owners may have made their estates the agricultural schools of the frontier. In any event, the villas played a major role in the agricultural development of frontier lands.

The extension of the villa system to the frontier regions of the empire was relatively rapid. There are remains of substantial villas in Gaul and elsewhere on the continent dating from the mid second century and even earlier. Even in Britain, where growth was generally slower and later, there were a number of villas prior to the third century.[19] There were great variations in the physical attributes of such villas, due to differences in local factors such as market availability, access to transport and communication, the relative abundance of local resources, and the characteristics of existing native economic and social organizations and institutions.[20] Another source of differentiation among the villas of the frontier lay in the fact that not all were derived from the same model. The immigrants to the frontier rarely came directly from Italy; the majority were natives of those pacified and Romanized provinces adjacent to the frontier regions. They came with institutions that had already been modified during the period when their own areas had constituted the frontier of the empire. Thus the villas of Pannonia were versions of Illyrian villas adapted to local circumstances. The Illyrian villas, however, were in turn versions of Dalmatian villas that had been adapted to the special needs of Illyria and the Illyrian people.

Because of these variations, the villas and their systems of cultivation, like other Roman civil institutions, assumed different forms in different parts of the frontier. Individual districts displayed widely differing degrees of Romanization in rural areas. Extensive villa building took place in some frontier districts, but in others the local population continued to live in native-style farms or villages. Whatever the extent or variant of the villa system employed, however, archaeological evidence indicates that the majority of the estates within a given frontier region had clearly been occupied by members of the native population. The model for technological and managerial advances was provided by a relatively small number of immigrants. The character of the local agrarian economy was determined largely by what use the local population made of these techniques in adapting to its new role within the imperial system.[21] This being the case, it is necessary to evaluate the agrarian economy of each of the frontier regions in turn. Since the main building was the core of the villa, and numerous examples have been excavated, consideration of the villa floor plans popular in the various frontier districts helps to provide initial insight into the character of the agrarian societies influenced by the example of the villa system.[22]

Native Adaptation along the Rhine

The hall-type villa was popular on the continent for a considerable period, and in several regions it was the dominant form of villa architecture throughout the Roman era. The characteristic of the hall-type floor plan was that it consisted of a rectangular hall of considerable size. Place-names such as Salamanca in Spain, derived from the Latin *sala magna* (great hall), suggest that the Romans themselves regarded the hall as the defining component of such structures. In time, this basic design was elaborated by the addition of a corridor with flanking rooms and other refinements. The remains of many villas of this type have been discovered in Lorraine, along the Moselle, and in the Rhineland.

The hall-type plan is similar to buildings at both Celtic and German sites dating from before as well as after the advent of the Romans in the region. It has been suggested that the popularity of the hall-type villa may have been the result of strong native elements coexisting with or beneath the Romanized social structure. If so, the large single room at the heart of the native-owned hall-type villa may have provided group living and sleeping quarters. The commonality and basic egalitarianism of such an arrangement has suggested to some historians and archaeologists that the native society that lived in such a fashion was organized more by kinship than by social class.[23] This is an attractive hypothesis, but is weakened by place-names that indicate that hall-type villas were built over a relatively wide area of the empire.

The fact of the matter is that the large hall could have been subdivided in many different ways through the use of screens and curtains when serving as private quarters, and that these could have been removed when the owner wished to use the hall as public space. Later German and Celtic literary evidence portrays the great hall as the place where the owner would receive visitors, distribute gifts, and hold entertainments. Sheer size can impress, and it is likely that this was an important function of the great hall. The size of the hall established the power and wealth of the owner in the eyes of the visitor, and allowed the owner to enhance his prestige by providing him with a setting in which to display his liberality by offering food, drink, and sleeping quarters to a large number of visitors and followers.[24] Place-names based on *sala magna* suggest that it was the great hall that impressed the villa owner's neighbors.

The hall-type villa thus may have been a tool for its owner to achieve or maintain status and social power. Such tools are largely unnecessary in societies where status and power are firmly established by law or custom, which would suggest that hall-type structures appealed to the Celts and Germans because their societies were in a state of flux in which status had to be won and defended. It would appear that in the Rhineland and adjacent regions, the Roman hall-type villa plan coincided with the traditional native architecture and met the peculiar social needs of the local population. The large single room may have reflected a lack of distinction between private and public space, and both Romanized immigrant and resident native villa owners may have gained prestige and social power through the sheer size of their great halls.

The archaeological investigation of large numbers of rural sites in the Rhineland and adjacent districts reveals that, in the first century, a dichotomy existed between large landowners possessing numerous dependents on the one hand and small independent landowners on the other.[25] The average-size villa in the Rhineland, the Saar, and Lorraine contained approximately 400 *jugera*, or about 260 acres.[26] This is a surprisingly low figure, and other regions were characterized by substantially larger villas. If one estimates that one-third of the lands of an average villa were forest and waste, one-third fallow, and one-third tilled, the average villa of the Rhineland and its hinterland would have had no more than eighty-seven acres under cultivation at any one time. Given a plowing season of about a month, such a villa would have required four plow teams for tilling and would have had a gross production of less than a thousand bushels of wheat. The surplus for sale would have been quite small.[27] The rural districts of this region were densely populated and intensively cultivated,[28] and one wonders why such fertile land, convenient to substantial military markets, was not controlled by large landowners.

Several explanations for this development are possible. The traditional Germanic system of hereditary law, known as *gavelkind* in historic times, dictated that each son, or sometimes each child regardless of sex, should receive an equal share of the parents' property. Such a system, when employed by a growing population with a fixed amount of land at its disposal, inevitably leads to morselization of tenure and a steady decrease in the size of the average land holding. Such a development would not have displeased Roman administrators. The system would have created a surplus population valuable to the empire as a source of recruits for the *auxilia* and later for the legions themselves. Also, catastrophic mortality through plague and war was a common feature of the Roman world. Heavily populated and extensively cultivated districts were best able to continue high levels of production under such conditions. Although a sizable portion of a large population might die, the remaining members would still be numerous and could concentrate their efforts on the most productive lands. The loss of productive capacity would thus be minimized. Finally, it should be remembered that the Romans taxed individuals rather than income. The greater the population of a district, the more revenue it produced for the state.

If this evaluation is correct, the bulk of the rural population of the Rhineland were relatively small farmers, producing barely enough surplus to pay their taxes. A few large estate owners stood out from their neighbors by the size of their holdings and houses, but they had little actual power in their districts apart from their personal influence. Although the general distribution of land and wealth in the area could be temporarily disrupted in the wake of a plague or civil war, the system was generally stable. There was a large population available to serve as agricultural workers at relatively low wages, and there was thus no need for slave labor even if the average villa owner could have afforded it. The stability of this state of affairs was secured by a relatively steady emigration from the countryside, with some people perhaps entering trade and manufacturing in the urban centers of the region, but the majority entering the military. Nevertheless, there were no great opportunities for individual advancement in the region, and a general dissatisfaction of the native population may have been partially reflected in the notorious readiness of the Rhine legions to rebel.[29]

Britain and the Fenlands Project

The villa system of Britain, and presumably rural conditions in general, differed in certain significant respects from that of the Rhineland.

In Britain, the evolution of the hall-type villa continued after the addition of a corridor and side rooms. Even in quite early sites, the great hall had disappeared, leaving an expanded corridor as the dominant feature of the floor plan. At the same time, the outbuildings that had formed part of the villa complex vanished, and the side rooms presumably filled their functions. It has been claimed that this basilica-type villa plan represents a specifically Celtic adaptation of a basic Roman model. The prevalence of the self-contained basilica-type villas in Britain may imply the growth of a class of native landowners who employed the villa system but adapted it to their own particular character and needs.[30]

Other possible explanations also exist. The basilicas, numbers of which were built in the new Roman towns of Britain, were the buildings in which edicts were read, court cases decided, and contracts registered. Before the advent of the Romans, local chieftains had served their people as judges. The basilica that formed the dominant feature of the Roman villas in Britain was a public space that may have served to remind visitors that the traditional powers of the local upper classes had survived into the Roman world, although in altered guise. At the same time, the Romanized immigrant estate owner may have felt more comfortable contracting with his employees and sharecropping tenants in a room that evoked the spirit and power of Roman law.

The legions and auxiliaries represented the vast majority of immigrants to Britain. Other than military personnel, the actual number of newcomers was probably rather small, although their influence on the native population was out of proportion to their actual numbers. It was primarily the British who had to develop the means to supply the Roman garrisons, and this was a substantial task. The British population was not numerous, and the occupying force was large in relation to the island's resources. It has been estimated that the army in Britain required about 530,000 bushels of grain a year as rations for men and horses.

A simple calculation of the labor needed may put this requirement in perspective. A Roman plow team, consisting of an ox and two workers, could till twenty acres in a plowing season of thirty days. The average yield per acre of reasonably good grain land was, up to early modern times, about eight bushels. Two bushels of seed were required to yield eight bushels, however, so the net yield per acre would have been about six bushels. This means that the net production of a plow team was about 120 bushels. The annual cereal ration for a Roman soldier was eleven bushels, and one might assume that the consumption of the farm worker was not much lower. The two-man plow team, their wives, and two children may have needed about sixty-six bushels for their own sustenance. This would mean that each plow team produced a surplus of fifty-four bushels, or the cereal rations for about five soldiers. The total military grain requirement of 530,000 bushels would thus have represented the surplus production of 10,000 plow teams, or about 60,000 people.[31]

Considered from another point of view, these 10,000 plow teams would have cultivated 200,000 acres of land. Another 200,000 acres would have to be tilled even though fallow and nonproductive.[32] A minimum of 30,000–50,000 additional acres would have been needed for grazing and winter feed for 10,000 draft animals, and a similar amount for roads, plowing headlands, field divisions, drainage ditches, houses and cottage gardens for the work force,[33] and similar purposes. The provision of the cereal ration for the Roman army in Britain would thus have required the tilling of about eight hundred square miles by a population of 60,000 people or more.

During the early stages of the occupation, imports supplied much of the military's needs, although this was doubtless only a temporary measure. It would appear that the imperial government took the initiative in developing the local resources necessary to fill this need. In a great project begun perhaps around A.D. 60–70, the marshlands of the Fens of eastern Britain were drained and put under cultivation. At the height of the Fenlands' agricultural development, probably during the reign of Hadrian, half a million acres had been developed for agricultural use, and the entire district possibly served as an imperial estate.[34] An elaborate system of canals served to drain the area and to furnish inland water routes or access to seaports from which commodities could be shipped to the frontier districts in northern England. Straight boundary lines, an elaborate road and track system, and a "Roman" angularity provided a sense of order and, coupled with the scarcity of Celtic field patterns in the northern Fens,[35] illustrate the degree to which this development was the product of Roman direction.[36]

The impact of this particular project upon the native population can only be imagined. Half a million acres, or 750,000 *jugera* of arable land, was an immense amount. Given the probability that the Fens were an imperial estate, it is likely that the agricultural workers moved there were levied from neighboring tribes, and that part of their labor was in lieu of taxes.[37] Their condition cannot have been happy. The Fens were damp and short of fuel, and the residents were doubtless troubled by sickness and high infant mortality. Moreover, the only economic pursuit traditionally valued among free Germans and Celts was the raising of cattle. Wealth and status were reckoned by the size and quality of one's herds,[38] and cultivation was the province of slaves and servants. The workers in the Fens had not only been moved to an unhealthy district, but had also been stripped of status.

It is intriguing to note that the total amount of land finally brought under cultivation in the Fenlands was quite close to the area we calculated would be necessary to provide the grain ration for the entire Roman army in Britain. The totals become even closer when one considers that a substantially greater amount of area in the Fens would have to be devoted to drainage ditches and shipping canals. It seems quite possible that the Fenlands were developed by imperial authorities over a period extending from about A.D. 70 to 140 for the specific purpose of filling the army's complete requirement for cereals.

This vast imperial project had a fundamental effect on the development of Roman Britain. One could argue that it led indirectly to a Roman failure to integrate the British provinces fully into the empire as a whole or to leave any lasting impression on the island. In order to appreciate the consequences of the Fenlands project, one must remember that Roman Britain consisted of two quite different regions. The Southeast had been the wealthiest, most sophisticated and culturally advanced, and most densely populated portion of the island prior to the Roman conquest. Nevertheless, it had been the most easily conquered and had quickly become a zone of civil, rather than military, administration. The North and West, by contrast, were mountainous, relatively poor, and thinly populated. These regions, however, had doggedly resisted Roman occupation.

The West, the Welsh peninsula, was finally occupied by Roman forces, who built a system of forts and military roads throughout the district. The North of the island, the area of Scotland, was never conquered, and a permanent frontier district developed between the legionary forts at Chester and York, and Hadrian's Wall some one hundred miles to the north. Both Wales and the northern frontier district remained under a military administration that made little apparent effort to win the frontier tribes over to the Roman way of life.

Freed by production in the Fenlands from having to concern themselves with supplying grain to the army, the civil authorities of the Southeast interfered relatively little with the agrarian economy of the region. The greatest Roman influence on this sector of the economy lay in the introduction of new crops, such as cabbages, peas, parsnips, turnips, carrots, plums, apples, cherries, and walnuts. Archaeological evidence suggests that the native British agricultural system and agrarian society continued relatively unchanged in many districts. With the loss of independent political power, tribal chieftains began to assume the role of an upper class of large estate owners. Similar transformations of native society had occurred elsewhere along the frontier, but in other areas the need to increase agricultural production had driven such rural aristocrats to lead their people in agricultural development. The native aristocracy of the Southeast of Britain was spared that responsibility by the Fenlands development.

The large landowners had little stimulus to adopt Roman agricultural methods, and the establishment and expansion of the villa system of exploitation progressed sporadically in Britain. In some districts, in fact, it did not progress at all. The Roman civil administrators were apparently unconcerned by this. Their plan of Romanization was directed not so much toward improving the British agricultural technology as changing the native pattern of living. The Roman administration of the island made a conscious effort to modify traditional, diffuse Celtic society into a more centralized system focused on urban life, and they concentrated their efforts on winning over the native aristocracy. The effect of this program of social engineering was to transform the native British aristocracy into a Romano-British elite, and to divorce them in great degree from the bulk of the native population and its traditional patterns of life.

This may in fact have been the objective of the imperial administration from the beginning. A people separated from their leaders constitutes relatively little threat, and their inability to advance technologically is a small price to pay for such inexpensive security. The improvement of local productive capacities occurred only after many years of development, and in some districts such improvement was never successfully realized.[39] The bulk of the Celtic population of the southeast did not develop the ability to produce surplus farm produce for trade, and, as a consequence, was unable to participate in many of the benefits of Roman life.

In other frontier districts of the empire, the combination of taxation and military markets had both driven and led the native populations to adopt Roman agricultural technology and organization in order to produce the agricultural surpluses necessary to supply the army of the frontier. The mass of the population was thus absorbed into the greater economy of the Roman world and came to adopt, if only imperfectly, other aspects of Roman society and culture. In Britain, however, imperial projects involving more or less forced labor met the basic needs of the army and spared the rest of the native population the necessity of pursuing economic development. The provincial authorities instead attempted to win over the local elite to Roman social and cultural standards of life.

They succeeded in doing so to a large extent. The archaeology of the civil zone of southeast England has uncovered numerous and extensive villas, palaces, and local capitals. In the long run, however, the Romanization of the province was only a veneer. Since they no longer commanded the allegiance of the lower classes, the Romano-British upper classes depended upon the protection and markets provided by the Roman army and administrators. When Roman forces were withdrawn, the upper classes could neither govern nor protect themselves. Many fled the island in the face of invaders, and the bulk of the population, which had never been absorbed within the greater Roman economy, soon demonstrated that traditional Celtic patterns of speech, culture, and political and social organization had persisted in British rural society, largely unaffected by the Romanization of their traditional leaders.

By the late second or early third century, the Fenlands project began to be abandoned and the land given over to sheep and cattle raising.[40] The reason was not simply that the district was admirably suited to such pursuits or that the army's appetite for meat was increasing, but that the native population of the northern frontier districts was beginning to produce surpluses of grain and other goods that filled a growing portion of the army's requirements.[41] Archaeological remains allow one to trace the evolution of this northern agricultural frontier and to gain some sense of the agrarian society that evolved there.

The agricultural transformation of the frontier districts of Roman Britain was the result of their residents' responding to nearby military markets and to the availability of Roman manufactured goods. The earliest signs of the growth of the northern agrarian economy are found in native farms in the immediate vicinity of military bases, such as Carlisle and Corbridge on Hadrian's Wall. Roman manufactured goods have been found in almost all farmsteads of this kind. Their ability to acquire Roman factory-made goods suggests that these farmers produced a surplus to sell. It has often been suggested that taxes, requisitions, and military levies combined to reduce the standard of living among the native population of the frontier districts of the empire. However, the archaeological evidence from this particular district suggests the contrary. It would seem that the native population of the district along Hadrian's Wall and in the Cumberland Plain increased in both numbers and prosperity. It is probable that the material prosperity of the frontier district was the result of an economic pattern in which the native farmers sold agricultural produce to the army and bought manufactured goods imported from the Continent and the Southeast of Britain. The importance of Carlisle derived in part from its position as a center of exchange.[42]

This northern agricultural frontier moved rather quickly from the immediate vicinity of the border forts into the Cumberland Plain, some twenty miles to the south. The remains of numerous native farm sites have been found in this area, and allow one to form a general picture of the society and economy there. Although no grain-storage pits or drying kilns have yet been found, there were hand mills for grinding grain. Pollen analysis shows that a large amount of grain had in fact been grown in the district. Few of the farmsteads have the remains of any enclosures suitable for penning cattle or sheep, and it is therefore unlikely that stock raising was an important activity. Many of the farmsteads appear to have been surrounded by large fields laid out with the irregularities characteristic of traditional Celtic farming techniques.

The archaeological evidence clearly indicates that the farmsteads of the northern frontier were devoted to the raising of grain. Moreover, the absence of any storage facilities or drying kilns suggests that the growers raised their grain for sale, and may have marketed most of it to the army directly after harvest.[43] The northern farmsteads tended to concentrate around military centers, and the army undoubtedly served as their major customer.[44] Near Old Carlisle, and in the western portion of the district generally, there were a large number of native farmsteads concentrated along the military roads, situated like Roman villas at favorable locations within a short distance of the highway. This intense exploitation was most probably the result of the combination of uncommonly good land, the security provided by the proximity of the fort at Old Carlisle, and the market facilities provided by the nearby town. It may also be that the local garrison collected grain levies from the farmsteads and villages itself.[45] In any event, the military roads provided transport routes for the district. The use of military roads for such purposes was rather unusual and no doubt contributed to the growth of the local economy, since these roads allowed the northern farmers to exploit good lands even if they were relatively far from procurement centers.

A similar reliance upon road transport of bulk commodities was an important factor in the development of another grain-raising center in the eastern portion of the frontier district. Farmsteads here tended to cluster along a civil road serving the agricultural lands near Old Durham. Modern settlement is rather dense in the area and has made archaeological exploration relatively difficult. As a consequence, fewer farmsteads have been uncovered here than in the vicinity of Old Carlisle. Remains have been found, however, of what were probably two Roman-style villas. Nothing of this sort has been found around Old Carlisle, and there may have been a greater degree of Romanization in the eastern portion of the frontier district. The evidence suggests that the region around Old Durham not only developed a grain-growing economy based upon markets of the frontier forts, but may also have supported the life of a Roman country estate.[46] The archaeological evidence also suggests that integrated economic systems existed in restricted locales in the northern frontier districts. Celtic farmers concentrated along the roads passing through arable lands lying in the vicinity of major northern military posts and devoted themselves to the raising of grain. This grain was transported by road to the frontier forts and to market centers immediately after harvest, perhaps being carried by military procurement troops and civilian wholesalers. Such an arrangement saved farmers the costs and labor of drying, storage, and transport, and allowed them to farm at a greater distance from their markets than would otherwise have been the case. Integrated local economic systems developed in which native farmers supplied grain to army units and wholesalers, who paid in transportation and either cash or credit. The farmers then purchased supplies and manufactured goods in small market centers, such as Old Carlisle and Old Durham, perhaps purchasing from the same merchants who had bought their grain. We shall find that such integrated local exchange systems were a common feature of the economies of the frontier districts, and involved many other commodities besides grain.

The development of this local northern production had its effects as far south as York. The military headquarters for the northern frontier had been established there, a hundred miles south of the actual frontier line. The main reason for this unusual arrangement was that the primary function of York was to serve as a supply center for the troops to the north. Shipping from the Fens could reach York by water via the Car Dyke canal zone, the Trent, and the Ouse; and North Sea shipping could simply use the Humber Estuary. By the early third century, however, the northern districts were requiring less and less bulk shipping of the sort that had been prevalent when their grain had come from the Fens. At the same time, local economic development in the vicinity of York itself had increased to such a degree that the civilian settlement associated with it was able to become independent and receive a municipal charter. Excavations have revealed that civilian York was sizable and possessed rather imposing buildings. While the military functions of York had declined, a vigorous civilian economy had developed in its vicinity. The military headquarters of York was eventually left in a civilian hinterland, while the true frontier lay well to the north.[47]

The unusual imperial attempt to supply the army in Britain through a massive governmental agricultural project had significant effects on the history of Roman Britain. It spared the native population of the rural southeast the necessity of meeting massive grain levies and, in doing so, it denied them the long-term benefits of being an integral part of the Roman frontier. It allowed the Roman authorities to cultivate the aristocracy of the region and to introduce them to Roman society and culture. The effect was to separate them from the population they were supposed to lead. The long-term result was that, although Roman remains in England are impressive, Roman influence left no lasting impression on the island or its inhabitants. In a relatively short time, the emergence of highly productive local economies in the northern military regions rendered the Fenlands grain project obsolete, and the area reverted to grazing land, with the resultant waste of the incredible human effort it must have taken to turn that environment into productive farmland. The north fared well under Roman occupation; its population increased and its newly acquired material prosperity appears to have been widely distributed.

We know little of the social and cultural relationships established between natives and Romans in the northern district, but we do know that the army in Britain became famous for its propensity to mutiny and for setting up its own emperors. It is interesting to note, however, that this generally occurred when the central administration failed to maintain peace and security not only in Britain, but in the western provinces in general. The British troops appear to have been more concerned with conditions in Gaul and the Germanies than in the heartland of the empire. They seem to have identified themselves with a Rome that lay on the periphery of the Western Empire rather than in Italy.

Later legends suggest that this particular sense of being Roman may have run deep in the local population of the North. Long after Roman forces had withdrawn from the island and the aristocracy of the southeast had fled to the continent, a leader called Arthur opposed the advance of the Germanic Anglo-Saxon invaders. Although later romances place him in the South of the island, early accounts have him fighting in the North, and imply that Old Carlisle may have been his stronghold. There is much that is Roman about the figure of Arthur in early accounts. He was named as the son of Uther Pendragon, or "dragonhead." Cloth dragon banners served as auxiliary standards in the late empire, and a "dragonhead" could have been an auxiliary commander. Arthur himself is portrayed as the military commander of the equally shadowy Ambrosius Aurelianus, leading a mixed group of cavalry not unlike a later imperial auxiliary wing. Early accounts place his death sometime around 530.

One of the characteristics of the frontier cultural environments is the frequency with which they give rise to frontier epics. *Martín Fierro*, *Digenes Akritas*, *The Song of Roland*, and the *Mahabharata* are only a few of these. They seem to arise when the frontier is ending, and look back upon the glories of the past. It may well be that the origin of the Arthurian cycle had been an epic of the Roman frontier, arising in the frontier districts of northern Britain, the farthest removed corner of the empire. The epic of Arthur recalls and glorifies a time when the militia of these districts made one last effort to beat back the waves of invaders and to preserve that last corner of an empire that had already fallen.

The Rise and Fall of the Small Farmers on the Danube

The establishment of a frontier on the Danube was motivated primarily by the emperor Augustus's desire to control an additional route connecting the eastern and western portions of the empire and to create a buffer zone to protect the passes through the Julian Alps into Italy. Broad imperial considerations, rather than a desire for new territory, led to the Roman advance to the Danube River. Although the Romans initiated an intensive program of economic development immediately after the conquest, military concerns dictated official policy in this region for the entire period of Roman occupation. The Danubian provinces of Dalmatia, Pannonia, Dacia, Upper and Lower Moesia, Thrace, and the neighboring Black Sea Coast shared a common pattern of historical development and played similar roles in the Roman strategic system. Nevertheless, due to disparate economic, geographic, or social factors, each region had its own special character.[48]

The history of Pannonia during the Roman era was conditioned largely by its geography. The region is watered by three major rivers: the Danube and its tributaries, the Save, and Drave. Both of the latter run eastward from the foothills of the Alps and afford easy access to passes opening into northern Italy. This was perhaps the most practicable land route into the Italian peninsula and certainly the most dangerous from the Romans' point of view.[49] The defense of Italy required the occupation of Pannonia, and that occupation was begun by Augustus as early as 35 B.C. The legions advanced from the province of Dalmatia on the Adriatic coast, first establishing fortresses on the Save and pacifying the territory behind them. They then advanced to the Drave and repeated the process. It was not until A.D. 6 that Roman forces had firmly established themselves on the middle Danube.

One of the difficulties in the conquest of Pannonia lay in the degree to which pacification lagged behind occupation. In 12 to 9 B.C. and again in A.D. 6 to 9, the Pannonians rose in revolts that the Romans had great difficulty suppressing. The elimination of the threat of further uprisings, the security of the overland route across the Balkans, and the need to supply the troops posted on the Danube all required that Pannonia be pacified and that the agricultural production of the region be increased as much as possible. Such considerations practically dictated that Italian settlers be established in at least a few strategic locations. Forest covered much of the land, but there were some open and arable tracts suitable for agricultural settlement. Archaeological evidence indicates that villas were established in these locations during the first century A.D., and that general settlement had been achieved by the beginning of the second century.[50]

Data from the early villas of these districts indicate that, unlike most of the districts of the Roman frontier, the majority of the early agrarian population of Roman Pannonia were immigrant settlers. As early as the reign of Tiberius (A.D. 14–37), retired veterans and north Italian traders were resident in the district of Scarbantia, some thirty miles south of the main Danubian legionary fortress of Carnuntum (Deutsch-Altenburg). By the reign of Domitian (81–96), similar settlers had established themselves on the shores of Lake Pelso, one hundred miles further south. The villa settlement of the upper valley of the Drave was begun under Trajan (98–117), who provided military veterans with land grants in the vicinity of Poetovio, a former legionary fortress.

The chronological progression of these settlements is suggestive. Rather than moving out from the Italian heartland toward the frontier districts of the Danube, the frontier of Roman agricultural development in Pannonia moved south and west from the major legionary fortress on the middle Danube, following the main road leading to the passes through the Julian Alps. Further settlement expanded from these centers and from Illyria on the Adriatic coast. Villa cultivation spread from the early settlements on the upper Save and Drave to fill the triangle between Poetovio on the Drave, and Emona and Siscia on the Save. Early villas also appeared further along the Save as far as Sirmium, not far from the confluence of the Save and the Danube. Villa agriculture along the river valleys not only exploited the most fertile lands of the region, but permitted the shipment of farm commodities by boat to the troops on the frontier. It is clear that the early agrarian development of Pannonia was a process aimed at the defense of the approaches to northern Italy, and that it was probably financed by the military markets of the middle Danube and manned by retired veterans of the army of the frontier. The lands of the lower Save and Drave, which lay within the military zone of the frontier districts, were opened up later, in a process perhaps aided by the Pannonian fleet.

The physical characteristics of the early villas have not yet been fully investigated, but there is better evidence for the later period. The pioneering villas of the region eventually developed into prosperous, but not lavish, farms,[51] and the entire area possessed a healthy mixture of many small villas and a few large ones. This general situation began to change in the end of the second century. By the early third century, a number of the smaller villas had been abandoned, and the region was dominated by the greater estates, such as the huge villa complex at

Parndorf. These great estates continued to be occupied into the late fourth century, although with substantial alterations.[52]

A number of events in the late second century had probably combined to transform the agrarian society and economy of Roman Pannonia. Around A.D. 160, a great plague swept through the empire, and many districts were almost depopulated as a result. As in the Black Death of the Middle Ages, family farms probably suffered more than larger establishments, since it was quite possible for an entire family to die and its property to be abandoned. This rarely happened to large estates simply because of their greater populations. There were yet other problems. Immediately following the plague, in the period 166–175, the powerful frontier tribes of the Marcomanni and Quadi crossed the upper Danube and devastated wide areas. They attacked again in 178–180, with much the same result. In 193, the Pannonian legions rebelled and declared Septimius Severus emperor. The troops left their positions along the frontier for the next four years to fight in a civil war between Severus and two other claimants of imperial power. At the victorious close of this struggle, Severus found himself obliged to devalue the currency regardless of the economic hardships this caused small property owners throughout the empire. It is little wonder that many of the small villas of Pannonia were abandoned. Under such conditions, only large, well-defended, and mostly self-sufficient enterprises could survive. Many of the independent farmers of Pannonia died in the plague, others were killed and scattered by barbarian attacks, still others were taken into the legions of Septimius Severus, and many of those remaining doubtless turned to their more powerful neighbors for protection and assumed the role of tenants. Thus the great villas of Pannonia came to resemble the quasi-feudal estates of the later empire.[53] Many of these great estates apparently were, or became, imperial property. If so, imperial policy may have had a great deal to do with the transformation of the agrarian society of the interior of Pannonia from one characterized by numerous small, independent landowners to one dominated by great estates.

The situation in the frontier districts along the Danube was quite different. The military occupation of the Danube frontier rapidly caused increased settlement in the vicinity of the legionary fortresses of Aquincum (Budapest), Brigetio, Carnuntum, Vindobona (Vienna), and Singidunum (Belgrade). This population increase is clearly reflected in the remains of villas concentrated in these areas. These villas functioned primarily as economic enterprises and generally lacked the refinements of the typical Roman estate, although many were furnished with heated rooms, mosaic floors, and other luxuries. Villa development tended to occur in the immediate vicinity of the legionary towns, and these villas undoubtedly supplied local military and civilian markets. Many of these villas date from about A.D. 200, and their numbers apparently increased throughout the third century.[54] Part of the reason for this development lay in the military reforms of Septimius Severus. The emperor not only raised army pay, but also allowed the troops to contract legal marriages and to live with their wives outside the forts. Moreover, the troops were permitted outside pursuits during their spare time, and it is not unlikely that many of them bought farms or set up small part-time businesses.[55] This soon led to the growth of substantial and permanent civilian settlements immediately adjacent to the frontier fortifications, and encouraged many veterans to remain on their property after their retirement from the ranks.

The frontier zone formed the economic and political center in the Danubian regions during this period. The interior of the frontier provinces possessed a certain wealth and prosperity, but the continued economic growth of these areas was frustrated by the troubles of the last half of the second century. The great estates that came to dominate the interior districts during the third century did little to increase population, urbanization, or agricultural production in those areas. The districts lying immediately adjacent to the frontier offered greater opportunity for small-scale producers and therefore developed a more diversified and productive economy.

This economic diversification resulted from the need to provide a wide assortment of merchant, military, administrative, and civilian services, as well as for the tribes beyond the frontier, for whom not only agricultural products, but processed goods, manufactured items, and services were required. The dense population and the varied economic pursuits of the inhabitants of the Danubian frontier districts effectively impeded the growth of the economic and social polarization that was occurring throughout the heartland of the empire. The upper classes of the frontier were unable to monopolize great tracts of land within such densely populated territories, and the produce of the great estates in the interior of the region offered poor competition for local goods.[56] At the same time, wealth along the frontier could be obtained through commerce and manufacture, and there were no doubt many frontier merchants who were richer than the local landowning aristocrats. Finally, much of the social and economic power of the upper classes in the interior sprang from their ability to offer their neighbors protection. The army performed this function along the frontier, and social distinctions in the frontier districts were therefore much less rigid than in the interior.

The interpenetration of the military and its civilian neighbors was so extensive along the Danubian frontier that any firm social or economic distinctions between the civil and military populations were relatively meaningless. The municipal upper classes and the military were so closely connected that the sons of city officials sometimes chose a military career, and, in some cities, retired veterans regularly served in the exclusive municipal legislatures. Individual soldiers, now allowed to pursue business in their free time, could be as wealthy as prosperous civilians.

The local civil population freely furnished recruits for the locally stationed military forces, and military service contributed a constant and a considerable monetary income for small family units.[57] This was perhaps a major reason why the aristocracy was unable to establish large villas in the frontier districts. The small estates of the frontier districts were able to compete with the large ones in the interior because their owners could rely on a steady supplementary income from military service. The aristocratization of the interior districts was averted on the Danubian frontier due to the protection afforded by the legions and the diversification of the local economy. This situation persisted as long as the troops in service could draw income from outside endeavors. For the frontier population of these districts, military service provided the means of preserving the prosperity of their estates and funding other undertakings.

The prosperous and generally egalitarian societies of the frontier districts of the middle Danube did not endure. In fact, the decline of the entire army of the frontier was already foreshadowed in Severus's reforms of 197. The emperor had raised the army's pay, but he had also devalued the currency. In 211, the emperor Caracalla again raised military pay, but he, too, devalued the currency. Later emperors devalued the currency without raising army pay, and the men of the army of the frontier found themselves with a steadily decreasing real income. In the districts of the middle Danube, this meant that the troops had fewer resources with which to finance their personal enterprises, and that there was less real currency to maintain the level of activity of the local economies. The entire machinery of these districts began to grind slowly to a halt. At the same time, the social egalitarianism that had been characteristic of the frontier districts began to decay. The local populations had furnished recruits to a frontier army that had offered good pay, economic opportunity, desirable living conditions, political power, and, perhaps most attractive of all, status and respect. This was no longer the case.

In the course of the civil war of 193–197, Severus had raised three new legions of elite troops. At the end of the conflict, the emperor stationed one of these legions near Rome and increased the size of other units posted near the capital so that he eventually had a mobile field force of some 30,000 men at his immediate disposal. This was, in many ways, a return to the pre-Augustan Roman offensive army, and the establishment of such a force inevitably meant a loss of prestige and power by the frontier units. The newly established mobile field force, stationed near the larger urban centers in the interior, now received the political deference and economic privileges earlier afforded the frontier legions. The reduced status of the frontier troops was reflected in part by Severus's policy, continued by his successors, of drawing military commanders from the equestrian middle class, rather than from the senatorial aristocracy. Thus, the same emperor whose reforms had made possible the economic prosperity of the frontier districts at the close of the second century also initiated the processes that ended that prosperity by the middle of the third century. The peculiar diversified economy and egalitarian society of the frontier districts of the middle Danube did not last out the third century. Instead, the period saw the increased formation of large estates in both the interior of Pannonia and near the frontier. By the fourth century A.D., the focus of wealth had shifted from the military regions along the Danube to the agricultural estates located in the interior.[58]

In many ways, Dacia was the frontier region that most resembled the American West. The reasons for its conquest were complex. The native inhabitants of the region were hostile and more than once had raided across the Danube. There was constant apprehension that the several tribes of the Dacians might unite to form a serious threat to the frontier, and in the period 101–107 it appears that they might have done so. At the same time, Dacia possessed extensive mineral resources, particularly gold, that had long been coveted by the Romans. In 101, the emperor Trajan concentrated thirteen legions on the lower Danube and invaded Dacia. In two bitter campaigns, the Dacians were defeated and their territory annexed to the empire in 107.

The garrisons placed in the region, as well as the miners who quickly moved in, needed supplies. This led to the rapid establishment of villas and an accelerated program of increased agricultural production. Those Dacian villas that have been excavated were working farms consisting of a small main house and wooden outbuildings, with the entire complex surrounded by a wooden stockade.[59] The general impression conveyed by the limited archaeological evidence is that of the settlement of an incompletely pacified area by small groups, or perhaps even single families. These villas tended to concentrate along the roads Roman troops had built through the region, and it is easy to suppose that the initial purpose of the settlers was to meet the supply needs of the military and mining populations of the region.

The immediate results of the acquisition of this new territory were striking. Since there was no longer any need for defenses in the area, the entire lower Danube from Belgrade to Stukten was demilitarized. Free land, new gold and other mineral wealth, and the opening of trade with the interior of Russia led to an economic boom throughout the lower Danube region and extending to Thrace and the towns of the Black Sea coast. The Dacian frontier was not a permanent possession, however. In the year 270, 163 years after its conquest, the emperor Aurelian decided that it could no longer be defended. The Dacian provinces were abandoned, their troops withdrawn, and their inhabitants resettled in the province of Moesia. The middle Danube was, of course, regarrisoned, and the episode closed.

Upper Moesia differed significantly from other districts of the Roman frontier in that there was virtually no integration between the native inhabitants of the district and the military units stationed there. The region was made a province in A.D. 6, but local recruitment for army service was not introduced until the reign of Marcus Aurelius (161–180). The frontier districts were small and their population scant. As a consequence, the military units stationed on the frontier of Upper Moesia were recruited from the interior of the region and from neighboring provinces.[60] The army remained an alien and intrusive element among the native population of this section of the frontier and could not serve, as it did elsewhere, as a bridge between the native population and the administrators, artisans, merchants, and farmers who had followed the army to the frontier. A permanent state of tension between these two groups prevented any fruitful exchange of technology or skills. The Roman occupation of the Upper Moesian frontier was in some ways reminiscent of its occupation of Wales; the army performed its duty of defending that portion of the frontier, but appears simply to have ignored the possibility of inducing the native population of the district to accept the benefits of Roman life.

The Danube frontier as a whole differed greatly from that of the Rhine. The establishment of the Rhine frontier was an earlier and more gradual affair. During the process of Roman occupation, the Gallic aristocracy found it easy to adapt the Roman villa system to their own traditional social and economic institutions. An extensive pattern of villa cultivation arose in the broad and fertile Gallic provinces that formed the hinterland of the Rhine frontier. Moreover, the villa system proved a point of entry for increasing Gallic participation in the culture and society of the greater Roman world. The Romanization of the Gallic provinces was a permanent achievement. Centuries after the fall of the Western Roman Empire, it was Charlemagne, a Frank from the old Rhenish frontier region, who attempted to restore the Roman empire in the West.

The settlement of the Danubian frontier occurred later and was dictated by pressing political and military needs. It was necessary to establish an adequate agricultural base in these regions as quickly as possible, and the native populations were not as receptive to the villa organization of agriculture as were many other frontier peoples. Italian settlers were brought into the Danubian countryside in order to speed the development of its agricultural base and to police the rebellious natives. Thus, the villa system was a foreign and intrusive element in Danubian lands and led to the growth of a more or less artificial society lacking the integration with the native population that was characteristic of the Rhine frontier.

Some General Observations

Extensive comparisons could be drawn between the various frontier districts. In each of them, however, there was an intricate interplay among the native peoples, the native aristocracy, the Roman military forces, and the civil populations that had been drawn to the frontier.

This process of mutual adjustment centered at first on the necessity of developing the agricultural resources necessary to supply the army, and later on the competition between the frontier districts and the hinterlands for control of these markets. The integration of the various groups of frontier residents was not allowed to proceed in a gradual and natural manner. There was constant barbarian pressure on the military frontier, portions of which sometimes broke. In addition, the military units on the frontier were involved in more than local concerns. They were an active political force in the empire and occasionally assumed the roles of emperor-makers or emperor-breakers in a game in which defeat often had disastrous consequences for the frontier districts where their home bases were located. Finally, the emperors were constantly tinkering with the frontier system, building a fortress in one place and abandoning one in another, moving a cohort here and a legion there, raising pay or debasing the currency, or devising vast new projects involving the investment of tens of millions of man-hours and changing the face of the landscape.

Under such complex circumstances, it is not surprising that the various frontier districts should have developed such different characteristics. But these differences should not be overemphasized, since there were also many similarities. All of the frontier districts were dominated by the military and its concerns. All had agrarian societies with inadequate technologies, struggling to increase farm production so that individuals could meet their taxes and levies and so that the soldiers could be fed. Moreover, all had grain as their staple farm commodity, whether their traditional way of life had emphasized cereal production or not. The frontier districts shared the common experience of living in danger of attack from the tribes beyond the frontier and at the same time trading for the valuable goods the tribesmen possessed. All were relatively free, since slaves were too valuable to be wasted on the frontier, and all were more or less egalitarian, since the common situation of the inhabitants of the frontier districts led to a greater commonality of interests than existed in the interior of the empire.

In the background of all of this, perhaps unperceived by most, was the great water route uniting the frontier from the Black Sea to Hadrian's Wall. Private boats and the ships of the river fleets constantly passed from district to district, distributing supplies, maintaining communications, and carrying men and ideas. Considering the whole panorama of the societies of the frontier districts, one is reminded of the various societies of Mark Twain's *Huckleberry Finn*. As Huck and Jim drifted down the Mississippi River, they came to know various groups of people, each possessing different social organizations, attitudes, customs, and turns of speech, but all united in the common experience of living on the river.

Notes

1. The processes by which the presence of Roman garrisons influenced local economies are complex and varied. The general issue is considered by Lothar Wierschowski, *Heer und Wirtschaft: das römische Heer der Prinzipatszeit als Wirtschaftsfaktor*, while particular cases are considered by N. J. Higham and G. D. B. Jones, "Frontier, Forts, and Farmers," *Archaeological Journal* 132 (1975): 16–28; and P. A. G. Clack, "The Northern Frontier: Farmers in the Military Zone," in *The Romano-British Countryside: Studies in Rural Settlement and Economy*, ed. D. Miles (Oxford: Oxford University Press, 1982), pp. 377–402.

2. It is unlikely, however, that there was anything like a Roman colonization of the countryside. In the North of England, Belgium, and northern France, where rural archaeology and aerial photography has been most intense, it would appear that the development of large estates and small farms was equally the work of natives, although immigrants from the interior provinces may well have provided the immediate stimulus. See J. Mertens, "The Military Origins of Some Roman Settlements in Belgium," in *Rome and Her Northern Provinces*, ed. Brian Hartley and John Wacher, p. 116, for Belgium and northeastern France, and p. 127 for the North of England; and Edith Wightman, "The Pattern of Rural Settlement in Roman Gaul," in *Aufsteig und Niedergang der römischen Welt*, ed. Hildegard Temporini and Wolfgang Haase, vol. 2, part 4: 584–657.

3. Since many of the goods shipped were bulk items such as hides, grain, timber, and metals, water routes were preferable to the slower and much less efficient land routes.

4. This could include bulk shipment over considerable distances. It should be remembered that large transfers of goods between Britain and the lower Rhine were common throughout the frontier period.

5. The basic unit of Roman government was the *civitas*, or city, and its surrounding *pagus*, or countryside. Administration, public works, maintenance of law and order, and the administration of justice were the responsibilities of the leading citizens of such a district and were concentrated in the *civitas*. The *civitas* was thus somewhat similar to the American county, although some were of considerably greater area.

One might also note that the population of the *civitates* in the heartland of the empire was frequently a combination of Roman, Romanized, and native people. In this regard, the social structure of the frontier *civitas* did not differ significantly from that of the interior of the empire.

6. This characterization is true only of the short run. The long-term situation of frontier settlements was, of course, much more complex. The history of the frontier is filled with local revolts, army mutinies, "barbarian" raids and invasions, and the permanent transfer of military units.

7. See Wightman, "The Pattern of Rural Settlement in Roman Gaul"; and H. C. Bowen, "The Celtic Background," in *The Roman Villa in Britain*, ed. A. L. F. Rivet, p. 28. A volume by Roger Agache, *La Somme pre-romaine et romaine: d'après les prospections aeriennes à basse altitude*, is the result of a massive campaign of aerial photography carried out during a severe drought that revealed building foundations with unusual clarity. These large-scale mappings corroborated the impression that traditional Celtic villages and land use persisted alongside more characteristically Roman exploitations.

8. N. J. Higham and G. D. B. Jones, "Frontier, Forts and Farmers," *Archaeological Journal* 132 (1975): 16. See also Peter Salway, *The Frontier People of Roman Britain*, p. 57.

It must be remembered also that the Romans introduced new crops into northern areas. The vineyards of the Moselle and the Rhine are famous examples, but there were other importations, including root vegetables like carrots, beets, celery, and radishes, as well as asparagus, lettuce, cucumbers, caraway, parsley, anise, onions, mustard types, and coriander. Roman grafting techniques improved native strains of apples and spread the cultivation of the famous Mattiana. They also added pears, plums, sour cherries, apricots, and peaches to the orchard crops. The effect of such a variety of new foodstuffs must have been nothing short of revolutionary both for farming and for the daily life and general health of the frontier populations. See Herbert Schutz, *The Romans in Central Europe*, p. 141.

9. Roman agriculture is a much-studied subject. Several works of K. D. White—*A Bibliography of Roman Agriculture*; *Roman Farming*; *Agricultural Implements of the Roman World*; and *Farm Equipment of the Roman World*—together with Sian E. Rees, *Agricultural Implements in Prehistoric and Roman Britain*, provide a full overview of agrarian technology. Pat Morris, *Agricultural Buildings in Roman Britain*; and Geoffrey Rickman, *Roman Granaries and Store Buildings*, offer an overview of Roman farm buildings. The villa was a different and more complex matter, and will be considered later.

10. One might consider that, given an acre of 43,560 square feet and furrows one foot apart, the plowman must guide the plow a total of over sixteen miles to double till a single acre. A yield of seven to eight bushels of wheat per acre was regarded as quite respectable even in the eighteenth century, and, in medieval times, one bushel of seed was required to produce four bushels of grain. Thus, a very full day's labor for plowman and draft animal, on good land and in a good season, would have netted a total of four bushels of wheat. Furthermore, considering that the plowing season lasts little more than a month, the net annual production of wheat by a single farmer would have been in the neighborhood 120 bushels.

11. Other technological limitations precluded the development of heavier plows. Such plows would have needed multiple draft animals, and the Romans had not developed the techniques of tandem harnessing that would have made team plowing a practicable affair. Moreover, since the Romans did not employ horseshoes or horse collars, their draft animals were restricted to slow-moving oxen and light asses.

12. Indeed, the words *village* and *villa* come from the same root. The word *vicus* was, for the Romans, a synonym for *villa*, and meant either "estate" or "village."

13. Roy W. Davies, "Social and Economic Aspects," in *The Roman Villa in Britain*, ed. A. L. F. Rivet, pp. 177–178.

14. Considerable archaeological work is being done on villas, and there are several general studies of this important institution. See Harald Mielsch, *Die römische Villa: Architektur und Lebensform*. John Percival, *The Roman Villa: An Historical Introduction*; and several articles in *The Economy of Romano-British Villas*, ed. K. Branigan and D. Miles, offer useful introductions to the subject. Keith Branigan, *Gatcombe: The Excavation and Study of a Romano-British Villa Estate, 1967–1976*, provides an excellent example of the many archaeological studies of individual villas.

15. Taxes were collected either in money or in kind and were an individual responsibility. The individual who could not meet his tax obligations usually turned to a moneylender, offering his lands or even his person as collateral. The fact that these were generally head and land taxes, and were not based upon wealth or income, must have served as a constant incentive to individual effort.

16. H. H. Scullard, *Roman Britain: Outpost of the Empire*, p. 125. This was not true everywhere, of course. In both Britain and Belgium, there is little evidence that Roman farming methods caused the increased agricultural production and intensity of exploitation. It would rather appear in these areas that the appearance of a Roman military market simply accelerated a process of development that was already underway. The generally favorable climate of the period and the peace and security established by the Romans were contributing factors. See J. Mertens, "The Military Origins of Some Roman Settlements in Belgium." In many other areas, however, the remains of early Roman villas suggest that Roman agrarian organization played a large part in local agricultural development.

17. Not a few Roman military campaigns had been financed on the expectation that a victory would secure the investors with large numbers of marketable slaves.

18. This observation touches upon the much-debated question of the transformation from "classical" slavery to "medieval" serfdom. Many historians, primarily Marxists, regard this development as the alteration in the mode of production that marked the definitive break between ancient and medieval European history, but cannot agree on when and why this change took place. The old classic of R. H. Barrow, *Slavery in the Roman Empire*, is still worth reading, while K. R. Bradley, *Slaves and Masters in the Roman Empire: A Study in Social Control*; the recent *Classical Slavery*, ed. M. I. Finley (London: F. Cass, 1987); and M. I. Finley, *Ancient Slavery and Modern Ideology* (London: Chatto and Windus, 1980), provide more modern treatments. William W. Buckland, *The Roman Law of Slavery: The Condition of the Slave in Private Law from Augustus to Justinian* is the standard study of the legal institution of slavery.

19. Percival, *The Roman Villa*, p. 120. Keith Hopkins, "Taxes and Trade in the Roman Empire (200 B.C.–A.D. 400)," *Journal of Roman Studies* 70 (1980): 101–102, emphasizes the effect of the reciprocal flow of taxes and trade in this development.

20. See Davies, "Social and Economic Aspects," pp. 178–179; also Percival, *The Roman Villa*, pp. 14–15.

21. Edith Wightman, "Cultural Factors within a German Province," *Comparative Frontier Studies* 10 (Spring 1978): 10, characterizes institutional advances

within Gallic society under imperial domination as being primarily "the effects on Gaulish culture and society of the absorption within the wider political and economic framework of the Mediterranean-based Roman Empire."

22. Such an approach has numerous advantages. Floor plans, like any other type of design, evolve over time and can clearly illustrate the influence of various styles at work. Moreover, those interested in semiotics will be well aware that a floor plan constitutes a set of signs and symbols that tell much about the people employing them.

23. Percival, *The Roman Villa*, pp. 134–135.

24. See, for instance, the Anglo-Saxon *Beowulf*, the Irish *Cuchulain*, Bede's *Ecclesiastical History of the English People*, or any number of medieval romances.

25. Percival, *The Roman Villa*, pp. 134–135.

26. The Roman *jugerum*, or "yokeland," consisted of 28,800 square feet, compared with the English acre of 43,560 square feet. The figures almost certainly represent the amount of land that one could expect to plow in a single day, and 151 percent would be the ratio of efficiency between medieval English plowing techniques and those of the Romans.

One should note that the average villa size was considerably larger in some districts of the frontier, particularly under military control.

27. If the seed-to-yield ratio were comparable to medieval times, about one-fifth, or 200 bushels, would have been reserved as seed. If the personnel of such a villa consisted of the proprietor and eight laborers, together with their families, and each family consumed twenty-five bushels of grain annually, an additional 225 bushels would have been needed for home consumption. This would have left a net production of only 475 bushels for sale. The net may have been even smaller, since an average yield of 11.5 bushels would have been rather high. In medieval and early modern times, yields of eight to ten bushels per acre were considered above average. A harvest of eight bushels to the acre would have left only 330 bushels surplus.

28. Percival, *The Roman Villa*, p. 363, claims that in less densely populated regions, such as the Ardennes, the average villa size ran to over 4,000 *jugera*. Aerial photography of the Somme basin has produced evidence for villa sizes ranging from 200 to 2,000 *jugera*. The smaller figures appear in regions heavily exploited for their cereal productivity. It is likely that small villas predominated in the Rhineland, but it is not yet possible to assess this with any precision.

29. As the legions came to be drawn increasingly from provincial populations, many of the emigrants from the countryside may have entered local units, and those units would have been influenced by local civil concerns.

30. Percival, *The Roman Villa*, pp. 135–137. See also Sheppard Sunderland Frere, *Britannia: A History of Roman Britain*, p. 135.

31. Other calculations have been advanced. See Davies, "Social and Economic Aspects," pp. 195–198.

32. The purpose of leaving land fallow for a year was only secondarily to allow the soil to rest and regain fertility. The main reason was to control weeds. Weeds grew in the fallow fields, of course, but these fields were plowed just before the weeds seeded, and animals, preferably sheep, were put in to graze down any late-growing plants until the end of the summer. For this reason, all land, regardless of its fertility, had to be put to fallow on a regular basis.

33. It is probable that farm laborers in preindustrial Europe derived a substantial share of their food from small household gardens of one to three acres tended by their wives and children.

34. David Hall, "Survey Results in the Cambridgeshire Fenlands," *Antiquity* 62 (June 1988): 313, states that as the Romans became aware of the geographical nature of the region, the area switched from one of agricultural emphasis to one dominated by salt production and animal rearing.

35. The Celtic field pattern differed from the Roman one primarily in its lack of regularity. Such field patterns may still be seen in the West of Ireland, where great numbers of stone wall–enclosed patches of varying sizes and shapes form a crazy-quilt pattern across the landscape.

36. Bowen, "The Celtic Background," pp. 29–30. The dates of this project are obscure. It may have begun soon after the conquest, but probably reached the height of its agricultural output around the reign of Hadrian (117–138). If so, it would rank with the other vast projects completed under his regime. See Davies, "Social and Economic Aspects," p. 198.

37. It is also possible that the first workers moved in to clear and drain the marshlands may have been prisoners from the unsuccessful British revolt of A.D. 61.

38. This characteristic of the German and Celtic societies is reflected in their epics and folklore. It is also preserved in the etymology of many words. *Vieh*, the Old German word for "cow," provides the root for the modern word "fee," and the legal term, "chattels," meaning possessions generally, has essentially the same root as "cattle."

39. Davies, "Social and Economic Aspects," pp. 176–178, feels that the geographical distribution of villas and towns shows their close relationship. This connection accounts for the consistent clustering of villas around towns and for their scarcity in regions without towns.

40. It is possible that the abandonment of the Fenlands may have been one of the consequences of the support the army in Britain gave to the opponent of Septimius Severus in the civil war of 193–197. Severus punished his opponents severely, and it is not unlikely that the British economy was dealt a severe blow. At the same time, it must be remembered that the Fenland salt marshes were extraordinarily well suited for livestock. During the Middle Ages, the fine fleeces of Fenland sheep would become famous throughout Europe, and their wool would become the most important single commodity in England's overseas trade. It may well be that the profits to be gained from turning the land to pastoralism led the imperial administration finally to shift the burden of army supply to the local population.

41. Higham and Jones, "Frontier, Forts, and Farmers," 19; Frere, *Britannia*, pp. 273–274, claims that the demand for agricultural products, especially by the military, on the frontier served as an impetus for local production.

42. Frere, *Britannia*, p. 114; Hopkins, "Taxes and Trade in the Roman Empire," pp. 101–102.

43. It is also possible that this lack of evidence may be the result of insufficient excavation in the district.

44. Peter Salway, *The Frontier People of Roman Britain*, pp. 113–114.

45. Ibid., p. 119.

46. Ibid., pp. 142–143.

47. Frere, *Britannia*, p. 276.

48. Percival, *The Roman Villa*, pp. 87–88. For the development of the several Danubian provinces, see Theodor Mommsen, *The Provinces of The Roman Empire*, ed. T. Robert S. Broughton; Andrés Mócsy, *Pannonia and Upper Moesia: A History of the Middle Danube Provinces of the Roman Empire*, trans. Sheppard Frere; and *The Archaeology of Roman Pannonia*, ed. A. Lengyel and G. T. B. Radan.

49. It was through this route that the fifth-century invaders of the empire finally gained access to Italy.

50. Percival, *The Roman Villa*, pp. 89–90.

51. Mócsy, *Pannonia and Upper Moesia*, p. 169.

52. Mócsy, ibid., pp. 173, 175–176, maintains that the richest native aristocrats, who were buried in wagon-graves accompanied by numerous Roman luxury goods, enjoyed a Roman standard of living. Scant evidence exists to evaluate the influence of Roman farming techniques among these people, but native dress and names continued among natives in northeast Pannonia much longer than among the Boians. Only the richest aristocrats of this district appear to have Romanized to any significant degree, and it is unlikely that there were appreciable numbers of native-owned villas in the area.

53. See L. H. Nelson, "The Place-Names of the Val Ancha and the Fall of Roman Spain," *Locus* 2 (1989).

54. Percival, *The Roman Villa*, pp. 89–90, states that the conquest of Dacia proved an important factor in the development of Pannonia. Pannonia gained both from the security provided by Dacia and also indirectly from the latter's mineral resources. The development of villas of substantial size and luxury took place in the interior of Pannonia during the time of Roman control in Dacia. The development around the Neusiedler See to the north might on its own seem an extension of the frontier region, but the comparable, more concentrated settlement of Lake Balaton reveals that it actually constituted a new departure. The area contained truly large villas with impressive residential quarters and whole ranges of outbuildings. The size of these villas suggests imperial ownership, and, although the evidence remains mostly circumstantial, it is quite possible that imperial estates of considerable size and number existed throughout this part of the empire. See also Klaus Randsborg, "Between Classical Antiquity and the Middle Ages: New Evidence of Economic Change," *Antiquity* 64 (March 1990): 123.

55. Peter Garnsey, "Septimius Severus and the Marriage of Roman Soldiers," *California Studies in Classical Antiquity* 3 (1970): 45; R. E. Smith, "The Army Reforms of Septimius Severus," *Historia* 21 (1972): 481. Since some of the legionary troops were specialists in various crafts and trades, they could easily have formed the core of a diversified local economy.

56. The basic reason for this was the cost of transporting bulk commodities from the interior. It should be remembered that the cost of land transport was some twenty times that of water transportation. See Jozef Mertens, "The Military Origins of Some Roman Settlements in Belgium," in *Rome and Her Northern Provinces*, ed. Brian Hartley and John Wacher, p. 40. It is also probable that the small-scale operations of the frontier were cultivated more intensively than the large estates of the interior and that their general productivity was therefore greater.

57. Frere, *Britannia*, p. 239, points out that a large number of tombs were set up by active or discharged legionaries in the frontier regions. The frequency of

legionaries' family gravestones demonstrates the regularity of local recruitment and the close connection between the local population and the garrison.

58. Frere, *Britannia*, pp. 307–308.

59. Percival, *The Roman Villa*, p. 91, states that the common villa pattern in Upper and Lower Moesia resembled that of Pannonia, with villas appearing initially behind the frontier and around such urban centers as Serdica (Sofia) and Adrianople (Ederne).

60. Mócsy, *Pannonia and Upper Moesia*, p. 154, claims that apart from Scupi and Ulpianum, the towns of the interior of Moesia were all established by either Marcus Aurelius or the Severi. They never developed a municipal life of their own, in spite of the apparent attempts of the administration to involve the local upper class in the municipal government. The administration of the earlier towns rested with foreign settlers and businessmen who remained somewhat isolated from the native population. Percival, *The Roman Villa*, p. 91, maintains that the reign of Marcus Aurelius marked the beginning of regular recruitment of Upper Moesians into auxiliary units. Even when Upper Moesia became a province, levies were not raised locally, and, later, conditions stayed so unstable that the government excluded Upper Moesians from the army. Mócsy notes that the Upper Moesian army of the second century A.D. was composed of legionaries, about half of whom were foreigners and the rest natives, and of auxiliaries who were usually foreigners.

IV PASTORAL PURSUITS: RANCHING AND GRAZING ON THE FRONTIER

We have concentrated on agricultural development in our discu sion of the economies and societies of the Roman Empire's frontier distr cts for a number of reasons. The supply of wheat was the first and most pressing need in feeding the army, and the villas that increased cereal production along the frontier left remains that can be uncovered and analyzed by archaeologists. It is possible in this way to fix the sites of agricultural exploitation and to trace their evolution over time. The same cannot be said for husbandry and ranching. These activities, even if practiced on a large scale, leave few detectable marks on the landscape; nor are they fixed in place, as agriculture is fixed to sites with arable land or capital improvements. Ranching sites can be shifted with ease over great distances. Although one can determine a great deal from the study of animal remains, such as bones, found at centers of consumption, these remains offer little information as to their origin. Since animals can walk, ranching is far less affected than agriculture by the need to locate near existing transportation routes. Nevertheless, no discussion of the economic development and social structure of the empire's frontier districts would be complete without a consideration of pastoral pursuits. Agriculture and pastoralism, together with mining and forestry, were the principal means of both exploiting of the resources of the frontier and filling the basic needs of the army for supplies and materials.

Military Demands for Leather

It is difficult for the modern reader to imagine the variety of uses to which animals and animal by-products were put in Roman times. If one were to imagine a world in which there were no plastics, rubber, canvas, epoxy, crates, nylon, paper, oil, cotton, coal, cardboard, natural or artificial gas, barrels, vinyl, or aluminum, and in which animal by-products were used in place of all these materials, one would only begin to grasp the importance of pastoralism to the economy and life of the Roman frontier. It is perhaps more revealing to consider the various animal materials needed by the Roman army of the frontier and to attempt to estimate how much of them the army consumed.

At the beginning of the second century, the European sector of the Roman frontier was garrisoned by a total of seventeen legions: three in Britain, four on the Rhine, and ten along the Danube. The total number of legionaries was therefore about 102,000, and there were probably an equal number of auxiliary troops in addition to units such as the fleets and special weapons and reconnaissance detachments. Considering that there are always some understrength units in an army, the army of the frontier nevertheless numbered at least 200,000 men. Although numerical calculations can become tedious, it is enlightening to esti-mate some of the requirements of these fighting men for animals and animal by-products in about the year A.D. 100. It is perhaps easiest to begin with leather and leather goods.

Each of these soldiers had his own suit of armor.[1] It had been the practice under Augustus for a legionary to serve twenty years of active service, and five years of light standby duty before retirement. Even then, veterans could be recalled in case of dire need. For this reason, it was customary for the soldier to take his armor with him when leaving the ranks, and this practice continued even after the original rationale had disappeared. Since the term of service in A.D. 100 was twenty-five years, this meant that the army of the frontier had to be prepared to replace annually some 8,000 suits of armor lost to retirements from ranks of both the legions and the auxiliaries.[2]

In the legions, these suits of armor consisted of a covering for the upper body made of a number of light iron plates riveted to an complex internal system of leather straps. Shoulder guards were constructed in the same fashion and secured to the main body with yet more straps. Officers wore, in addition, a number of leather straps hanging from their waists and protecting their thighs.[3] Accouterments included belts, straps and scabbards for swords, and a leather cap and chin straps to be worn with an iron helmet. The shield was an oblong affair, measuring about three feet tall by two feet wide. It consisted of a body of laminated wood (it should be remembered that the glue of the period was derived from horns and hooves), encased in leather, with an iron or bronze facing sewn to the body with tough rawhide. It was furnished with a strong leather carrying strap. The soldier wore a tunic reaching to the knees that was usually made of linen, but could be made of leather for greater protection. Finally, the heavy military sandals consisted of several thicknesses of tough leather, studded with hobnails, and secured to the ankle and thigh with a complex set of leather thongs.[4] While the amount of leather needed for a replacement was not great, it was obviously necessary. At least in a figurative sense, the Roman soldier was held together by leather straps,[5] and these leather straps were always breaking, fraying, cracking, and wearing out. So while the leather required for armor and accouterments was perhaps a relatively small quantity, its importance illustrates the steady appetite of the Roman military for tanned hides. However, there were other uses that demanded a far greater amount of leather.

The standard military tents of the period, whether for legionary or auxiliary troops, were ten feet square, with an additional two feet in width for guy-ropes. The tents of the centurions were considerably larger, partly because the offices of the century were located there and partly because rank had its privileges. The remains of turf screens, used to keep the tents dry, have been discovered at Cawthorn, England, and reveal that the centurion's tent was about twenty feet square. The tents of tribunes were probably even larger, and the legate's tent the largest of all.[6] There were probably other tents, such as the surgeon's and the infirmary, but little is known of their number and size.

Tents were composed of a number of standard-sized leather panels. Fragments of such panels have been uncovered in the archeological excavations of a number of military sites in Britain and provide a good deal of evidence about their nature. The only leather used was natural calfskin. A calf hide, counting back, neck, and belly, generally yields about ten square feet of usable leather. Roman military tent leather, however, was only of the finest quality. Only the back hide was used, and this was cut in two pieces each measuring about two by one-and-a-half feet. Each calf hide thus yielded about six square feet of tent leather,[7] or two panels. Each standard tent required forty-two panels, and the centurion's used 168.

The standard tent was not designed for comfort and was expected to accommodate eight soldiers within its 100 square feet of floor space. If we can assume that auxiliary troops were furnished with the same quality of shelter, it is possible to calculate the total amount of leather used in the frontier army's tents. Each century of eighty men would have had ten standard tents and one larger centurion's tent.[8] Every eighty men, rounding off for the fact that we are not including the other military tents, would have required 588 calfskin panels. The frontier army in Europe numbered some 200,000 men, using approximately one-and-a-half million calfskin panels cut from the hides of 750,000 calves for shelter.[9]

These figures represent the initial investment in the frontier units, and do not include the number of animals that would have been necessary to provide the leather for mending or replacing worn tents. The usable life of such tents cannot be calculated. By A.D. 100, most units of the frontier army were quartered in permanent forts and barracks, and their tents would have been used only on training exercises and during campaigns. Nevertheless, Roman tents represented a great deal of livestock: for the army in Britain some 132,000 head; for the army on the Rhine, 176,000; and for that on the Danube, 440,000.

Transport required a second large investment of leather. The transportation of bulk goods was a particular problem during imperial times. Containers were absolutely necessary since Roman transport technology was limited in many ways. The technology of tandem harnessing, eveners, and pivoted front axles had not been developed,[10] and so most overland transport was by small cart or pack animal. Ancient boats invariably leaked, and cargos had to be kept dry. Clay jars were often used in the Mediterranean for such commodities as wine and grain, but they were bulky, heavy in proportion to their contents, and breakable. Although the remains of barrels have been discovered in the lower Rhine districts, they are apparently of a relatively late date. In any event, the barrel did not come into general use until the early medieval period. In the year 100, most goods such as grain, beer, preserved meats, and fruit and vegetables were shipped in leather bags.

The amount of leather used in transportation was enormous. If one assumes that grain was shipped in leather sacks holding about two bushels,[11] sack leather would have measured at least ten square feet. A full hide could not have made more than four such sacks. If we consider just the amount of grain that had to be carried to the frontier units, the importance of ranching to Roman transport can be appreciated. Each soldier received a ration of eleven bushels annually. The frontier army in Europe needed yearly shipments of 2.2 million bushels of grain that would have required 1.1 million leather sacks, the products of the hides of 275,000 head of cattle. Such sacks could have been reused a number of times, of course, but they would also have worn out quickly and have needed replacement. In addition, these calculations do not take into account the transport necessary to fill the needs of the civilian settlements that had arisen near the army forts. If one accepts that there were enough sacks to handle the entire annual grain ration for the army, the army in Britain utilized the hides of about 50,000 cattle, the army on the Rhine those of about 65,000 head, and the Danubian forces around 162,000.

Considering only tents and sacks, Britain had to supply over 180,000 hides; the Rhineland, 241,000; and the Danubian lands, over 500,000. In short, the army required a basic investment of close to five hides per man for shelter and food transport. Such calculations as these are always open to debate and recalculation, but, in point of fact, tents and sacks represented only a fraction of the leather required by the army of the frontier. An even greater amount was needed to supply the numerous small uses to which leather was put.

Normal legionary dress included a linen tunic next to the skin, and often a leather outer tunic reaching to the knees. The auxiliary troops normally wore skintight leather trousers, and legionary troops were allowed similar attire in cold weather. Each soldier carried a leather water-skin on the march; in addition, a pack mule, needing harness, pack saddle, and carrying bags, was allotted to every eighty men in a legion.[12] Many of the artisan troops had leather aprons, shoulder protectors, or gloves, and the 120 cavalry mounts assigned to each legion needed saddles and other gear. Buckets were often made of leather, as were the legate's document cases. The troops carried their money and dice in leather purses, and the surgeon carried his scalpels and probes in a leather box. Leather was essential even to the troops' leisure pursuits.

Extensive and meticulous archeological excavations have been carried out on a fort in northern Britain called Vindolanda.[13] Dating from the period before Hadrian (117–138), the remains of this frontier fort have yielded a great deal of information about Roman army life in the second half of the first century A.D. Among the areas excavated within the fort was one that appears to have been a tannery and leather-working shop. A number of items were left strewn on the floor when the fort was abandoned. These included a large assortment of leather goods, among them shoes, wearing apparel, belts, thongs, and a purse. The most common items, however, were the shoes, and over two hundred of them have been recovered. It is striking that over 70 percent of these shoes are so small that they can only have been worn by women or children.[14] It would appear that the army workers in this establishment used their spare time and army equipment (and perhaps materials) to make shoes for local sale.

On at least one occasion, the army's appetite for leather led to a border war. Much of the area of the modern Netherlands had been conquered by the Romans in 12 B.C., and the Frisians, the tribe inhabiting the region, had submitted to Roman authority. Being confined to a marshy region, they were not a very prosperous people, and their sympathetic Roman conqueror had decided that they could pay their taxes by delivering a number of ox hides for the use of the army. He neglected, however, to specify the size of these hides. Native tribes in the frontier region were normally placed under the direction of a Roman representative called a prefect, and, after some time, an eager centurion named Olennius was assigned as prefect of the Frisians.[15] It may be that Olennius was trying to make a name for himself and gain promotion, or he may have arranged to get a cut of any increased revenues from the district. At any rate, he ordered that the tax was to be paid with the hides of aurochs, a very large, rare, and costly relative of the buffalo. In order to meet this ruinous assessment, the Frisians were forced to sell first their own cattle and then their lands. In A.D. 29, after many had sold their wives and children into slavery, and had found that their complaints and appeals to the army and to the government were getting them nowhere, the Frisians declared their independence. Soldiers sent to collect the taxes that year were hanged from the nearest trees, and Olennius fled to the nearby fort of Flevum.[16]

The Frisians followed Olennius to Flevum and laid siege to it, and the governor of Lower Germany, Lucius Apronius, had legionary detachments quickly shipped down from Upper Germany to lift the siege. He then assembled a large force, including both legionaries and numerous auxiliary infantry and cavalry, and marched into Frisian territory. In the battle that followed, the Frisians beat off every attack launched by the Roman troops. The governor finally retreated from the battlefield without bothering to bury his dead and having lost many of his best centurions. In fact, it would seem that the governor and his staff ran. About 900 Roman troops, almost certainly auxiliaries, were cut off by this sudden withdrawal and were killed in a battle to the death in a nearby forest. Four hundred others, also probably auxiliaries, had escaped to a nearby villa owned by an auxiliary veteran named Cruptorix.[17] Fearing that they would be betrayed, perhaps by the native workers on the villa, and deciding that it would probably be better not to be taken prisoner by the Frisians, the entire 400 troops killed each other.

Apronius apparently withdrew across the Rhine, and news of his defeat soon reached the emperor in Rome. Apronius may have had some powerful friends or relatives, since the emperor decided to hush up news of the defeat. No new commander was appointed, nor were any troops assembled to avenge the defeat and retake the lost territory. The Roman frontier in Lower Germany was now fixed on the left bank of the river, and the territory of the modern Netherlands was permanently lost to the empire. All this because an overeager centurion had tried to increase leather shipments to the local military units.[18]

Consumption of Other Animal By-Products

We have not yet considered the many other animal by-products needed by the troops and the civilian settlements that lay near their forts, but a few examples may serve to indicate the extent and variety of such materials and their uses. We have discussed how much leather the army used, and it must be remembered that leather dries and cracks. The army must have needed tons of lard and millions of man-hours of greasing and kneading to keep its tents, belts, bags, straps, sandals, caps, and other paraphernalia supple and usable. Additional fats were needed to grease wheels and axles, waterproof clothing, and protect the wooden parts of buildings, tools, weapons, siege engines, and the like from rot.

For proper storage, metal items such as armor, swords, helmets, and lance points required a light coat of grease to protect them from rust. Even the surgeon needed at least some fat for his salves and unguents. Tallow candles and fat-burning lamps provided illumination.

Important ropes, such as those used by the cavalry, siege artillery, and naval units, were braided from animal hair, goat hair being favored in the navy and horsehair being widely used among land forces. The artillery used quantities of hair, and also tough sinew, for the springs that powered their machines. The archers would have demanded good gut, well waxed, and the finest wing feathers for their weapons. Thousands of horns and hooves would have been needed to provide the armorers, carpenters, and leather workers the glue they required for their work. Bone was used for knife handles, bow and lance grips, and dice. Capes and cloaks, winter undertunics, blankets, horse blankets, and most civilian clothing, from the finest to the roughest, were made of wool, and the demand for woolen textiles, particularly among auxiliary units, was very great.[19] This list could be extended almost indefinitely, but two facts should be evident. The Roman army of the frontier used a great variety and vast quantity of animal by-products. Moreover, these materials were absolutely essential; there were no substitutes.

Meat for the Legions

The army had other uses for animals than merely leather and other by-products, since it would appear that frontier service may have altered army appetites considerably. The diet of the Roman army in the early empire had consisted primarily of cereals, supplemented with a little meat. Meat was certainly not considered a daily requirement. The historian Tacitus relates how a Roman force under the command of the legate, Corbulo, ran short of rations while on campaign in Armenia. Unable to have bread, pasta, or porridge, they barely managed to avert starvation by supplementing their short rations with what for the troops was a sickeningly large quantity of meat. The tale illustrates that the soldiers of the early first century not only did not receive much fresh meat, they did not want it.[20] This was, of course, the basic reason that the frontier districts had to increase their cereal production so quickly.

Barley was extensively cultivated as animal fodder and food for the poor, but the Roman troops preferred wheat. It is interesting in this respect that the standard punishment for a unit guilty of cowardice was for every tenth man to be beaten to death with clubs and for the rest of the unit to have barley substituted for their wheat ration.[21] This may demonstrate how important a regular supply of wheaten food was to a

Roman; 60 percent of his food intake was cereal, most of which was wheat.[22]

Numerous frontier forts have been excavated by archaeologists, however, and large numbers of bones of food animals have been discovered at these sites. The bones of virtually every animal that is eaten have been found: mostly cattle, but also sheep, goats, pigs, chickens, ducks, geese, dogs, and horses, as well as game, wildfowl, and fish. Not only the number, but the variety of these remains suggests that the frontier troops had become avid consumers of meat.[23]

A fragmentary tablet from Vindolanda listing food disbursements provides an excellent indication of the diet of Roman soldiers in about the year A.D. 100, and illustrates the degree to which the appetites of these troops differed from those of the beginning of the century. In these accounts of commodities, barley is mentioned most frequently, whereas wheat is referred to only once. The apparent popularity of barley is perhaps the most surprising aspect of these lists, since this grain still usually served as animal fodder. The references to barley consumption occur under the month of June, however, just before the wheat harvest. It may be that the garrison had run out of wheat and were simply waiting out the time before harvest. It is also possible that the troops were accepting their cereal ration to devote it to other purposes, such as the feeding of fowl or the brewing of beer. The Vindolanda tablet also mentions the disbursement of fish sauce (*muria*), pork fat (*axungia*), spices (*condimenta*), salt (*sal*), wine (*vinum*), sour wine (*acetum*), Celtic beer (*cervesa*), goat's meat (*caprea*), young pig (*porcellum*), ham (*perna*), and venison (*cervina*). The diet of the Vindolanda garrison was clearly varied, and more than a little meat was consumed at the fort.[24] If Vindolanda, the only site for which we have precise information, was not completely atypical, the military diet had altered considerably. The troops in the permanent frontier forts ate not only cereals, but also bacon, cheese, lard, vegetables, sour wine, salt, olive oil, and a considerable and varied quantity of meat. Fixed amounts were frequently deducted from the soldiers' pay in order to pay for nonration supplements to the unit's menu, and a soldier with particular tastes could buy extras off-post or write home for specific items.[25] If the evidence from Vindolanda is representative, Roman frontier troops were eating meat in substantial amounts almost from the very time they arrived on the frontier.

What had happened to alter the diet and appetite of the Roman soldier to such a degree? One of the first considerations to present itself is that the wheaten diet of the early legionaries was adapted to a Mediterranean climate. The colder climate of northern Europe demanded a higher caloric intake, and the troops may have found it difficult to accomplish this simply by eating more porridge. Also, there is little evidence as to what the troops of an earlier era may have used to supplement their grain ration, but one suspects that they may have eaten considerable quantities of dried fish, sausage, and fowl.[26] Meat was a good deal more plentiful along the frontier and may gradually have substituted for the more expensive supplements previously favored. One must also remember that garrison life can become quite boring, and that troops living under such conditions become much more concerned about the quality of their mess. It is probable that the troops, particularly in smaller and more isolated forts, derived some of their entertainment from hunting and fowling. A greater taste for meat might have been introduced gradually among the troops by these means.

Perhaps the most important point to consider, however, is that the natives of the frontier districts were recruited into the army from the very beginning, and those with Roman citizenship soon entered the legions. In time, the Roman army of the frontier became composed almost entirely of Celts, together with some Germans. It is probable that the alteration in the Roman military diet reflected the change in the composition of its ranks from Italians to residents of the western frontier.

Whatever the reasons, at least some members of the frontier army appear to have been meat eaters. As a consequence, they and the civilians associated with them were probably healthier than the inhabitants of the interior who depended upon grain as the mainstay of their diet. Not only is wheat protein inferior to that of milk, eggs, cheese, and meat, but much of it is lost in the process of cooking.[27] The addition of quantities of meat to the military diet produced troops with greater stamina and resistance to illness. As such, meat was an essential military commodity. If one were to assume that the military consumption of meat were as low as one pound per week per man,[28] the army in Europe would still have needed over 5,000 tons annually.

Cavalry Remounts

The Roman army's needs were not restricted to dead animals. Although commonly pictured as an infantry force, the army in Europe actually had an unusually large cavalry component.[29] By the year A.D. 100, the Roman army included approximately 80,000 mounted auxiliaries. In addition, each legion deployed a cavalry unit of 120 horses, and a pack mule was generally assigned to each century-sized unit. There is some evidence that allows us to estimate the number of mounts in the army of the western frontier.[30] The army in Britain would have had 8,500 auxiliary cavalry and 360 legionary horse; the army on the Rhine would have included 11,300 auxiliary and 480 legionary cavalry; and the Danubian forces would have deployed 28,300 auxiliaries and 2,040 legionary mounts. The cavalry contingents of the Roman army in Europe would have totaled 50,140. Fully a quarter of the army of the frontier in Europe were cavalry.

The totals just given are only those of cavalry mounts, and, since the quality of these animals often spelled the difference between life and death and victory and defeat, they were carefully chosen. Only mares and geldings were employed, since stallions could not be kept together without fighting or pursuing the mares, and stallions tended to be too high-strung for the cavalry. Cavalry mares were valued highly and were not used for breeding since this would have made them unfit for military action for too long. What this meant was that the army was choosing the very best horses available, both mares and stallions, and permanently removing them from the breeding pool. Unless that pool were very large and constantly infused with new blood, the quality of its members would quickly have begun to deteriorate. The army needed a number of large and independent herds from which to select its mounts, since this would not only guarantee continued quality, but would also afford procurement officers the widest possible selection of animals. These factors effectively precluded the army from establishing its own breeding herds. This particular situation greatly stimulated horse breeding throughout the frontier regions, but also virtually required the importation of horses from barbarian territories.[31]

Although some of this demand for cavalry horses was satisfied through imports into the frontier districts and by confiscation from defeated enemies, the army needed a reliable local system to furnish remounts. Horse dealing with the barbarians was too uncertain for an organization that had to be sure of a steady supply of high-quality remounts. The cavalry in particular needed remounts when preparing for war and while on campaign, a time at which the barbarians were more likely to be preparing for war themselves than furnishing the

Roman cavalry with fresh horses. Confiscation was equally uncertain; and neither confiscation nor local levies provided any effective method of quality control.

In order to overcome these problems, the army of the frontier established a highly organized system of remount procurement in which the procurement officers routinely purchased their mounts from civilians. The army set high standards for such animals, and a veterinary examination of each horse was required before it was purchased. Imperial stud farms in Cappadocia, Thrace, and Spain were later established to breed horses for the army. A papyrus bill of sale has survived for a Cappadocian horse purchased in A.D. 77. The animal cost 675 *denarii*, more than twice the annual pay of a Roman legionary. It had passed its veterinary examination, and had even had some training for its future tasks. Yet this horse was not intended for the cavalry; it was a pack animal. In the late Roman Empire, precise stipulations were established regulating the size, shape, and age of military horses, and their training was intense.[32]

The turnover of army horses was probably quite rapid. Unlike in motion pictures, where the horses seem never to be killed, many horses were lost and wounded in battle. A favorite defensive tactic of both Romans and barbarians along the frontier was to prepare a position with numerous "lilies," small holes about two to three feet deep and covered with sod. They then tried to lure the enemy cavalry into attacking over this prepared ground. The leaders of both sides fell for this trick far too often, and tens of thousands of horses over the years had a leg snapped at the knee. In any cavalry attack, the defenders tried first to kill the horse, which was of course the larger target, and then slit the throat of the fallen rider. Frontier warfare used up good horses at a rapid rate.

Although cavalry units took the best possible care of their horses, they lacked modern vaccines, and in the close quarters of a frontier post perhaps originally designed for infantrymen, equine fever or a number of other sicknesses could quickly kill off many of a unit's mounts and leave the rest so weakened as to be useless. In addition, compared to modern horse breeds, the horse of Roman times was small, and her load was heavy. Training was constant and wearing, and food sometimes in short supply. The frontier cavalry horse aged quickly, and no cavalryman who valued his life would have been satisfied with an overaged or jaded mount.

Military service constituted only a part of the demand for horses. Many civilians also rode horses and were as eager as the army to have the finest and healthiest mounts possible. Mules and donkeys were employed extensively by both the army and civilians as pack animals. To transport goods by land, Romans generally put them in a cart or on the back of a pack animal. Hence, the number of animals necessary to satisfy the requirements of commercial transport in the frontier regions must have been substantial.

The Importance of Imperial Pastures

Roman legions and auxiliary units possessed tracts of land, designated as *prata* or *territoria*, assigned to their forts. These pastures served as grazing grounds for cattle and horses belonging to the unit. Certain soldiers were designated as *pecuarii* (cattlemen) and tended the animals that grazed on these lands.[33] These Roman *vaqueros* apparently herded the cattle used by the unit for food. An inscription from Cumberland in Britain refers to individuals called *venatores* who quite likely supervised the provisioning of fresh meat.[34] The substantial demands of the troops for ranching products were met partially by local military herds, but the animals in these herds had probably been bought from local stockmen.

A military *pratum* on the lower Rhine brought about a confrontation between farmers and ranchers of the sort beloved by writers of Western fiction. The Roman army of the frontier had been quiet for some time and had never avenged their defeat at the hands of the Frisians in A.D. 29. In the year 58, the Frisians had grown tired of scratching out a living in the marshes, and had learned of some excellent farmland located on the left bank of the Rhine. The entire tribe picked up their goods, fought their way through marshes and forests, forded the Rhine, and arrived at an extensive *pratum* reserved for the army of the lower Rhine. They liked what they saw, built houses, plowed fields, and generally settled down.

The new imperial governor of Lower Germany, Lucius Duvius Avitus, learned of the Frisians' squatting on army land and sent them word to clear off. They instead decided to appeal to the emperor Nero and sent two of their leading citizens, Verritus and Malorix, as delegates. Upon arriving at Rome, they were assigned a guide and taken to see all of the usual tourist sights. They went to a play at

Pompey's Theater, a prime attraction for sightseers, but knew too little Latin to understand what was going on. They became interested in the various reserved seats, however, and their guide explained that some were general admission, some reserved for members of the equestrian class, and the best held for members of the senatorial order.

Gawking at the senators, they saw that there were men in foreign clothes seated in that section and asked their guide who the foreigners were. The guide explained that these were delegates from peoples distinguished for their courage. Verritus and Malorix thought that over for a moment, and bawled out that nobody was braver than the Frisians. They then shoved various important people aside and seated themselves in the midst of the senators. The audience immediately began applauding this old-fashioned patriotism. Nero quickly did them both the honor of making them Roman citizens. He also told them to clear off the army's *pratum*. When the Frisians did not move, they were attacked by auxiliary cavalry and driven off. Those who failed to move quickly enough were either killed, or captured and sold into slavery.

Shortly afterward, a landless tribe, the Ampsivarii, moved onto the same land. Their leader, a long-time ally of the Romans named Boiocalus, pleaded with the imperial governor for permission to settle there.

> How little of this land will ever be used for the grazing of Roman soldiers' flocks and herds! Hold back pasture for your cattle if you have to, even though people are starving, but do not think that such wastes are more valuable to you than friendly tribes. Heaven belongs to the gods and the land belongs to man; men can take land that is not used.

The governor was impressed by the rhetoric, but told Boiocalus to get his people off the *pratum*. The Ampsivarii wandered among the German tribes, trying to gain allies to help them seize these pasture-lands, but the Romans intimidated every tribe the Boiocali approached. They finally decided to fight other German tribes for land. Their men were killed, their women and children were taken as slaves, and the Ampsivarii ceased to exist.[35]

All of the evidence and anecdotes point to the same set of conclusions: that the Roman army that defended the European frontiers of the empire was absolutely dependent upon a wide variety of animals and animal by-products and had to be able to draw upon vast reserves of flocks and herds to meet its needs. It is clear that the constant demands of the army must have been met by an increased breeding of horses, sheep, goats, and cattle in the frontier regions. In short, ranching and animal husbandry must have been stimulated much as agriculture had been. We have not yet considered where these animals came from or how ranching was conducted along the frontier.

Ranching

A large rectangular portico once stood immediately behind the legionary fortress at Carnuntum on the Danube. Archaeologists have discovered that there were several wells located inside and have concluded that chief function of this building was to serve as a livestock market. This would fit with what we know of the frontier line. The fortifications did not obstruct traffic across the frontier, but channeled and controlled it. Just as Roman traders crossed over into barbarian lands, so too the barbarians brought their goods in for sale and trade. The areas near the entry points in the frontier must have been lively places, with barbarians, legionaries, local natives, and various civilians jostling as they inspected each others' goods and renewed old acquaintances. The most important of the trade goods brought in by the frontier tribes appear to have been hides and cattle.[36] The Romans probably restricted this trade to specific sites near fortresses and under the supervision of the military. The market at Carnuntum was almost certainly one of these sites, and there must have been many more. This practice undoubtedly fostered the growth of the fortresses as trading centers and promoted the emergence of the civilian settlements that sprang up near many of the forts and fortresses of the frontier.

A second source of animals was no doubt the farms and villas that lay immediately behind the frontier. With the passage of time, the great estates that emerged in some regions of the frontier, particularly in the Danubian area, replaced the smaller-scale family farms that had previously dominated the rural landscape. At the same time, the districts immediately along the frontier began to develop a surplus grain production capable of satisfying the local military markets. Considering the competition in grain production, and the profits that were to be gained from horse and cattle raising, it would be surprising if the owners of some of these very large estates had not converted the arable lands they were acquiring into pasture. Indeed, the increased profitability of rangeland was perhaps a contributing factor in the disappearance of the small villas of Pannonia and Illyria. There may have been ranching villas in these regions, but none has been identified and excavated so far, and so their character and methods of operation are unknown.[37] It is known, however, that the large estates of Pannonia and Moesia were exporting significant quantities of grain and cattle by the end of the third century.[38] The army's requirements were thus served by trade with barbarian tribes and both large- and small-scale enterprises along the frontier and in its hinterland. The Fenlands of Britain provide some idea of how large-scale ranching may have been conducted by the Romans.

The Fenlands, which we have previously discussed as a great imperial agricultural project, also provide an excellent example of the development of an interior ranching district designed to supply the frontier.[39] The development of the Fenlands probably began relatively soon after the conquest and may have been connected in some fashion with the revolt of the Iceni, the native tribe of the region, in A.D. 61. The initial development consisted primarily of digging canals. Numbers of them appear to have been constructed for transport, while many others appear to have been designed to drain the land water off to the sea. The organization and planning necessary for the development and maintenance of a project of this scale almost presupposes that it was conducted under governmental direction and control.[40] Excavations conducted at Stonea, in the Cambridgeshire Fens, have uncovered the remains of a complex of buildings that may have been the administrative center for the southern Fenlands.[41] The region was characterized by numerous small and simple farms and villages. The complete absence of villas suggests that the area was imperial land, and that the small holdings were assigned to tenant-farmers who operated them under the direction of an imperial official.[42]

By the close of the second century, the agricultural exploitation of this area was being slowly abandoned. A number of factors may have contributed to this. The frontier districts of the North had begun to develop a system of agricultural exploitation sufficient to meet the army's needs with locally grown produce. At the same time, Britain had opposed Septimius Severus in the civil war of 193–197. Severus took savage revenge upon his opponents, and the economy of Britain, as well as Gaul, was probably badly disrupted as a result. Finally, the maintenance of the works necessary to sustain agriculture would have been an expensive and time-consuming business, and the pastoral value of the Fenlands was no doubt continually increasing.[43]

There is ample evidence that ranching became the primary economic activity of the Fenlands. There were wide expanses of open land between settlements, and large quantities of animal bones have been discovered in the remains of Fenland villages. This would suggest that cattle were the most likely stock, and that the villages served as processing centers, butchering a number of the animals and using the abundant local sources of salt to preserve the meat either by salting or by pickling in brine. Live cattle were driven north, and preserved meats shipped over the canals that had once been the main arteries for the army's grain supply. The extensive imperial estates, the availability of satisfactory water communications, and the presence of a significant supply of salt combined to make the Fenland especially attractive to cattle raising and meat packing.[44]

A number of the cow and sheep bones found were those of older animals, strongly suggesting that the villagers were also engaged in the raising of sheep for wool and of dairy cattle. The quality of the Fens environment is such that it can produce fleeces of extremely high quality. The discovery of loom weights in the Fenland villages indicates that weaving was practiced locally. This makes a good deal of economic sense. Both agriculture and husbandry are highly seasonal in nature, and during much of the year, there is little for the workers to do. Local processing would better distribute productive labor over the year, increase the value of the commodities exported, and decrease the weight of the material to be shipped. It is not improbable that the villagers also processed their milk and cream into cheeses.[45]

If this was in fact the management policy of the Fenlands, it may provide the key to understanding the nature of the operation of other large ranching and pastoral enterprises. After a certain period of economic growth of the frontier, a point would have been reached when the military markets, which were remarkably constant in terms of demand, could have been filled from a number of different sources, the production of which had been generally increasing. A period must have followed in which the small farms of the local frontier districts, the large estates of the hinterland, and barbarian traders from beyond the frontier competed in selling to the military. Each of these groups would have had its own advantages. The small producers of the frontier districts would no doubt have had good relations with procurement officers, and the transportation costs of their goods would have been relatively slight. The production costs of the barbarians would have been low, and they would have been able to rely on more than grain and animals for trading purposes. Thus barbarians could afford to sell their leather, cattle, and horses relatively cheaply. The large estates of the interior could have become competitive by processing their goods, thus maximizing the efficiency of their labor force, increasing the value of their goods, and decreasing their shipping costs by decreasing the weight of their goods.

The ranching enterprises of the interior would, then, have also been processing centers. They may have raised cattle, but a portion of their sales would have been preserved meats, polished horn, and dressed leather. They would have raised dairy stock in order to make and ship cheese, and sheep in order to weave and transport finished cloth. Horse breeders would have enhanced the value of their stock by breaking and training their mounts before offering them to the cavalry. Such an organization would have been perfectly in keeping with the basic concept of the villa, and it is easy to imagine the owner of a large villa expanding his stock-raising activities and decreasing the labor devoted to pure agriculture. At the same time, he would have secured the services of men and women trained in the various forms of processing. It would have been unusual if such establishments as we find in the Fenlands did not also supplement their shipments to the military with dried fruits and nuts, pickled cabbage, and salt and fermented fish. The strengths of the villa system were its adaptability and capacity for rationalizing farm production. It is probable that much of the Roman ranching industry was managed on such a model.

The demand for animals and animal products on the Rhine and Danube frontiers was similar to that of Britain, but there is less archaeological evidence of how this demand was satisfied. Animal bones from numerous sites in southern Germany, Austria, and Switzerland reveal that horses, cattle, sheep, pigs, goats and chickens were raised throughout the area. There is also literary evidence that the region became famous for its breeding of horses.[46] As in Britain, the production of woolen cloth and cheese also bulked large in the local economy. On the other hand, these regions were particularly suited for ranching based on transhumance, the regular shifting of livestock from summer to winter pastures and back. Since the pastures are generally considered common lands under this system, it is routine for a number of owners to assemble their animals in a single herd or flock and place them in the charge of a master drover and his assistants. This pattern was the basis of Celtic herding from prehistoric times and has continued into modern times in many regions of Europe where the geography is suited to the practice. In fact, many of the routes presently followed by herds and flocks are apparently the same as in pre-Roman times. The system affords small-scale stockowners the ability to pasture their animals without owning rangeland and, in Roman times, would have supported small-scale, village-based producers. It is quite probable that village-centered stock raising based on transhumance and collective pasturing competed with the practices of the large villas, based as they were on large herds, private ownership of rangeland, and the administrative and processing center of the villa. In the long run, however, it was the villa system that exercised the greater influence on later ranching practices. The stock-raising practices of the great Spanish estates, heirs to the late Roman villas of the peninsula, were exported to the New World and formed the models for American ranching.

The steady demand of the 200,000-man frontier army in Europe for animals and animal by-products was easily of great enough magnitude to require the frontier regions to increase their livestock production substantially. A significant immigration of civilians and the growth of the local population under the protection of the army contributed still further to an increased demand for animals and animal by-products along the frontier. Although some of this demand was satisfied through trade with the tribes beyond the frontier, the effect of these expanded markets was to stimulate the growth of a ranching industry along the frontier and in its immediate hinterland. Although a full range of archaeological data is lacking, it would appear that ranching on the frontier developed as some of the owners of large villas concentrated their efforts on the raising of stock. This appears to have been combined with an attempt to concentrate various processing activities in the villa itself. Such policies would have been merely modifications of the traditional practices of the large agricultural villas. Villas of this sort probably began to assume many of the characteristics of an American *hacienda* or *estancia*.

An Old Dilemma: Ranching versus Farming

One would normally expect that an agrarian economy based upon both agriculture and husbandry would lead to an efficient, integrated system of land use. Ranching and herding would use land unsuitable for agriculture, and agriculture would convert its wastes into straw and silage for winter fodder.[47] Although our examples are limited, it would appear that this did not happen along the frontier. The pastoral industry of the Fenlands arose only when the agricultural production of the area began to decline as a result of the domination of military markets by the northern frontier districts. Fenland stock raising expanded over lands previously employed for cereal production. A similar process took place in Pannonia and Illyria, and probably in Moesia. The numerous small farms and villas of the interior of the frontier regions began to be absorbed by great estates when the districts immediately along the frontier became able to supply the local military demand for grain. Some of these great villas of the interior turned to ranching and herding for the military market. Thus again, pastoralism spread over abandoned agricultural lands or perhaps even displaced cultivation. Along the lower Rhine, both the Frisians and the Ampsivarii were desperate to be allowed to cultivate some of the lands set aside for military grazing.[48] Here, too, arable land was being used to support stock animals.

It is difficult to imagine why ranching and agriculture did not develop a complementary pattern of land use along the Roman frontier, but the present state of the evidence indicates that they did not. Such a failure could not have benefited either the economy or the society of the frontier regions. Agrarian development in the third century generally saw the disappearance of small farms and independent farmers, and the growth of great villas and conversion of plowlands into range. The great disparities of wealth and status characteristic of the heartland of the empire began to appear among the frontier societies. Thus, the rise of frontier ranching may have played a significant role in the decline of the cultural interchanges and social integration that had previously characterized these regions.

Notes

1. The equipment used by the auxiliary troops is a matter of some dispute. It seems unlikely that they would have worn a full *lorica segmentata* like that of legionary troops (see below, note 3), but it is clear that the distinctions between

legionary and auxiliary units were constantly decreasing. Graham Webster, *The Roman Imperial Army of the First and Second Centuries A.D.*, pp. 150–151, claims that many of the auxiliaries were equipped differently, but most wore some kind of body armor.

2. The actual number was probably considerably smaller, since a number of troops would not have lived to see retirement.

3. This particular armor was a relatively new piece of equipment, having been developed in the arms factories established by imperial order in the West. It would seem to have been a version of Celtic body armor modified to meet the needs of a Roman legionary. The name for such a suit was *lorica segmentata*, and *lorica* was not a native Latin word. Earlier armor had consisted simply of a series of plates riveted to a leather jacket.

4. H. Russell Robinson, *The Armour of Imperial Rome*, p. 174. Webster, *The Roman Imperial Army*, pp. 124, 128–129, states that every legionary owned a suit of body armor fashioned with metal strips and plates. This armor was designed to provide total freedom of movement and so must have been held together by leather straps in order to allow for the necessary mobility. The outside surface of the Roman shield was covered in leather upon which were fastened gilded or silvered decorations, probably in bronze. Tacitus, *Annales*, 1:17, maintains that the legionaries had deductions taken from their pay for food, clothing, and arms replacement. See also Sheppard Sunderland Frere, *Britannia: A History of Roman Britain*, p. 227, and Ian A. Richmond, *Trajan's Army on Trajan's Column*.

5. A well-illustrated, although brief, account of the arms and armor of the imperial period may be found in Peter Connolly, *Greece and Rome at War*, particularly pp. 228–239.

6. Connolly, ibid., pp. 62–63.

7. James McIntyre and Ian A. Richmond, "Tents of the Roman Army and Leather from Birdoswald," *Cumberland and Westmorland Antiquarian and Archaeological Society* 34 (1934):73–76, point out that the Birdoswald deposit has yielded panels of leather strikingly like the panels shown forming tents depicted upon Trajan's column. The leather found at Newstead not only included panels resembling those from Birdoswald, but far outnumbered them.

8. It has been suggested that each legionary century occupied only eight leather tents because a group of sixteen men per century was constantly posted on guard duty. See Anne Johnson, *Roman Forts of the First and Second Centuries A.D. in Britain and the German Provinces*, p. 166.

9. Two hundred thousand men divided by an eighty-man century equals the equivalent of 2,500 centuries; 2,500 centuries multiplied by 588 tent panels equals a total of 1.47 million.

10. See Christoph Wilhelm Röring, *Untersuchungen zu römischen Reisewagen*, for details of the structure of Roman wagons.

11. Two bushels would weigh about 120 pounds, a convenient weight for two men to handle. Also, older sacks might easily break with heavier contents.

12. Auxiliary troops presumably had a similar arrangement.

13. The literature on this site is large; some of the more recent publications are Anthony Birley, "Vindolanda: New Writing Tablets 1986–89," in *Roman Frontier Studies: 1989*, ed. V. A. Maxfield and M. J. Dobson, pp. 16–20; Robin Birley, *Vindolanda: A Roman Frontier Post on Hadrian's Wall*; Alan K. Bowman,

Vindolanda: The Latin Writing-Tablets; and three works by Alan K. Bowman and J. David Thomas: "A Military Strength Report from Vindolanda," *Journal of Roman Studies* 31 (1991): 62–73; "Vindolanda 1985: The New Writing Tablets," *Journal of Roman Studies* 76 (1986): 120–123; *Vindolanda: The Latin Writing-Tablets*.

14. Robin Birley, *Vindolanda: A Roman Frontier Post on Hadrian's Wall*, pp. 123–124, states that complete skulls of oxen, sheep, goats, horses, and dogs were discovered at Vindolanda along with vast quantities of foot bones and hooves. This is typical of the kind of refuse to be found at a tannery. Several wooden items possibly associated with leather working have also been found. Half-moon-shaped pieces of wood, similar to the instruments employed in more modern times to remove the fat of skins, have been discovered along with more than twenty fine boxwood combs. A large vat stirrer, an iron punch, several knives, and numerous leather scraps provide further evidence that the site was that of a tannery.

15. The prefects' duties included advising tribal chiefs, overseeing the collection of taxes, arbitrating disputes between Romans and the natives, and generally representing Roman authority at the local level.

16. The fortress of Flevum was at the site of the modern Schiermonnikoog in the Netherlands.

17. Although Tacitus calls Cruptorix "a veteran of ours," the name is clearly either Celtic or German. Cruptorix was probably a retiree from an auxiliary unit, perhaps from the fort at Flevum. The -rix ending of his name is the Celtic root meaning "king," and suggests that this veteran had been a member of the Celtic aristocracy.

18. Tacitus, *Annales* 4:73. Tacitus favored continued imperial expansion, and the inference to be drawn from this passage may be that Tiberius suppressed the news of this frontier defeat because if it were known there would have been a popular outcry to reconquer the land.

19. K. D. White, *Roman Farming*, pp. 310, 315. Toward the end of the first century A.D., linen began to advance in popularity. Also see J. P. Wild, *Textile Manufacture in the Northern Roman Provinces*; and Joan M. Frayn, *Sheep-rearing and the Wool Trade in Italy during the Roman Period*.

20. Tacitus, *Annales* 14:24. Johnson, *Roman Forts*, p. 195, mentions that the daily grain ration for each soldier during the late Republican period was approximately one kilogram. The grain was milled and then baked into bread or made into pasta or porridge dishes.

21. See Peter Connelly, *Greece and Rome at War*, pp. 13–14.

22. Geoffrey Rickman, *The Corn Supply of Ancient Rome*, pp. 5 and 7; also see the discussion of the Roman diet in chapter 1 above.

23. Robin Birley, *Vindolanda: A Roman Frontier Post on Hadrian's Wall*, pp. 75, 123, states that dog bones discovered in association with butchered meat and mutton suggests that the dog was sometimes eaten. Strabo, *Geographica*, 3 vols., ed. A. Meineke, vol. 1, 4:5, claims that Britain exported corn, cattle, gold, silver, iron, hides, and hunting dogs.

24. Robin Birley, *Vindolanda: A Roman Frontier Post on Hadrian's Wall*, pp. 154–155, maintains that other items besides grain may have been stocked in the military granaries located in every fort. Possibly hams, muttons, bacon, and other smoked meats were hung in the bins so as not to reduce floor space. Hams averaging

five pounds each would run to approximately fifty to seventy pounds per yard, and in a 450-yard granary this would allow for up to ten to fifteen tons of meat, enough to provide the garrison about one pound of meat weekly for each soldier for the entire year. See also R. G. Collingwood and F. Haverfield, "The Provisioning of Roman Forts," *Cumberland and Westmorland Antiquarian and Archaeological Society* 20 (1920): 141; Anne P. Gentry, "Roman Military Stone-Built Granaries in Britain," *British Archaeological Reports* 32 (1976): 1–95.

25. Johnson, *Roman Forts*, p. 196.

26. These were popular dishes in the civilian meals discussed in literary sources.

27. Rickman, *The Corn Supply of Ancient Rome*, p. 7.

28. This is the estimate of Johnson, *Roman Forts*, pp. 142–143.

29. The Greeks usually regarded the horse as a luxury; Ann Hyland, *Equus: The Horse in the Roman World*, provides an excellent account of the role and status of the horse among the Romans.

30. The Romans had three legions in Britain, and some 8,500 mounted auxiliaries. Stanwix, the main cavalry post on the northern frontier, could accommodate some 5,500 regular auxiliary cavalry and 3,000 light cavalry of *cohortes equitatae*. This would suggest a ratio of 2,833 auxiliary cavalry per legion. This same ratio, applied to the twenty-nine legions of the imperial army, yields a total of about 82,157 auxiliary calvary, close enough to other estimates to justify the use of the ratio in fixing the cavalry contingents in Europe.

31. Roy W. Davies, "The Supply of Animals to the Roman Army and the Remount System," *Latomus* 28 (1969): 429–431, points out that horses were generally acquired from civilians. Louis C. West, *Roman Gaul: The Objects of Trade*, p. 74; Geza Alföldy, *Noricum*, pp. 108, 112; Andrés Mócsy, *Pannonia and Upper Moesia: A History of the Middle Danube Provinces of the Roman Empire*, p. 246, all point out that horse breeding was a very important economic activity in many provincial areas, and especially in northern Gaul, Noricum, and Pannonia.

32. Arther Ferrill, *The Fall of the Roman Empire: The Military Explanation*, pp. 79–81.

33. *Corpus Inscriptionum Latinarum* 12:8287 (hereafter cited as *CIL*), refers to a soldier of *Legio XX* from Cologne. See also Webster, *The Roman Imperial Army*, pp. 254–255. As a slight digression, it has been suggested that *pecuarius* might be translated as "cowboy," but *pecus*, or cow, was not originally a Latin word, so one should employ a foreign term in place of "cowboy." *Vaquero* is a good translation for *pecuarius*, particularly since they are the same word.

34. *CIL* 7:830. S. Applebaum, "Roman Britain," in *The Agrarian History of England and Wales*, ed. H. R. R. Finberg, p. 209, states that the British legions maintained cattle ranches in order to supply their needs. The place-name of *Bovium*, which might mean (place) of cattle, appears in the *Itinerary of Antoninus* as situated near Chester and has been identified with Heronbridge on the south bank of the Dee, or possibly with Holt, Denbigshire.

35. This story is found in Tacitus, *Annales* 13:53–56. The quotation is a loose and partial translation.

36. *Dionis Cassii Cocceiani Historia romana* 71:2. See also M. Teichert, "Size Variation in Cattle from Germania Romana and Germania Libra," in *Husbandry in Europe*, vol. 4 of *Animals and Archaeology*, ed. C. Grigson and J. Clutton-Brock, pp. 93–103.

37. The probability of the existence of ranching villas is based partially on what is known of the economic situation of the era, and partially upon the verified existence of imperial stud farms in the region at a somewhat later date. The difficulty of identifying the remains of a ranching villa lies in the fact that the rangeland of such an operation would have consisted of previously tilled soil and that the immediate environs of such a villa would probably have been devoted to wheat and barley agriculture. This would make it difficult to determine the land-use pattern at any given date.

38. Mócsy, *Pannonia and Upper Moesia*, pp. 127–129.

39. H. C. Bowen, "The Celtic Background," in *The Roman Villa in Britain*, ed. A. L. F. Rivet, p. 37. A. L. F. Rivet, "The Rural Economy of Roman Britain," in *Aufsteig und Niedergang der römischen Welt*, ed. Hildegard Temporini and Wolfgang Haase, p. 347, commenting on the growth of settlements in the Fenland, states that by the second century A.D. settlements including four or more homesteads accounted for at least 27 percent of the population. See David Hall, "Survey Results in the Cambridgeshire Fenland," *Antiquity* 62 (June 1988):313. It is currently argued that agriculture never constituted the primary land use of the area. Little of the Fenland lies more than fifteen feet above sea level, and it is thought that frequent flooding probably restricted agriculture to the periphery of the area. It is now generally accepted that pastoralism was undoubtedly a more rewarding land use than agriculture. Although this is undoubtedly true, the evidence would suggest that the original intention was to develop the Fens for agriculture. An immense amount of human labor was spent in constructing shipping canals in the area, as well as the great Car Dyke and Foss Dyke canal systems that provided an inland water route from Cambridgeshire all the way to the military supply base at York, some 150 miles to the north. Such a great investment would have been unnecessary for a ranching area, since the animals could have walked to York.

40. Peter Salway, "The Roman Fenland," in *The Fenland in Roman Times: Studies of a Major Area of Peasant Colonization*, ed. C. W. Phillips, p. 10.

41. Hall, "Survey Results in the Cambridgeshire Fenland," p. 312.

42. Salway, "The Roman Fenland," p. 10. T. W. Potter and R. P. J. Jackson, "The Roman Site of Stonea, Cambridgeshire," *Antiquity* 56 (July 1982): 111, state that the Roman site at Stonea was the headquarters of a provincial procurator administering perhaps the whole of the southern Fens as imperial land.

43. Britain was not able to draw on the great reserves of barbarian trade available to the continental provinces and was thus more dependent upon its own resources. As population, and meat consumption, increased, the profits to be gained from ranching would also have increased.

44. Salway, "The Roman Fenland," p. 13.

45. Bowen, "The Celtic Background," pp. 44–45. See also Salway, "The Roman Fenland," p. 13.

46. Alföldy, *Noricum*, pp. 107–108.

47. Sown grasses were not employed in Europe until the early modern period. The availability of winter fodder therefore set the upper limit on herd size.

48. These tribes were driven away from the army pasture not so much because of an inflated view of the value of the pastureland as from a disinclination to allow native tribes to establish themselves on the left bank of the Rhine.

V TRADING ON AND BEYOND THE FRONTIER

The Frontier Traders

During the reign of the emperor Nero (A.D. 54–68), a young Roman serving as the agent of the merchant Julianus undertook a trading expedition to the Baltic. Leaving from the great legionary fortress and trading town of Carnuntum on the Danube, he and his men traveled some 600 miles north along one of the most well known of the trade routes into free Germany. This route led northward up the valley of the March, through the Moravian Gates, and into the German plain. From the upper Oder, the trail proceeded toward Kalisz in upper Poland, where it reached the lower Vistula and the famous "Amber Coast" of the Baltic. The trip from Carnuntum along the amber route to the Baltic took about two months, although a merchant passing this way could spend considerably longer if he stopped to bargain at the numerous trading posts that lay along the route and offered travelers accommodations and the opportunity to purchase local wares.[1] Needless to say, this was not a new trail, but one that had existed from prehistoric times, joining Baltic and Mediterranean lands. The young Roman trailblazer's adventures were well publicized, however, and the large amount of amber he brought back helped to focus Roman attention on this and other products of the North.

Amber quickly became an object of fascination for the Romans, and gladiatorial, circus, and theater performances sometimes featured displays of crude amber, amber jewelry, and amber-colored accessories. Amber, the fossilized resin of prehistoric forests, possesses a number of unusual qualities that particularly intrigued the Romans. Soft to the touch, it grew warm when held in the hand. Hair and bits of lint were attracted as if by magic to a cloth that had been stroked by a piece of amber. If one were to rub a piece of amber against a pin or needle and then float the needle on some water, one would find that the needle pointed always north, as if pointing the way to the lands from which the amber had come. The Roman populace, a superstitious lot at best, seized upon amber as a sovereign defense against the dangers of the evil eye. There were few Roman parents who felt that they could not afford at least a small piece of amber for a bracelet or necklace to protect their children from the envious and malevolent witches who seemed to abound in the early empire. For this and many other reasons, there continued to be a steady and significant demand within the empire for northern amber. The amber route became a well-traveled path upon which a wide variety of Roman and northern goods passed back and forth among the numerous middlemen who took up residence along the road.

These Roman traders did more than pass goods from hand to hand. They went out from the amber route to trade their wares with nearby tribesmen for local products such as honey, beeswax, furs, rosins, and even the luxuriant hair of German women to make wigs for the noble ladies of Rome. It was not a secure life; when a tribe began to feel that life, the gods, or their neighbors were treating them unfairly, their first reaction was often to kill the Roman merchants who dwelled or passed among them, usually in the most unpleasant manner they could think of. Other Roman traders soon came to take their place, however. For many Romans, the frontier was not a barrier, but rather a point of departure from which to seize the opportunities that German trade presented. Many lost their lives in the pursuit of profit far beyond the frontier of the empire, but the hope of riches and the assurance of adventure lured others to replace them.

The basic geography of the frontier virtually ensured that Roman trade and commerce would be carried far beyond the lines established by the Roman army and that such commerce would eventually stimulate the manufacturing potential of the frontier districts themselves. The Romans had sought defensible military positions and had found them in the Rhine and Danube rivers, but these rivers were also the hearts of great watersheds, and the tributary waters of the frontier led north, into free Germany, as well as south into the border provinces of the empire. These water routes northward made trade not only possible, but almost inevitable. Indeed, trade beyond the frontier was well developed even before the frontier itself was firmly fixed; Roman merchants had established themselves far beyond the Rhine by the mid first century A.D.

Tacitus reports that there was a concentration of Roman traders by this time among the Marcomanni, who inhabited the region of Bohemia. They had been encouraged to settle in the Marcomanni capital by the leader of the tribe, and had stayed on because of the profit possible in supplying the Marcomanni with Roman export goods. By the end of the century, they appear to have lost their Roman identity and adapted to German ways.[2] The abundance of Roman goods found in archaeological sites in this region indicates that this early merchant colony was quite active,[3] and the entire account suggests the complex nature of commerce beyond the frontier. It was not a simple matter of Germans and Romans; the trading network often developed its own peculiar population, a half-German, half-Roman merchant folk who acted as intermediaries between the two cultures. There is no history of these people, but incidental references by Roman historians make it quite clear that they existed and that they played an important role in carrying Roman goods and influences deep into German lands. One wonders if the German killings and mistreatment of Roman merchants may not sometimes have been the result of these Germanized traders' attempts to eliminate unwanted competition.

The trade routes were often as complex and varied as the people who traveled them. In the west, for instance, Roman trade goods were apparently carried from the frontier to the lands of the Elbe, but some of these goods were apparently transshipped down this and other rivers of northern Germany to markets established at the rivers' mouths.[4] The merchants from the German interior, carrying a mixed cargo of Roman exports and German goods, were met here by other traders, most probably Frisians, who were carrying Roman goods by sea for trade all along the German and Norwegian coast.[5] Still other merchants attending these northern markets bought Roman wares from both Frisians and the traders from the interior and carried them into the Baltic. Archaeologists have traced such wares across the base of Jutland and have discovered several concentrations in the Danish islands. It would appear that Danish merchants traded their Roman wares along the Baltic coast, often in competition with similar goods carried from the region of the Elbe across to the Vistula and then northward to the coast.[6]

Such complex systems indicate that Roman imports were important goods in a large and far-flung German trading economy.

This fact was of major significance to the Roman government. Roman traders supplied frontier tribes the wares with which those tribes carried on commerce with their neighbors, and this gave the Romans a certain degree of control over their German neighbors. They could reward a friendly tribe by increasing its access to Roman export goods and thus allow it to expand commerce with its neighbors and increase its wealth. Conversely, pressure could be placed upon a tribe by limiting the Roman wares it could acquire, thus putting it at an economic disadvantage in obtaining the materials it needed from other tribes. Finally, on those rare occasions when a tribe attacked the frontier, trade with the Romans was automatically ended, and the whole tribe soon began to feel the effects of the lack of exchangeable commodities. Although plunder could remedy that deficiency for a time, the disruption of normal commerce could not help but soon alienate the hostile tribe's neighbors, who were, after all, gaining no profit from the situation.

The inhabitants of the frontier districts were probably less concerned with the value of the German trade as a device for controlling the frontier tribes than they were with the profits to be gained from its pursuit. For the frontier districts, there were three distinct aspects to this commerce: the trade by which Roman goods were carried beyond the frontier for exchange among the Germans; the trade by which the Germans, usually border tribesmen, brought their goods to frontier stations for exchange with local merchants; and the local production of export wares to supply both types of commerce.

Generally speaking, trade beyond the frontiers of Britain appears to have been negligible, although a certain amount of Irish goods probably found their way to British markets, particularly in the western part of the island.[7] There was little that the Picts and Scots of the North could offer in the way of exchange, and there is little evidence of any attempt on the part of the Romans to stimulate a desire for Roman wares among them.[8] The result was that Roman influences were very slight among the northern tribes, and, since the Romans could not influence them through the control of commerce, the natives of the North of the island remained particularly unpredictable and hostile. Elsewhere along the frontier, however, traders were active in carrying their wares to markets beyond the frontier. From the Rhine districts,

Roman merchants generally moved up the Rhine's eastern tributaries. The Lippe, with the fortress of Vetera (Xanten) at its base, the Ruhr from Asciburgium, and probably the Sieg from Bonn all facilitated trade with the Germans, but the Lahn and the Main rivers, the latter overlooked by the fortress at Mainz, were probably the most important routes for long-range trade. These streams provided easy access to the broad lowlands near the Elbe and, eventually, the Baltic. Trade in the Danubian region appears to have been just as extensive as along the Rhine and perhaps even more important to the empire. Roman traders ranged along the amber route to the Baltic, as well as its western branch that led to Bohemia and the region of the Elbe. Some from the lower reaches of the Danube may have used the Black Sea route to reach southern Russia and even penetrate up the great rivers of the region, although there is less solid evidence for this than for the other routes mentioned.

The Control of Trade as a Defensive Weapon

Although trade with the border tribes occurred all along the Rhine– Danube frontier, and many frontier fortresses had special facilities to accommodate this activity, it was of greatest significance along the Danube. The border tribes of the region—the Marcomanni, Quadi, and Dacians—were numerous, well organized, and relatively sophisticated. They were also dangerous adversaries, and the most desperate struggles in the history of the Roman army of the frontier were waged against these peoples. It was because of their presence that the bulk of the army of the frontier was garrisoned along the Danube. Nevertheless, it was important to the Roman government that commerce be maintained with these peoples. Not only did the Roman frontier districts depend heavily upon German imports of leather, horses, cattle, and the like, but it was essential that the government have control of commerce as a possible implement of foreign policy. Several treaties made with the Germans testify to the Roman government's concern with this commerce. Trading immediately along the frontier posed a clear danger to military security, but its continuation was necessary.

The imperial government maintained a policy of encouraging frontier trade generally, but strictly controlling its conduct. Tacitus remarked that the Hermundiri, a frontier tribe dwelling north of the upper Danube and allies of the Romans, were the only Germans who trade with us, not only on the riverbank, but deep inside our lines, in the brilliant colony that is the capital of Raetia [Augsburg]. They come over where they will, and without a guard. To other nations we only show our arms and our camps; to them we expose our palaces and our country-mansions and they do not covet them.[9]

This policy of controlling trade was continued until the disintegration of the western frontier. As late as 369, an agreement between the Emperor Valentinian and the Goths restricted German traders to two locales on the Danube.[10] By and large, the policy was effective. Although the frontier tribes along the Danube were dangerous and restive, and serious wars had to be waged against them, the fact that war interrupted commerce and ended their ability to acquire Roman export goods tended to act as a brake upon their hostile tendencies. After the battle of Adrianople in 378, for instance, the victorious Visigoths found all their opportunities for trade with the Romans had been cut off. Without their accustomed Roman imports, they soon found themselves in such straits that they sued for peace.[11]

The Role of Transport

The empire's restrictions on frontier trade and its extending or withdrawing trade as a means of controlling the border tribes must have had an unsettling effect upon the merchants of the frontier districts.[12] A number of factors no doubt made the German trade unpredictable enough without adding imperial manipulation of the merchants' activities. The complex of trade routes and the existence of various independent groups of shippers could mean, for instance, that a merchant carrying a load of glassware, at a great investment of time, expense, and personal danger, to a market at the mouth of the Elbe, might find the market glutted by similar shipments brought in by Frisians to sell to Danes who had already bought such wares from Danubian merchants at the mouth of the Oder. Or he might find that the entire trade route system had been closed by a war breaking out between two far-off tribes, fighting to the death for some typically incomprehensible German reason. Despite such uncertainties, however, the German trade continued along the frontier, and eventually encouraged the growth of a considerable manufacturing potential in these districts along the edge of the empire. The German trade, and the manufacture of export goods to supply it, became a virtual monopoly of the frontier.[13]

The basic reason for this development lay in the fact that there was no effective all-water route from the heartland of the empire to its European frontier districts. Overland transport was both expensive and slow in the ancient world and was avoided when possible. Transport and packaging technology was, as a consequence, poorly developed. The Romans generally employed pack animals when possible, but when the weight of the load demanded, they would use carts. Such carts were drawn by oxen, which served as the primary draft animals prior to the adoption of the horse collar in the early medieval period. Since the Romans had not developed such basic wagon technology as tandem harnessing, eveners, wheel bearings, and pivoted front axles, their carts were limited to light loads and were both clumsy and easily worn out. They were poorly suited for rough roads or cross-country hauling, and their maximum traction was two animals. Pack mules could cover about fifty miles per day on a relatively regular basis, but their loads were necessarily light and they required grain while traveling. Ox-drawn carts could carry more freight, but could manage only about twenty miles in the same time.[14]

Given the small maximum loads and the great time required to cover any appreciable distance, the costs of land transport were exorbitant. Long-distance hauling and the shipment of bulk commodities were simply not cost-effective, nor could any enterprising merchant afford the excessive turnaround times required by overland freighting. The result was that whenever possible, the Romans relied on water transport. Roman traders could never view the Rhine and Danube as limits or barriers when their tributaries offered clear water access to the interior of Germany. Throughout the history of the Roman frontier districts, they served as jumping-off places for traders ranging deep into the interior. While the imperial administration may have viewed the frontier districts as the boundaries of the empire, their inhabitants saw them also as the fringe of the vast lands of free Germany. The contrast between the government's view of the frontier as a static line and its inhabitants' perception of the frontier as a dynamic region contributed to the existence of a sentiment for continued imperial conquest, as opposed to the government's official anti-expansionist policies.

The limitations of overland transport had other profound effects on the frontier districts and their inhabitants. The basins of the Rhine and Danube were separated from that of the Mediterranean by short, but costly and time-consuming, overland routes. As a consequence, trade and commerce between the heartland of the empire and its continental frontier, although extensive, was not unlimited, and the two tended to form separate economic regions. At the same time, the importance of the North Sea, Rhine, and Danube as water routes uniting the frontier districts was accentuated. Divorced by overland barriers from their heartland and connected closely to each other by their water routes, the frontier districts could easily develop and maintain a sense of separate identity. The relatively high cost of goods imported from the imperial heartland provided an opportunity for small-scale local manufacturers and producers to compete successfully in the regional military market as well as in the production of export goods for the German trade. Some luxury goods, such as fine wines, were of such great value per unit of weight that their export from the imperial heartland continued to be a profitable pursuit.[15] By and large, however, as time passed, an ever-greater portion of production for both local consumption and export came to be concentrated in the frontier districts.

The significance of the fact that the frontier districts were separated from the empire by an overland barrier was not lost on the Romans. In A.D. 58, Lucius Antistius Verus, an energetic governor of Upper Germany, developed a plan to link the Saône and the Moselle by a canal, using army engineers to provide the planning and frontier troops to furnish the labor. In reporting this event, Tacitus enthusiastically noted that this would have allowed goods from the Mediterranean to be shipped up the Rhone and Saône via the canal to the Moselle, and thence to the Rhine and North Sea, thus eliminating the need of overland transport.[16] Strikingly enough, Aelius Gracilis, the governor of Gallia Belgica (modern northern France and Belgium), where the canal would be built, refused to allow the frontier troops to enter his province. Tacitus attributed his action to jealousy, and quoted his argument that the project would please the inhabitants of Gaul and cause the emperor concern. Tacitus implies that this was merely an excuse, but it is more likely that Aelius Gracilis realized that an all-water route from the Mediterranean would benefit the producers and manufacturers of southern Gaul to the detriment of the inhabitants of his own province. It is not improbable that other such schemes were frustrated by the same type of resistance. The inhabitants of the frontier regions must have realized that their isolation from the large-scale production centers of the South worked to their advantage and that it was in their interests to keep it that way.

The Rise of a Money Economy among the Germans

The goods and wares involved in the German trade were varied, and provide important insights into the needs of the parties involved. We have already observed the apparently insatiable demand of the army of the frontier for leather, horses, and stock animals. In terms of volume, these consumable items, brought by the border tribes to trading stations along the frontier, constituted the bulk of the imports from free Germany, and the supply of these commodities was the most important aspect of the German trade from both the German and the Roman point of view. The needs of the frontier military were too great to be supported by the relatively small frontier districts even when these districts had increased their agricultural production to its maximum. The German trade allowed the imperial administration to tap the resources of Germany to supplement local production in supporting the army of the frontier. By so doing, it gained several advantages. It obtained needed supplies for relatively low prices, avoided the costs of shipment to the frontier, and enjoyed the benefits of German dependence on peaceful commercial relations.

The Germans apparently sold their goods and stock for money, for coins are the Roman objects most frequently uncovered in the area that was free Germany. The border tribes accepted both gold and silver coins to use in their trade with the interior, and were conversant enough with Roman coinage to be able to recognize and prefer certain types.[17] Tacitus emphasized that the tribesmen did not value gold and silver for its own sake, as did the Romans, but only for its utility in trade. Farther from the frontier, the major coin finds are silver rather than gold, confirming Tacitus's observation that the tribes of the interior preferred silver coinage as being a more convenient medium of exchange given the relatively low prices of the regions.[18] Both archaeological and literary evidence confirms that by the first century A.D. Roman silver coinage had become the standard medium of monetary exchange among the tribes of Germany.[19]

Although there were tribes still farther removed from the frontier who did not use money, but traded only by barter, most of free Germany was integrated into a money economy based upon Roman coinage. This meant, in turn, that the Germans were dependent upon a regular supply of high-quality Roman silver coins since it was inevitable that there was a steady loss of coins from the German trade system. Despite Tacitus's contention that the Germans did not value gold and silver for its own sake, Romans coins uncovered in free Germany often appear as grave offerings and in coin hoards. Still more coins were no doubt beaten out to provide the silver for native manufactures of jewelry, armor ornaments, religious vessels, and the like. Given this steady drain, it is clear that the Germans had to sell more than they bought, and that any prolonged interruption of trade with the Romans would have disrupted the monetary base of their intertribal commerce and led to widespread inflation.

At the same time, many of the tribes coveted Roman manufactured goods, and it would appear that Roman traders generally sold their wares for money, so that the Germans needed Roman coins to pay for imported goods. In A.D. 107, the imperial government recalled all coins struck before the reign of the emperor Nero (54–68). These coins, which had been widely circulated in the empire and free Germany, disappeared from both areas, for very few have been found in coin hordes dating from after the year 107.[20] This would suggest that most of the money that flowed into Germany in exchange for German commodities eventually flowed back into the empire in exchange for manufactured wares. The balance of trade clearly seems to have been in favor of the empire, which gained numerous advantages from the German trade at no cost to itself.

Frontier Exports and German Imports

A large amount of Roman wares were exported into free Germany between the first and fourth centuries. Metalware, arms and armor, pottery, and glassware were among the leading Roman exports, and metalware appears to have been the most popular commodity among the Germans. A substantial amount of Roman silverware has been uncovered in free Germany, and more than 850 bronze vessels have been found in Germany and Scandinavia.[21] Over 500 bronze vessels and 300 glass vessels have been found in Scandinavia, the vast majority of them in Denmark.[22] As might be expected, several examples of Roman arms and pieces of armor have been found in Germany. The

Roman short sword briefly influenced the style of the German sword, although, interestingly enough, the German long sword later became the standard type used within the empire. Despite the prohibition in the later empire of the export of arms to the barbarians, a number of Roman swords, several dating from the fourth century, have been discovered in Scandinavia. Even Roman plowshares and agricultural tools have been found near Cassel and in Thuringia in Germany.[23] The German trade thus had technological implications for both the German tribesmen and the Romans, and this suggests the degree to which fashions, attitudes, and ideas may have passed back and forth between the Germans and the Romans through the frontier districts.

The industrial development of the frontier regions helped to bring about basic changes in the source of Roman exports to Germany. In the first and early second centuries, Italian goods dominated the trade, traveling by road to the Danube and then by the amber route to the Baltic, or, in the early part of the first century, to Bohemia.[24] In the West, Italian goods shipped to Gaul and western Germany were passed eastward by both land and sea.[25] By the third century, however, most export goods were produced in Gaul and the Rhineland, with some eastern production in the Black Sea districts. Gallic and Rhenish pottery, glass, metalware, and coinage began to spread eastward and northeastward into Germany.

This transformation is best illustrated in the export of pottery and glassware. The famous red-glazed pottery known as *terra sigillata* or "Samian" ware has been recorded in over 260 sites in free Germany and Scandinavia; some was carried from the frontier districts, but the bulk was shipped from the lower Rhine to the North Sea to supply the sea traders of Frisia. This type of pottery can be dated rather precisely,[26] and it can be stated with some certainty that pottery export wares did not appear in any quantity until the second century. Moreover, the great majority of the Samian pottery found in German lands was manufactured in the Rhineland. The earliest center of production appears to have been at Lezoux in Central Gaul, but by the end of the first century the bulk of the pottery exported originated in factories established at Heiligenberg, Rheinzabern, Buckweiler, Trier, and Westerndorf in the frontier districts of the Rhine.[27] It would appear that the production of Samian ware for export began in the region of the Rhine frontier during the course of the second century and continued as a thriving industry until the civil wars of the third century. A technological by-product of this trade was the introduction of the potter's wheel into Germany during the third century.[28]

Glassware was also an important Roman export. Several examples of first-century glassware have been discovered in Germany. Although some is clearly of Italian manufacture, the bulk was produced in the Rhineland. The frontier manufacturers attempted to appeal to German customers, who were accustomed to drinking from horns. The workshops of Cologne began making horn-shaped glass drinking vessels for the German market, and the product proved so popular that these models were soon employed throughout the empire.[29]

Much the same progression of events can be observed in the production and distribution of Roman export bronzeware. Italian products were dominant during the first century. Most were cast in workshops in southern Italy, and were carried primarily by traders from the Danubian districts, although a few of these Italian products have been found near the Rhine. By the second century, however, bronzeware produced in Gaul appears to have captured a significant portion of the German market.[30] Over eighty bronze statuettes, whole or fragments, have been discovered in the Netherlands, northwest Germany, and the Baltic islands. At least a third of these were produced in Gaul.[31]

The same pattern can be seen in other areas of export commodities. Even before the establishment of the military frontier, Roman traders had been opening up German markets and encouraging a taste for Roman manufactured goods among the tribesmen. The arrival of the army of the frontier was the catalyst that transformed a desultory luxury trade into a complex and far-flung commercial system. Military procurement enabled the Germans to obtain sufficient money to purchase Roman wares in far greater quantities than had hitherto been possible, but only by being able to provide the military markets established along the frontier with large quantities of bulk commodities. Roman coins permitted the Germans to develop a money economy that allowed the border tribes to acquire from their neighbors the leather, horses, mules, cattle, grain, and other products they needed for their trade with the Romans. In this fashion, however, buying power was spread widely among the Germans, allowing traders a more extensive market for their wares. Multiple trade routes, complex systems of transfer and transshipment, and the direct involvement of German traders became necessary to reach all of the areas with a taste for Roman goods and the means to purchase them.

The manufacturing centers of the heartland of the empire were not well suited to meet the needs of this expanding market. They lay far from the frontier, and their products had to be shipped some distance overland before they reached the export merchants. All this added to the cost of the goods without adding to their worth. Moreover, the merchants suffered by being so distant from their suppliers. Orders could not be filled quickly, and merchants could not control the quality of their wares, nor could they be assured that the large-scale producers of Italy would be responsive to their needs. The internal markets of the empire were far more important to Italian manufacturers than the relatively small and unpredictable needs of the German trade. Finally, the Italian manufacturers knew and cared little about German tastes and preferences. It was perhaps inevitable that frontier entrepreneurs, some of them perhaps retired army artisans, should establish small-scale operations to meet the immediate needs of traders with the Germans. By this time, the imperial administration was no doubt aware of the importance of the German trade in helping to supply the army of the frontier and in creating an economic dependence on Roman manufactured goods among the border tribes. The government therefore encouraged and protected frontier manufacturers, since their activities directly supported long-term imperial policies for the stabilization and self-sufficiency of the frontier. Frontier manufacture soon supplied a large portion of the export market.

Roman export goods discovered in Denmark illustrate the rapidity with which frontier and provincial production, once begun, came to dominate the export market. Italian-made glass and bronze are found in graves dating up to about A.D. 150, but the Roman goods found in graves after that date were all produced in the frontier districts. The transition was so rapid that both Italian and provincial wares have never been found in the same grave.[32]

German Exports

We cannot expect the same kind of physical evidence to illustrate the quantities and types of German imports and the routes by which they reached the Roman frontier. This is due in large part to the nature of the imports themselves. We have seen that German supplies of perishable and consumable goods to the army, such as leather, horses, and cattle, were an important aspect of the German trade. Fragments of leather and cloth, and large quantities of animal bones have been discovered, but there is no way to determine whether such things were originally Roman or German. There is sufficient literary and archaeological evidence, however, to prove that the Romans received such imports and that they were important elements in the supply of Roman military needs. Drusus's imposition of a tribute of ox-hides on the Frisians for the equipment of his army illustrates the Romans' need for imported leather. A wax tablet found near Leewarden attests to the properly witnessed sale of an ox by a Frisian to a Roman, and Marcus Aurelius, as part of a peace settlement, received a large number of cattle and horses from the Quadi and others.[33]

Even with the increased agricultural and pastoral production of the frontier districts, it would seem unlikely that the population would have been able to feed itself solely from local sources. Many of the frontier districts had restricted areas of arable land, and an unusually large portion of the local population consisted of groups such as soldiers, manufacturers, administrators, and merchants and traders who were not directly involved in the production of foodstuffs. German imports doubtless supplied much of the shortfall. In Britain, where a similar situation existed in the area of Hadrian's Wall, but where there was no extensive trade with the border tribes, extensive and costly works were undertaken to supply the frontier population from within the province. The lack of similar works on the Continent, and the failure of the Romans there to construct all-water routes to the frontier, suggests that German imports, combined with local production, were sufficient for the purpose and that the river routes allowed the transfer of necessary supplies between frontier districts when imports from the border tribes had been interrupted.

The importance of the Frisians as traders in Roman wares along the coast of northwestern Germany has already been noted, and the large quantities of Roman goods discovered in Friesland and Groningen indicates that they were large-scale consumers, as well as traders, of Roman exports. It has been suggested that the Frisians obtained these goods at least partially in exchange for North Sea fish.

After animals and grain, the second most significant import from Germany was no doubt the Roman coins with which the Germans bought the Romans' export wares. We have see above that the recall of early coins in the year 107 and their absence from graves and coin hoards in Germany after 107 suggests that most Roman money spent for German imports returned to the empire, probably rather rapidly.

This cannot be proven by the coins themselves, however, since there is no means of determining whether coins found within the lands of the empire had ever passed through German hands. Despite the difficulty of conclusively demonstrating the absolute dominance of animals, grain, and Roman silver, it seems clear that other imports were of relatively minor importance in the overall context of the German trade.

One class of import, live animals, is attested in numerous literary accounts and suggests an aspect of the German trade that may have done much to affect the Roman view of Germany and its inhabitants. The Romans employed large numbers of wild beasts in their imperial games, and several species of animals from the northern frontier appeared in the games at Rome. Among the wild beasts exhibited were bears, several species of antelope, elk, bison, and wild boars and oxen.[34] The *Historiae Augustae* provides a description of the shows given by the aristocrat Gordian in the reign of Septimius Severus. Among the beasts displayed were bears; stags from Britain; thirty wild horses, perhaps from the Danubian plains, Spain, or Britain; and ten wild elk, possibly from Germany.[35] An additional market for wild animals was doubtless provided by provincial games and shows.[36]

Some of the animals for these spectacles were doubtless imported from Germany, although there is little information as to how they were obtained. Imperial magistrates were often delegated this responsibility and apparently hired professional hunters, as well as purchasing directly from dealers in wild animals.[37] The Roman knight described earlier who journeyed to the Baltic was quite possibly acquiring wild animals and slaves as well as amber.[38] Roman troops may also have engaged in the trapping of wild beasts. Hunting would have been of practical benefit as a military training exercise, and Pliny mentions that commanders of auxiliary cohorts on the Rhine frontier had once been ordered to divert their troops from their usual duties and go fowling.[39] In any event, the closest contact many Roman citizens had with Germany was probably the savage animals featured in the public games. Their mental picture of Germany and the Germans must have been powerfully influenced by this rather limited vision.

One would imagine, given the richness of Germany in such products, that a substantial fur trade would have developed. However, it is difficult to find many indications that any such trade developed. Both Caesar and Tacitus describe the Germans as wearing furs, but there is no suggestion that this was a Roman custom. Furthermore, although the Roman satirists attacked virtually every form of luxury, none mention the wearing of furs as being among the vices demonstrating the decay of public morality from those former days in which the Romans led simple and austere lives and were filled with all the proper virtues. One suspects that if German furs had been at all widely used, they could not have escaped being grist for the satirists' mills. There are references to *pelliones*, dealers in skins and furs, but there is no evidence that their trade in furs was in any way significant. Trajan's Column depicts Roman standard-bearers wearing bear or wolf furs, but this tradition could scarcely have supported a substantial commerce in furs.[40] The Romans were wearers of wool, linen, and leather, and therefore had little interest in what might, under different conditions, have become one of Germany's most profitable exports.

Amber was probably the most famous of the German exports and, as we have seen, became quite fashionable in the early imperial period. Despite its popularity and the fame of the long and dangerous route along which amber shipments traveled, however, it represented only a minor element within the German trade as a whole. The majority of the amber objects found within the empire date from the first and second centuries. After the second century, the popularity of amber among the upper classes apparently waned, and literary references to it are quite scarce after that time. This is most likely the result of the unsettled conditions in free Germany during the third-century migrations of several tribes. The movements of the Goths, in particular, may have blocked the amber route and virtually cut off further imports of that particular product.[41] Nevertheless, amber continued into early modern times as a prized commodity in eastern Mediterranean lands, and served as one of the major trade goods shipped along the Varangian route of the medieval period.

The Romans generally referred to Germany as a great forest, and it is not surprising that they looked to Germany to satisfy some of their considerable need for timber. A large number of structures of the early frontier period have been excavated over the past century and they confirm the military's heavy demand for timber. The great majority of Roman fortifications were constructed of wood, and the timber was used with a lavish hand. A plank was seldom used where a beam would serve the same purpose.[42] Although timber lacks the defensive value of stone, fortifications of timber were more quickly constructed, more easily moved, and better insulated against the cold of the northern climates. Although we usually think of the fleets in connection with the need for adequate supplies of timber and timber products, the army actually used a far greater quantity of wood than did the navy.[43]

Roman troops had to construct their own camps, make their own weapons, build bridges, and erect substantial defensive works such as the *limes* in Germany, and these structures were generally built of wood. When Agricola was forced to abandon his campaign in Scotland in A.D. 83, he left behind some of the supplies he had assembled in the fort at Inchtuthil. When archaeologists investigated the site, they found a mass of about a million nails that had been hidden there. This offers some indication of the amount of wooden construction provided for in a relatively small-scale provincial campaign. It was not until the reign of Hadrian (117–138) that the wooden defenses of the frontier began to be replaced by stone forts. In the course of his frontier-building campaign, Hadrian also had two-and-a-half million trees felled in order to construct a timber palisade along a portion of the frontier.[44] Other military structures on the northern frontier that illustrate the massive use of timber for construction include the fort at Valkenburg near the Rhine in the Netherlands and the forts built in Scotland under Domitian.[45] Without even considering the fuel requirements of the population of the frontier districts, it seems evident that the army of the frontier required enormous quantities of timber, and that wood formed another of the absolute necessities of military life.

The acquisition of timber by both military and civilians was a complex procedure that included felling, transport, conversion, and marketing. Although there are few records of the timber industry, the Romans, like the American settlers, employed oxen to drag the large trunks from the forest to the nearest watercourse. The river systems tributary to the Rhine and Danube rivers were well adapted to rafting, and there is every reason to believe that springtime runs were made down the German streams and along the Rhine and Danube to collection and preparation points. The movement of timber overland to its point of use presented the Romans with the greatest of difficulties. They appear to have preferred to use mules when possible, despite their expense and high cost of maintenance. It was sometimes necessary to use as many as thirty to forty oxen, if the load was heavy. Given their lack of tandem harnessing, the management of such a team must have been an extremely difficult task. And yet, since a single fir of one hundred feet weighs over three tons, such operations must have been frequent tasks.[46]

Roman military and civilian requirements for timber caused a tremendous drain on the forest resources of the frontier districts. In addition to taking timber for construction, the troops would have been compelled to clear the trees for at least a bowshot in front of their works and lines. The legions must have cut down great swaths of trees as they built their barracks and defensive works. This may have had the accidental effect of opening up arable land in their immediate vicinity and providing the first base for the local expansion of agriculture. Although the army continued to prefer local timber because of the costs and difficulties of transport, the nearby German forests were no doubt exploited to supplement the depleted stands of the frontier districts.

Slaves from free Germany are often considered a significant element of the German trade, but the actual volume of that traffic is a matter of some debate. It cannot be denied that the government's policy of ending expansion must have reduced the number of war prisoners and captive populations available for the slave markets of the empire. Under these new conditions, slaves could only be acquired in the following ways: in the course of defensive wars, which normally yielded few captives; in aggressive wars demanded by defensive priorities; from border trade; or from placing inhabitants of the empire under bondage.[47] The major aggressive war of the frontier period consisted of the conquest of Dacia in 101–107 and led to the enslavement of numerous prisoners and inhabitants of the region. Nevertheless, there are few references to Dacian or Pannonian slaves during the long course of Roman dealings with the two regions.[48]

There is even less evidence for an extensive slave trade along the Rhine frontier. We have already discussed how the Frisians, after selling their wives and children into slavery to satisfy Roman tax demands, were finally driven into revolt. Tacitus relates the incident as an extraordinary circumstance, one that led directly to the empire's loss of all those lands that compose the modern Netherlands.[49] Elsewhere, he recounts how the emperor Domitian had purchased German slaves in order to exhibit them as war captives. This story, scurrilous as it may have been, indicates that German slaves were for sale along the frontier and that the Romans were still interested in the continued acquisition of war prisoners, as a sign of victory if nothing else.[50]

The evidence of slavery and an extensive slave trade in the frontiers of the West is very slight when compared to that for the eastern regions of the empire. A slave trade with the East had existed long before imperial times, but the situation there was far different from Germany. The population density of the East was relatively great, and the population was skilled in a wide variety of pursuits. The Romans enslaved eastern doctors, scholars, teachers, artists, singers, and actors, as well as trained agricultural workers and artisans. The German tribesmen simply did not possess the skills that would have made them useful slaves, nor were they of a temperament to have made docile servants or workers. A different system of the Roman use of human beings emerged very early in the West, where border tribesmen were recruited into the Roman auxiliary forces instead of being forced into slavery.[51] The need for manpower in the defense of the frontier was thus met by inexpensive mercenaries, who would have made very bad working slaves at best. Thus, the needs of the army of the frontier prevented the development of any extensive slave trade or the establishment of a substantial enslaved population in the frontier regions. In this admittedly relative sense, the Roman frontier was a land of free men and women.

The Significance of the German Trade

When we consider the overall balance of the German trade, it is striking how advantageous the entire arrangement was to the Romans. Many Roman military units found themselves stationed in areas where the local resources were insufficiently developed to provide them with adequate food, clothing, shelter, and other basic goods. Taxation and the stimulus of a cash market for their produce encouraged the local populations to increase their production, but this was often a slow process. While local development was under way, the army was forced to seek supplies elsewhere. If these could not be economically transported from the interior or shipped in from other frontier regions, they had to be acquired from the border tribes. The German trade thus enabled the army of the frontier to survive the difficult days when it was establishing itself, a time in which its needs for supplies and materiel were perhaps the greatest and in which local resources were least able to meet these needs.

Even when the resources of the frontier districts had been fully developed, many were still incapable of supporting the local garrisons and the settlements that had grown up around them. Such districts often became permanently dependent on trade with the border tribes to supply their shortfalls in necessary goods and supplies. Without the German trade, the Romans would have had to abandon a number of portions of the frontier, or supply reduced garrisons at exorbitant cost. The German trade made the maintenance of many sections of the Roman frontier possible.

The Germans were paid for their goods, and Roman silver coins provided the medium of exchange that created a great trade system stretching from the Danube and the Rhine to Scandinavia and the borders of Russia. Tribes far removed from the frontier were integrated into this system and thus became dependent upon the Roman coins upon which the German trading economy had come to be based. The border tribes soon realized that their economic prosperity depended on their trade with the Romans, and were more hesitant than they might otherwise have been to break the peace. The Romans soon found that they could use trade as a means of controlling the border tribes, increasing the trade of friendly groups and limiting the trade of those whom they wished to punish. Once the imperial government recognized the potential of such policies, the regulation of the German trade became one of the major functions of the army of the frontier. Specified fortresses served as points of entry for German imports, and the army and river fleets attempted to ensure that all trade passed through these selected points. The government could thus control the direction of trade while at the same time levying taxes upon it.

Roman traders ranged widely throughout free Germany, stimulating the appetite of the natives for Roman export goods. As the German market for Roman goods expanded, it promoted the development of small-scale manufacturing and processing in the frontier districts. This, in turn, increased the population and tax revenues of those areas, as well as creating new local economic opportunities. These opportunities encouraged retired veterans to settle permanently along the frontier, where they served as a reserve militia and reared sons who eventually replaced them in the ranks of the frontier army. The frontier districts, together with the border tribes, became prime recruiting grounds and relieved the empire's interior of the burden of manning its defenses.

It is true, of course, that the empire had to pay for the support of these garrisons, but the frontier itself contributed a significant amount to these expenses. The money spent on German imports was partly recaptured through customs duties. The Germans spent much of the rest on Roman imports for which they generally paid cash. This money was returned to the frontier districts, where it helped to pay the taxes levied on the local population. An incidental benefit of the system was that it sent traders and merchants throughout free Germany, providing the Romans with a superb, and cost-free, intelligence and reconnaissance service. All in all, the German trade was very much to the advantage of the Romans, who gained many direct and indirect benefits with very little expenditure. When this is understood, the greater significance of the German trade becomes clear. We have already considered how Augustus's original decision to stabilize the empire's frontiers was dictated largely by his realization that the empire's resources were no longer sufficient to maintain a massive offensive army. The civil wars that plagued the empire from A.D. 69 onward did nothing to increase the empire's ability to support a large army. When one surveys the establishment of the army of the frontier, one is struck by how much of it was accomplished "on the cheap." The troops were expected to build their own fortifications and barracks; make their own tools and weapons; build the necessary roads and bridges, ports and harbors of the region; operate factories, mines, and smelters to turn a profit; and use their massive manpower for public works and defensive lines. All of this was done on a sparse diet and low pay.

Meanwhile, the local populations were subjected to such heavy levies that they were forced into a rapid development of their resources in order to meet the demand of the imperial administration that they provide the necessary supplies to feed and equip the local garrisons. Recruitment policies were adopted that were designed to draw much of the manpower necessary to support the army of the frontier from the frontier itself. It seems clear that the Romans not only intended that their frontier defense be as cheap as possible, but that little of the cost be borne by the interior provinces of the empire.

It is difficult to say whether these parsimonious policies could have been continued on a permanent basis. The restiveness of the frontier legionaries, together with their growing identification with the local populations of their districts, would suggest that they recognized, and resented, the degree to which they were being exploited and neglected. It was at this point, however, in the latter half of the first century, that the German trade began to grow and to improve the conditions under which the frontier army was operating. Inexpensive German imports increased the supplies available to the military, while at the same time relieving the local populations of the full burden of attempting to produce those supplies themselves. German cavalry and other auxiliary units soon were joining the Roman army, and the pressure of recruiting levies among the frontier populations relaxed. The Germans soon had money that they were willing to exchange for products manufactured in the frontier districts. This provided the local populations with cash for taxes, with enough left over for investment in the local economy. Perhaps the Romans could have established and maintained their frontier without the assistance of the German trade, but in fact they did not. At each of the critical steps in the process of establishing the frontier, the German trade provided the vital margin of success.

In another sense, however, the growth of the German trade eventually frustrated Roman plans. The early emperors had seen the frontier as a line separating them from their barbarian neighbors. It never was. The presence of the Roman army of the frontier in fact helped to create a great, although turbulent, German trading system that was soon integrated into the Roman money economy and the markets and products of the frontier districts. The Roman border provinces and free Germany formed a single economic entity. In later centuries, as the productive capacities of the Western Empire waned and its frontier defenses were stripped, the Romans' trading partners—Ostrogoths, Visigoths, Vandals, Sueves, Franks, Alans, Burgundians, and other border tribes—would cross the frontier in attempts to restore the situation. A reunification of the old trading region eventually came about, but not until the expansion of Charlemagne's empire in the early ninth century.

Notes

1. Pliny, *Naturalis Historia* 37:45. Olwen Brogan, "Trade between the Roman Empire and the Free Germans," *Journal of Roman Studies* (hereafter *JRS*) 26 (1936): 196.

2. Tacitus, *Annales* 2:62. M. P. Charlesworth, *Trade-Routes and Commerce of the Roman Empire*, pp. 187–188, 208, 215, 217, states that even before Caesar, merchants had penetrated into the Rhine Valley. As early as Caesar's time, merchants were engaged in trade with Britain, and during the reign of Augustus, trade relations were kept up with this region. Among the items exported from Britain were gold, silver, iron, hides, cattle, sheep, wool, dogs, cloth, and slaves.

3. R. M. Wheeler, *Rome beyond the Imperial Frontiers*, p. 7.

4. Pliny, *Naturalis Historia* 37:45.

5. Brogan, "Trade," p. 196.

6. For German traders in the region of the Elbe, see Brogan, "Trade," p. 196, ˙who also suggests that some of the sailors of the lower Rhine, mostly Germanic, may have traded along the north German coast.

7. A few Roman coins have been found in Ireland, particularly in the Boyne Valley of Meath, which might indicate trade with Britain. The coins may have reached Ireland indirectly, however, through Welsh traders.

8. But see L. Macinnes, "Baubles, Bangles and Beads: Trade and Exchange in Roman Scotland," in *Barbarians and Romans in North-west Europe*, ed. J. C. Barrett, A. P. Fitzpatrick, and L. Macinnes, pp. 108–116.

9. Tacitus, *Germania* 41.

10. Ammianus Marcellinus, *Rerum Gestarum Libri Qui Supersunt* 17; 9, 10.

11. Wheeler, *Rome beyond the Imperial Frontiers*, p. 15.

12. Although, naturally enough, evidence is lacking, it would appear more than likely that such government restrictions would have led to extensive smuggling. It would have been difficult for the government to control such an activity along the entire length of the frontier, particularly when a sizable portion of the local population would have supported it. It was generally forbidden to trade armor or weapons to the Germans, but the numerous finds of such items in German burials and other archaeological sites indicates that this government regulation sat rather lightly on the shoulders of the frontier traders.

13. C. R. Whittaker, "Trade and Frontiers in the Roman Empire," in *Trade and Famine in Classical Antiquity*, ed. P. Garnsey and C. R. Whittaker (supplement vol. 8), considers the general phenomenon, while Brogan, "Trade," is dated but still worth reading as an introduction to the German trade. Otto Schlippschuh, *Die Händler im römischen Kaiserreich in Gallien, Germanien und den Donauprovinzen Ration, Noricum und Pannonien*, provides a general view of the activities of traders, while Jurgen Kunow, *Der römische Import in der Germania libera bis zu den Markomannenkriegen: Studien zu Bronze- und Glasgefassen*, confines himself to two important wares. V. Sakar, "Roman Imports in Bohemia," *Fontes Archaeologici Pragenses* 14 (1970), considers the extent and variety of Roman trading to a single region.

14. See Christoph Wilhelm Röring, *Untersuchungen zu römischen Reisewagen*, for a discussion of Roman wagon technology. J. Mertens, "The Military Origins of Some Roman Settlements in Belgium," in *Rome and Her Northern Provinces*, ed. Brian Hartley and John Wacher, p. 39, suggests that the failure of the Romans to develop more efficient harnessing indicates that their transport technology was sufficient for their needs. In northern Europe, the terrain would have impeded freight wagons in any event, so one may conclude that water transport and pack animals made the development of more efficient means of hauling unnecessary.

15. Wheeler, *Rome beyond the Imperial Frontiers*, pp. 47–48.

16. Tacitus, *Annales* 13:53. It should be noted that Tacitus was not only an expansionist, but felt that, while the imperial administration was concentrating its attention on the East, the real danger to the empire was from the Germans. The establishment of an all-water route to the frontier would have been an important

step in launching major efforts at the conquest of the North of Britain, the Frisian coast that the Romans had once held, or the interior of Germany. It would also have allowed additional troops to reach the Rhine frontier much more rapidly in the event of a German attack.

17. This was not a contemptible skill; many different coinages were in circulation, particularly on the frontier, where new issues arrived from the interior of the empire and antique coins would return from many years of circulation among the German tribes. Due to debasement, clipping, and wearing, Roman coins of the same denomination could in fact be of quite different values. The ability to identify and select the correct type of coins was a sophisticated and important mercantile talent.

18. Tacitus, *Germania* 5.

19. Brogan, "Trade," p. 203.

20. Ibid., pp. 205–206. The date of a coin hoard can be determined, of course, from the date of the latest coin found in the treasure. It is extremely rare to find, in either Germany or old Roman territories, hoards containing coins from the period 54–68 and after 107.

21. For some discussions of Roman bronze- and glassware, see L. Kraskovska, *Roman Bronze Vessels from Slovakia*, British Archaeological Reports International Series, 44; Kunow, *Der römische Import in der Germania libera bis zu den Markomannenkriegen*; Hans Norling-Christensen, "Danish Imports of Roman and Roman Provincial Objects in Bronze and Glass," in *Congress of Roman Frontier Studies. 1949*, ed. Eric Birley; and Friedrich Fremersdorf, *Von Römischen Gläsern Kölns*.

22. Wheeler, *Rome beyond the Imperial Frontiers*, pp. 68 and 72, credits the combination of warfare and diplomacy for the large numbers of silver vessels found in Germany.

23. Brogan, "Trade," pp. 212–214. Tacitus, *Germania* 15, refers to the use of splendid arms, metal discs, and collars as gifts between chiefs and various German communities.

24. In Bohemia, the Marcomanni were active for a time as both consumers and middlemen in the central and northern European trade, but after their defeat by the Cherusci and the exile of their Romanized king, Maroboduus, their prominence quickly diminished. Although there were numerous regional trading peoples, such as the Danes in the Baltic, no single German tribe became commercially dominant. This was perhaps due to Roman merchants attempting insofar as possible to serve even distant markets, thus garnering for themselves the profits that might otherwise have gone to middlemen.

25. Wheeler, *Rome beyond the Imperial Frontiers*, p. 91.

26. *Terra sigillata* means "stamped earth," referring to the fact that this type of pottery was usually stamped by the manufacturer. Since it was often placed in graves along with other goods, including dated coins, scholars have been able to identify the periods during which a number of the potteries producing Samian ware were in operation. The stamps occasionally give the location of the manufactory, and chemical analysis of the clay can establish the location of still others. The location and date of production even of unstamped Samian wares can often be deduced by their stylistic similarity to known and dated types. The added fact that Samian ware was quite common and used throughout the empire and beyond

makes it one of the archaeologists' most useful tools in establishing the date and commercial connections of any site in which it is found.

27. Wheeler, *Rome beyond the Imperial Frontiers*, p. 87.

28. Brogan, "Trade," pp. 214–216.

29. Ibid., pp. 216–218; Fremersdorf, *Von Römischen Gläsern Kölns*.

30. Louis C. West, *Roman Gaul: The Objects of Trade*. The origin of bronze items can be determined not only by their style and composition, but also because many of them are signed by their manufacturer.

31. See Brogan, "Trade," pp. 297–309.

32. Norling-Christensen, "Danish Imports of Roman and Roman Provincial Objects," pp. 76–78.

33. For leather, see Tacitus, *Germania* 5; *Annales* 4:72. The wax tablet of Leewarden is discussed by Brogan, "Trade," p. 219, and an account of Marcus Aurelius's treaties may be found in Tacitus, *Annales* 71:2.

34. Brogan, "Trade," pp. 62, 167, states that the European bison was extinguished in its last reserve in the Caucasus as late as World War I. The maned bison and the *urus* (a large, long-horned wild ox) are cited by Pliny, *Naturalis Historia* 8:15, 38, as two kinds of wild ox native to Germany.

35. "Gordiani Tres," in *Scriptores Historiae Augustae*, ed. E. Hohl, 3.

36. George Jennison, *Animals for Show and Pleasure in Ancient Rome*, p. 140. It should be noted, however, that provincial games were severely curtailed by Nero's ban upon their sponsorship by imperial governors.

37. Jennison, *Animals for Show and Pleasure*, p. 140.

38. Brogan, "Trade," p. 219.

39. Pliny, *Naturalis Historia* 10:22, 54.

40. Brogan, "Trade," p. 221. *Scriptores Historiae Augustae*, "Vita Severi Alexandri," 24, mentions that Alexander Severus imposed taxes on weavers of linen, glass-workers, silversmiths, goldsmiths, and furriers. It should be noted, however, that the reliability of information from this particular source is a matter of some dispute.

41. Brogan, "Trade," p. 220. Tacitus, *Germania* 45, describes the gathering of amber on the Baltic shore by the Aestiones.

42. One of the reasons for this was no doubt the fact that sawing planks was a laborious task. Military posts and settlements on the American frontier were usually constructed in the same fashion, as long as timber was plentiful and convenient.

43. David P. Davison, *The Barracks of the Roman Army from the 1st to 3rd centuries A.D.: A Comparative Study of the Barracks from Fortresses, Forts, and Fortlets with an Analysis of Building Types and Construction, Stabling, and Garrisons*; and Anne Johnson, *Roman Forts of the First and Second Centuries A.D. in Britain and the German Provinces*, provide a good overview of Roman fort and barrack construction. German reconstructions of frontier barracks provide a striking view of the Romans' lavish use of timber.

44. See chapter 2 for a discussion of this project.

45. Russell Meiggs, *Timber and Trees in the Ancient Mediterranean World*, pp. 173–174.

46. Ibid., p. 334. One might note that the difficulty of dragging heavy timbers from the forest was lessened by the fact that the track was generally downhill, and

hauling was often done during the winter, when snow and ice reduced the friction of the load considerably.

47. R. H. Barrow, *Slavery in the Roman Empire*, p. 15.

48. Ibid., p. 16. For the enslavement of Pannonians by the emperor Tiberius, see *Dionis Cassii Cocceiani Historia romana* 54:31. Further evidence for slave trading along the Danubian border is provided by a number of wax tablets dating from the middle of the second century A.D. and discovered in 1855 at Verespatak in Roman Dacia. These include a number of documents relating to the sale of slaves, including one recording the purchase of a woman called Theudote by Claudius Julianus, a soldier of the century of Claudius Marius in the Thirteenth Legion "Gemina" for 420 *denarii* on October 4, 160. See Thomas Wiedemann, *Greek and Roman Slavery*, p. 109.

49. Tacitus, *Annales* 4:72. Within Tacitus's general presentation, with its instances of how easily Germans could be roused to a fighting pitch or driven to desperation, his account of the causes of the Frisian revolt assumes the proportions of an admonitory tale.

50. Tacitus, *De Vita Agricolae*, ed. R. M. Ogilvie, 39; Brogan, "Trade," p. 219. Prisoners were a necessary feature of every Roman triumphal procession. Originally, they may all have been intended as sacrifices to the Roman gods. By imperial times, only one was so sacrificed, and the rest remained as hostages or were enslaved. It is difficult to ascertain whether the Romans saw them as representing the slaves that the victorious general had acquired, like the other war booty that graced the procession, or merely as a symbol of his victory. In any event, Tacitus's claim that Domitian had bought his "prisoners" was intended as a particularly scathing denunciation of the emperor's duplicity.

51. R. H. Barrow, *Slavery in the Roman Empire*, pp. 16–17. German mercenaries joined the Roman army in various capacities from very early times and in ever-increasing numbers. It is safe to assume that they did not all divorce themselves from their former homes and that at least some of their earnings found their way back to Germany. See Brogan, "Trade," pp. 221–222.

VI THE TOWNS AND CITIES OF THE FRONTIER

Borrowing their early traditions from their Etruscan neighbors to the north, and greatly influenced by Greek models of eastern Mediterranean life, the Romans were overwhelmingly an urban-minded people.[1] The empire as a whole consisted of an assemblage of city-states, or *civitates*, each surrounded by its dependent countryside, or *pagus*.[2] Each city-state possessed its own council drawn from the middle class residents (*curiales*) of the town. The council elected its own leaders, collected local taxes,[3] and planned and supervised the construction of local public works. Local courts were held in the basilica that was constructed near the forum in the center of virtually all of these towns, and, in theory at least, all trade and commerce was conducted within the city markets, where the proper taxes could be collected and legal forms observed. Most city-states either had or aspired to have their own circuses, theaters, and stadiums, and each had a municipal temple in which an official priesthood served the state deities and the deified emperors. Some councils subsidized public teachers of Greek and Roman rhetoric and philosophy, and wealthy citizens gained prestige by underwriting plays, horse races, and gladiatorial shows for their fellow citizens. In short, each city-state aspired to be a little Rome, and many of them contrived to provide their residents with an impressive array of public amenities. The government was content to allow the middle-class councilors of these city-states to manage local affairs, and the great bulk of Roman political and public life was conducted at this local level.

Despite this well-developed tradition, the Roman government appears to have had no clear policy for the urbanization of the frontier districts into which the army had been moved. While a great deal of planning went into the building of cities and towns in the civil areas immediately behind the frontiers,[4] it would seem that the imperial administration had little intention of making a major effort to Romanize or urbanize the frontier population.[5] Urbanization did come to the frontier districts, but it came as a result of the economic, commercial, and industrial development of those districts, rather than because of any deliberate planning on the part of Roman authorities. Nevertheless, the cities and towns that did emerge along the frontier showed considerable vitality, and many of them still exist, long after the frontier that gave them birth has disappeared.

The durability of the Roman frontier towns was the result of two basic factors. The Roman city-states of the interior were political entities, and their locations were often chosen for administrative reasons, rather than for the presence of local economic resources or accessibility to transportation routes. The cities of the Roman frontier were different in that they generally sprang up in the vicinity of Roman fortresses, and these fortresses were situated in positions commanding strategic water passages and overland transport routes, and often in proximity to areas of economic value. Moreover, the towns of the frontier districts were not artificial creations; they were economic entities that had evolved in response to nearby markets. They retained these basic attributes of good location and economic function even after the collapse of the Roman Empire in the West, while those towns that had been administrative centers disintegrated in the slow political decay of the fifth and sixth centuries. Trade continued in the tumultuous times that ensued, and the residents of the one-time frontier towns were able to pursue a precarious commercial life, seeking refuge in what remained of the nearby Roman forts in case of need. Still later, these same forts served as quarries for the construction of town walls during the early feudal age.

The Army Towns

The thought that they were laying the foundations of a thousand years and more of urban life in the frontier districts must have been far from the minds of the civilians who moved up to the frontier in the wake of the legions and auxiliary units. When the camp-followers arrived, the wooden fortresses were still only half finished, were surrounded by half-cut forest, and were in the midst of newly subjugated tribes who were feeling for the first time the pressure of merciless Roman levies of animals, foodstuffs, labor, and money. The troops themselves would have been hard-pressed to spare time from their duties to help the newcomers establish themselves, so the first camps were probably built by the prostitutes, gamblers, wine sellers, "wives" and children, and others who followed the legions. The initial days must have been hard indeed. The frontier was ill prepared to supply the massive demands of the garrison for food, drink, clothing, and materiel, and so supplies must have been short and prices high. Nevertheless, these camps were built, settlements without a plan, straggling out in various directions from a focal point near one of the fortress gates. Often built without adequate provision for drainage and sewage, and sometimes located half in one of the ditches that surrounded some of the fortresses, these ill-favored conglomerations of camp-followers, called *canabae*, were the first Roman towns of the frontier.[6]

The populations of these towns must have presented a strange assemblage. Senior officers, who were allowed to marry, were usually provided with substantial houses within the fortresses themselves. Their wives, children, and servants must have composed a small "proper" class. Frontier life could be hard for such women. Extended families were the general rule in the interior of the empire, and most upper-class Romans grew up surrounded by numerous relatives. The men probably felt the isolation and loneliness of their new situation much less than their wives, since they had the comradeship of their brothers-in-arms to support them. The women had no such solace; far from family, friends, and finery, it would have taken a strong woman to adapt to such conditions, and young legionary officers were usually more interested in marrying girls of family, wealth, and refinement than women of strength.

Centurions and the lower ranks were not supposed to marry during their term of active service, but this was widely ignored by the men, and their infractions of this regulation were rarely reprimanded by their officers.[7] Their women provided washerwomen, seamstresses, cooks, nurses, and rough confidantes for the officers' families, and their sons provided future centurions for the legion. Nevertheless, rankers were allotted quarters sufficient only for themselves. Their wives and children lived in the *canabae*, and the men probably spent what little free time they were allowed in the settlement, perhaps managing to fashion somewhat more comfortable quarters for their broods or helping their wives to establish some small-scale business to supplement a salary that was scarcely sufficient for themselves, much less a growing family. The histories of the time have little to say about the life of the legionary besides drills, duties, and punishments, but the soldiers' wives must have played a large role in creating an environment that made the hard life of a frontier posting more endurable both for their husbands and for others. In addition, when the men of the army of the frontier fought, they were fighting for more than the emperor and his honor; they were also fighting to protect their wives, children, and girlfriends in the *canabae*.

Not all the troops were married, of course, but, as is the case with most armies of the world, this does not mean that they were indifferent to feminine companionship. Women from all over the Roman Empire were found on the frontier, and many doubtless married and settled down there. Local women also were attracted to the *canabae*, and marriages between such women and the soldiers, even if they were contrary to regulations, soon began to weave a network of interrelationships between the men of the fortress and the local population.[8]

Some of the Roman soldiers even contrived to build up small businesses. The individual soldier was not allowed to buy land or pursue agriculture in the province where he was serving, nor was he allowed to go on leave for the purpose of conducting private businesses.[9] Business pursuits were not forbidden, however, and could easily be conducted through agents, particularly in places as close as the *canabae*. Part of the population of the *canabae* almost surely consisted of slaves, freedmen, and civilian partners of legionaries inside the fortress. Such a situation provided a great temptation for corruption; there were no doubt payments for exemptions from duty, and military materials were perhaps prone to vanish if not vigilantly guarded. Such things have been common at military bases for centuries, and, in the long run, provide productive outlets for the energies of those ambitious soldiers who would surely make trouble if it were not possible to make money instead.

There were ample opportunities for business in the settlements, since the troops provided a large and nearby cash market. The *canabae* no doubt had their share of drinking shops, gambling dens, brothels, and eating houses, but since both officers and soldiers bought much of their own equipment, there were also cloth merchants, armorers, leather workers, tailors, and a host of other establishments.[10] There were also the women of the fort to be provided with perfumes, fine clothes, cosmetics, and other luxuries. Many of the small-scale businesses and services were no doubt managed by the rankers' wives, but the small businessmen, artisans, slaves, and freedmen who also lived in the *canabae* provided for the army's unofficial needs. It would have been strange if young men from the vicinity had not come to the *canabae*, perhaps to find jobs, to offer their services as hunting guides or the like, to sell some local product or bit of game, or simply to see the sights. Thus, Romanization, at least at the level of the common people of the frontier, began in the *canabae*. The effectiveness of this process is attested by the survival of so much army slang in the post-Roman languages of these regions.[11]

With the passage of time, however, conditions changed in the *canabae*. The development of native farms and even Roman-style villa exploitation in the vicinity allowed the local residents to increase their grain production and to begin selling their surplus to both the military procurement officers and the residents of the *canabae*. This brought the local population a cash return, which it was more than willing to exchange for Roman manufactured goods. The tribesmen of the district soon formed a new and more extensive market that quickly attracted more substantial merchants and artisans producing a wider variety and greater quantity of goods than the residents of the *canabae* and the garrison of the fortress were prepared to absorb. At the same time, the increased local production of foodstuffs made possible a greater concentration of civilian population. The *canabae* slowly began to lose its character as a dependency of the fortress and assumed the proportions of an independent manufacturing and market center.[12] Its productive capacities were further enhanced by the skills of the military. At least some of the retiring veterans of the legions, having established relationships in their neighborhoods, chose to retire in the vicinity, and further increased the population of the *canabae*. They could now buy land and further increase local agricultural production, or they could employ whatever special talents they had gained in the army as cobblers, smiths, wainwrights, carpenters, or the like in private business.

The Civilian Towns

It may well be that the growing class of "solid" citizens that had come to settle outside the gates of the fortress were often less than happy with some of the more lurid and rowdy aspects of life in the *canabae*, but it is more likely that the lack of any town planning, poor drainage, inadequate road and water connections, and simply the greater attractiveness of some nearby location played greater roles in the movement of the population away from the fort. The security provided by the fortress and its garrison made such a move possible, and new, more purely civilian settlements were often established near, but not adjacent to, the fortresses. In most such instances, the importance of the *canabae* dwindled, and the dominant Roman frontier town became the civilian, commercial, and manufacturing *vicus*.[13]

Such predominantly civilian settlements arose in yet other ways. It must be remembered that the army of the frontier was almost continuously engaged in construction, if only to keep the men busy. One of the primary concerns of army commanders was to improve transportation and communication so that men and materiel could be concentrated quickly at whatever point of the frontier might be threatened. The troops constantly expanded an extraordinary system of all-weather roads, constructed massive bridges over rivers and streams, and cut wagon roads through hitherto impassable terrain. The navy, meanwhile, built river ports along the Rhine and Danube, and made even the smallest tributary streams navigable by dredging the streambeds and cutting practicable towpaths along the banks. The construction of canals opened up some new areas for economic development. The face of the landscape was altered in many ways, and the combination of improved transportation, military markets, and the introduction of Roman technology and organization stimulated the rapid development of the local native economies of most frontier districts. Native villages grew as a result of that development, and some became centers of the new transportation and marketing systems created by the military presence along the frontier.[14]

At the same time, the army had built extensive road systems intended to serve purely logistic purposes. The lower Rhine-North Sea route though modern Belgium was an example of such a supply road. The bases established along this route, perhaps originally intended merely to support the invasion of Germany, were insufficient to meet the demands of providing a continuous flow of supplies over the long term. The civilian personnel of the military supply service were soon supplemented by additional civilians, both in the villas that sprang up in the vicinity of the supply road and in the towns that soon lay along the road itself. The towns that sprang up along this route—Tongres, Bavay, Cassel, Tournai, and Therouanne—were new foundations, serving as collecting points for the produce of the surrounding country-side and as manufacturing centers producing military tools and equip-ment to meet the constant needs of the military.[15]

Many of the new settlers attracted to the centers that emerged along the new overland and water routes were either Romans or immigrants from the Romanized frontier provinces. Although the origins of such *vici* were different from those of towns that had evolved from *canabae*, the result was much the same. All constituted focal points for the integration of an intrusive Roman population and the local inhabitants of the district.

In still other areas, *vici* were established rather artificially at the direction of imperial administrators. At Canterbury in Britain, for in-stance, archaeological excavations have discovered that the irregular drainage ditches of a Celtic town were filled in shortly after the con-quest, and a Roman town with a typically symmetrical, right-angled street plan was built over the old settlement. The Romans did not always displace native settlements in establishing their new towns, however. A *vicus* was built immediately adjacent to the old Celtic town of Verulamium, the capital of the Catuvellauni tribe, and a short walk here took one from the typical Celtic culture of the old city to the order, symmetry, and prosperity of the new *vicus*. The Romans per-haps intended the contrast to be an object lesson in Roman superiority for their native neighbors.[16]

Such developments represent the exception, however. The majority of frontier towns arose in response to local economic needs and condi-tions. The *canabae* attracted local residents to Roman settlements, the growth of native villages attracted Romans to local population centers, and the supply towns merged local agricultural producers and Roman artisans into an integrated economy. In all cases, the Romans and natives shared a common interest in the pursuit of profit and quickly found the advantages of cooperation and integration.

There is no mention in literary sources of conflict between the fron-tier populations and Roman civilian immigrants. On the contrary, the Romans, often including the legions themselves, soon joined with the native residents in protesting the more extreme examples of arrogance and exploitation on the part of the imperial administrators. For their part, the imperial administrators soon began to treat the immigrants, most of whom came from the provinces anyway, with the same contempt that native peoples usually encountered. From their inception, then, most frontier towns were points of social integration and cultural exchange. Far from being artificial models of Roman life established by the government to impress and control the native population, they represented an empirical response to the realities of frontier life. A new frontier society emerged in these *vici*, neither purely Roman nor wholly native.

The integration of the frontier *vici* into the local economies was a source of long-term security for the inhabitants of these towns. The original Roman commercial settlements were dependent upon the market provided by the local garrison. Although this was a powerful attraction, it was also an uncertain basis for long-range planning. The frontier was relatively fixed, but there were constant adjustments in its lines and the location of its garrisons. In short, the garrison could be moved. Even if this were not the case, the military exigencies of the frontier often required that troops be transferred for a period of time. The traders and merchants of the period and region usually had a minimum of capital, and even the slightest interruption of business was a serious matter. Moreover, the military market had inherent limitations for the successful merchant in that the size of his market was fixed by military tables of organization. No matter how fine his wares or how low his prices, a trader residing by a legionary fortress could not increase the size of the legion.

As a result of such factors, there was a constant tendency of the merchants to lessen their dependence on military markets, and to invest their efforts and resources more intensively in the permanent opportunities offered by the local economy and the limitless possibilities of the growing trade with free Germany. Smaller traders were always ready to take their places in pursuing the quick profits offered by the garrisons, even if it meant following them on their detached duty or to a new posting. There were always camp-followers to jerrybuild a sorry collection of huts by the gate of a new station and people a settlement that, more often than not, would eventually evolve into a *vicus* and repeat the process of commercial growth, increased independence of the military market, and eventual integration into the local economy.

Not all *vici* survived the departure of the local garrison and the abandonment of its fortress, but many did. The civilian *vicus* of Nida developed near the headquarters of a cavalry wing located at what is now the town of Heddernheim in Germany. Under Hadrian, the wing was moved to new positions along the *limes* that the emperor had ordered established beyond the Rhine. Despite the loss of its military market, Nida continued to flourish and became the economic center of a prosperous market region. In the course of time, it became the *civitas Taunensium*, enjoying all of the rights and privileges that the empire granted its city-states.[17] Rottenburg (Sumelocenna) in Germany became the center of a *saltus*—an administrative area with city-state status—that extended at least twenty-nine miles. By the third century, Sumelocenna also had attained the status of a self-governing community. Even in the economic and military backwater of the Neckar Valley, a *vicus* survived the movement of the frontier eastward to the outer *limes*, and evolved into the modern town of Wimpfen. The towns of the Roman frontier displayed a vitality that not only carried them through the departure of the garrisons that had given them life, but even through the fall of the empire itself. When commerce and urban life began to revive around the year 1000, their first stirrings often enough occurred in what had once been Roman frontier towns.

The Towns of Roman Britain

Although many sites of individual frontier towns have been excavated and investigated, no frontier district has been so thoroughly studied as the northern frontier of Britain. In a sense, this is unfortunate, since this particular district was quite different from the Rhine and Danube, and even from the western frontier of Britain. Nevertheless, the information available for this district provides a unusually detailed and intimate glimpse of life along the frontier.

The Roman frontier in northern Britain enjoyed a stability unknown to the other sections of the European *limes*. It had been established in a lightly populated territory, with only a narrow front to defend against the Picts and the Scots. Although the Roman governor Agricola attempted to subdue Scotland in A.D. 77–84, his efforts were frustrated and abandoned.[18] By 90, the garrison in Britain was converted from an offensive footing; the number of legions was fixed at three, old legionary bases were converted into *vici* and *coloniae* (veterans' colonies), and much of the island was turned over to civil administration. In the years 122–127, the northern frontier was fortified. Its eighty-nine miles were spanned by a massive stone wall strengthened by great ditches, and a large garrison was established in permanent quarters in a number of small forts erected along its length. Except for a relatively short period beginning in 142–143, when an attempt was made to fix the frontier on a wall further north, the army of the frontier in the North of Britain was on station along Hadrian's Wall for the next 280 years.

Its district was lightly populated, and the territory behind it poorly suited for agriculture, and so, even from the beginning, it received many of its supplies from the South. A great tract of land there was developed at tremendous expense to produce the necessary grain, and a system of canals constructed to provide a water route to transport these supplies to a supply and shipment base established at York. It was not until well into the third century that the frontier district was sufficiently developed to begin to contribute significantly to the supply of the garrison. The local population appears to have consisted of Roman immigrants from Celtic provincial territories, and never did become very dense. There was virtually no trade with the tribes beyond the border. The local economy was relatively small in scale, compared with those that arose elsewhere along the frontier, and it remained almost completely devoted to the supply of military markets and the needs of the garrisons along the Wall.

Given such conditions, the civilian inhabitants of the *canabae* had neither resources nor reasons to move from the immediate proximity of the local fort. There was no local native economy with which to integrate, nor were there any routes leading to larger or more secure markets along which to settle. Urban growth along the northern frontier of Britain consisted primarily of the expansion of some of the *canabae* that lay beside the small forts that dotted the Wall. While this sort of urban growth occurred elsewhere along the frontier, nowhere was it as common a pattern as in this district.

The *vici* in northern Britain, like the *canabae* that formed their central districts, were unplanned. The typical town expanded haphazardly, with new buildings being situated along the various roads leading away from the gates of the fort, as was the case at Brougham, Maryport, Binchester, and Beckfoot. Sometimes a back lane grew into a secondary street (Housesteads, Piercebridge, and possibly Chesterholm). The main military road that led along the Wall often made loops to bypass individual forts, and, in such cases, isolated buildings were occasionally situated along the main road (Chesters and Housesteads). The opportunities for trade with passersby along the road caused the main concentration of settlement in some instances to shift away from the fortress in much the same way that a modern highway bypass sometimes attracts businesses from the old town center (Old Carlisle and Piercebridge). New buildings were sometimes constructed away from the major streets leading from the gate, and clung to the outer edge of the ditches that surrounded the fort (Greatchesters, Carrawburgh, and Chesterholm). Substantial concentrations of buildings also arose around the local bathhouses.[19] All of these variations suggest a heterogenous group of settlers, each following a different set of criteria in choosing a site for his house or shop. It is often held that the frontier breeds an independent spirit. The scattered pattern of settlement of the *vici* along Hadrian's Wall clearly indicates that these towns lacked any controlling authority and that their residents were making basic decisions of life each in his or her own way.

This does not mean that there was no rationale governing the growth of these towns. Although the streets of *canabae* responded to minor features of local topography, a general pattern in their layout can be observed. From an initial tight aggregation of buildings immediately outside the fort gate, a number of streets spread outward in a fan shape. As the distance from the fort increased, an irregular system of cross streets joined some of the main strands. Such features as streams, drainage ditches, or slight changes in elevation produced major distortions in that basic plan, leaving a general impression of haphazardness and lack of order. This was not true, of course; the street plans and building sites of the *canabae* were the result of a number of different people making independent decisions as to which locations would be most advantageous to them individually. If we knew enough about any single *canabae*, we would probably discover that the location and orientation of each street served a perfectly rational purpose. The apparent lack of order in these towns means only that there was no central authority to require individual residents to conform to an official plan.[20]

The general lack of order in the *vici* and *canabae* of northern Britain is only accentuated by a single piece of evidence that suggests that the *vicus* may have had some form of political organization capable of initiating enterprises under official auspices. The first instance is found at the site of the *vicus* of Chesters, where a system of sewers has been excavated. These sewers, which served the houses of the settlement, formed a regular system and were connected to the main sewer line of the fort. The existence of a unified and planned system of sewers within the town suggests that there was some form of community organization to design and execute the work, and its connection to the fort's main line undoubtedly required official permission. It is difficult to avoid the suspicion that the overall design may have been the work of military engineers, although it is clear that the cost of the system as a whole must have been met with some form of general levy. It would appear that although the siting of the houses of the *vicus* and even the line of its streets was usually unregulated, some sort of organization existed that could address pressing matters of public need.[21]

More than 175 town buildings have been investigated in northern Britain, and almost all are variations of a single type. The discovery of the remains of one of these long, narrow, rectangular buildings is generally regarded by archaeologists as a certain indication that they are dealing with a *vicus*. In the center of the settlement, these buildings were generally built with their long axes perpendicular to the street, although some lay parallel to the main path of traffic.[22] The basic design of a long, narrow building generally produces an inconvenient and inefficient floor plan, and its appearance anywhere is usually a good indication that the conservation of street frontage was a basic concern of its builders. This, in turn, is a good sign that the street for which the building was intended was a commercial thoroughfare with a predominance of pedestrian traffic.

The entrance to these buildings was generally from the street, but a number had doors in one of the long sides of the structure. The street side of some buildings was apparently unwalled and open to traffic. Some of these had a single central post in this open front, with indications that it served to affix swinging doors or shutters by which the front could be closed; other such buildings simply had an open veranda. This particular design suggests that such buildings served the public as shops, eating houses, taverns, and the like. The main street of a *canabae* or *vicus* along the frontier in northern Britain probably consisted of a line of such buildings, with shops along the street open to the public. Behind these front quarters were workshops or storerooms, and living quarters were either behind these, or in a second story. The side entrance perhaps led to a yard at the back of the property, served by an alley parallel to the street.[23] There were no public buildings in such a town, nor were there any clearly defined marketplaces. Virtually the only public spaces were the streets and the area in front of the fort gate that served as the focus of the entire settlement.

The lack of public amenities or any expression of civic institutions would have marked such population centers, in Roman eyes, as essentially uncivilized; they lacked the defining characteristics of urban life.[24] Nevertheless, these towns fulfilled their basic purpose of serving the garrisons of the Wall. There is some evidence that the distinction between fort and *canabae* or *vicus* may have become obscured with the passage of time. For example, at Vindolanda, perhaps the most intensively studied site along the Wall, the civilian settlement lay on the east side of a stone fort and must have qualified as a *vicus*; by the late third century, its population numbered between 800 and 1,500 inhabitants.[25] We have already noted that the soldiers working in the tannery and leather-working shop of the fort seemed to have been engaged in the manufacture of goods for women and children.[26] A large number of items clearly belonging to women and children have been found within the fort of Vindolanda, and much of it cannot be associated with the household of the commanding officer, the only person allowed by regulations to house his family within the fort. This and other evidence suggests that Roman army regulations were not rigidly enforced along the frontier in northern Britain.[27]

Thus, at Vindolanda, and presumably elsewhere along the Wall, women and children lived both within the fort and in the *vicus*, and manufacturing for trade was conducted at both sites. Relaxed regulations decreased the distinctions between soldier and civilian, and thus between fort and settlement. This was perhaps a major reason why the *vici* of the district did not divorce themselves from dependence upon the local fort; the interpenetration between the two was too great for the civilian population to disengage itself from the local garrison.

Although this pattern of development was anomalous within the context of the Roman frontier as a whole, the British *vici* met the needs of the district at least as well as urban centers elsewhere along the *limes*. With the passage of time, the district managed to increase its agricultural production to the point that it was able to supply much of the area's military market.[28] With this, the drain of army money out of this district was decreased, and the standard of living of its inhabitants began to increase. Local industries concentrated on supplying the basic needs of the district for manufactured goods. Although more elaborate items were imported, manufacture provided another means of keeping money within the developing local economic system.[29] The district was even able to maintain a small urban capital, Carlisle, which was initially constructed in the first century A.D. and remained a civilian center after that date. The cemeteries of the town, however, show that the site continued to be occupied down to the end of the Roman period and contained a substantial and prosperous civilian population.[30]

The Role of Veterans in Urban Life

In addition to the *canabae* and *vici*, settlements of retired soldiers, known as *coloniae*, played an important role along the frontier and in the border provinces. The Roman government frequently established urban centers in which it settled military veterans to assist in the Romanization and pacification of a selected area.[31] Each discharged veteran received a plot of land inside the town and another in the *territorium*, the area around the town and within its jurisdiction. Since the troops received citizenship upon retirement, the population of the *colonia* was Roman by law, although non-Romans were allowed to establish residence. These towns were provided by the government with a charter (*Lex Coloniae*) upon their foundation,[32] and their local governmental institutions began functioning without delay.

The government usually took care to establish relatively large populations in such towns and to provide them with ample lands. The *coloniae* were generally prosperous as a result, and quickly furnished themselves with the normal amenities of a Roman town. The veterans who formed the bulk of the population, having served up to twenty-five years in the Roman army, were still subject to military call and constituted an unusually stable and responsible citizenry. Moreover, many of them had developed special skills as artisans, accountants, engineers, and the like during their term of service. They thus brought an unusually wide range of expertise and economic skills to the new cities.

Coloniae were scattered throughout the western portion of the empire. Along the Rhine, they were established at Cologne in A.D. 50,[33] and at Xanten (*Colonia Ulpia Traiana*), among other sites. On the Danube, immigration into the border provinces created substantial civilian urban centers, but *coloniae* were also an important element in the urban development of the frontier districts. Under Trajan, the number of veterans' colonies in each province was set to equal the number of legions in the provincial garrison.[34]

The first *colonia* in Britain was founded in A.D. 49 at Colchester for veterans of one or perhaps more of the legions stationed in the province. Two additional colonies were established at Gloucester (*Colonia Nervia Glevensium*) for veterans of the Second Augustan Legion and at Lincoln (*Lindum Colonia*) for the Ninth Spanish Legion. At least two of these locations had originally been legionary bases. This perhaps accounts for the fact that they were larger and displayed a greater degree of town planning than most other urban centers in Britain. Colchester possessed a population of approximately 15,000, while both Lincoln and Gloucester had about 5,000 residents. A substantial *vicus* had developed outside the fort at Gloucester and had become a sizable population center by the middle of the second century. The choice of this particular site for a *colonia* would appear to have been at least partly a political decision designed to benefit the civilian residents of the *vicus*. The role of the discharged legionaries seems to have been that of furnishing the merchants of the *vicus* with a new and expanded market for their products and of gaining their settlement an official status through a colonial charter.[35]

Although the military *coloniae* played an important role in the border provinces and even along the frontier, they were not products of the frontier environment. They were, like the fortresses themselves, the results of government policy. Their size and location were not functional responses to economic opportunities or local needs, but were in fact simply a different expression of imperial military planning. Many of these *coloniae* became important cities and have survived down to the present day, but this is due to the fact that sites of strategic value are frequently also of economic importance.

The Role of Veterans in the Frontier Towns

The *canabae* and *vici* were the most numerous and characteristic forms of urban organization on the Roman frontier. Evolving out of a squalid settlement established by camp-followers at the gates of a legionary fortress, a typical frontier *vicus* often became largely independent of its limited military market by integrating with the local native economy. Once its independent economic identity had been established, its further growth was a reflection of the effectiveness of its residents in developing local resources, enhancing local production, and expanding its market area.[36]

The processes of growth of both the *canabae* and the *vicus* were often affected also by the degree to which they were able to attract military retirees as residents. The imperial administration usually did not compel veterans to settle in any particular place. On those occasions when the government attempted to locate retirees in areas not of their own choice, it failed dismally. Veterans frequently chose to settle close to the places where they felt strong bonds, and many moved into the *canabae* and *vici* near the forts and the units in which they had served.[37] A curious feature of the British frontier is that few veterans settled there except in the government-sponsored *coloniae* of the South. It would appear that the lack of amenities in the settlements along the Wall, coupled with the harsh climate, were more than sufficient to overcome the attractions of old friendships and long familiarity.

The frontier towns elsewhere, as well as those of the border provinces, were distinguished by their relatively large numbers of retired military residents. These veterans continued to be on call as a reserve military force to maintain local security in case of need and thereby free regular troops for action in the field. An incidental consequence of this policy was that those settlements in which a number of such retirees had settled enjoyed a higher degree of security as a result. Many of the frontier towns had militia in residence, and raiding tribes would have done well to give such settlements a wide berth.

Despite their role in local defense and their common military background, the veterans did not conduct themselves merely as an urban extension of the army. They considered themselves civilians and behaved as such. Many owned prosperous farms near the settlement and provided food and raw materials for the residents, while others set themselves up in business as artisans or shopkeepers. Whatever their pursuits, however, they integrated fully with the civilian life of their towns. Until citizenship was extended throughout the empire in 212, they were probably the only Roman citizens in some of the smaller settlements. Judging from the many dedications left by retired veterans in *canabae* and *vici* throughout the empire, they appear to have occupied a prominent place in public life. With their discharge grants and the skills and discipline they had acquired through long years of service, they were citizens of means and ability. Insofar as the *canabae* and *vici* of the frontier may be said to have had an upper class, it was largely composed of such men.[38]

One of the reasons for the influence of veterans lay in the fact that it was customary, at least in the larger towns and the *canabae* of the great legionary fortresses, for retirees to form ex-servicemen's clubs. Such clubs, each with a regular organization and elected officers, appeared as early as the first quarter of the first century A.D. They were independent associations, organized for the benefit of their members, and with no formal connection with the army. They may originally have been primarily social in nature, but they soon came to exercise a degree of political and economic power within the towns in which they were located. The clubs, which were closed to nonveterans, afforded their members a sense of group identity and a means of mutual support, as well as the opportunity to discuss matters of common concern and to form a unified front on such matters. Civilian associations of a similar nature played an important role in the public life of the towns, and membership in them was open to local military retirees. Many veterans joined and even became officers in these civilian associations, with whose members they were often connected in business and private life.[39] In this fashion, the attitudes and desires of the veterans, shaped in their clubs, gained even greater influence when allowed to dominate the civilian associations that more or less governed the towns.

The Cities

If the typical frontier town was a *canabae* or a *vicus*, a few towns were able to achieve a more elevated status. Some of these settlements, blessed with a location favorable for trade or the proximity of important natural resources, were able to attain one of the levels of municipal status and take their place among the other *civitates* that composed the empire. In order to reach such rank, a town not only had to accumulate considerable wealth, but also had to gain the favor of the imperial administration. The town had to be able to present a large number of solid, middle-class citizens, usually at least thirty, who had the resources and probity to serve as municipal councilors. Councilors were expected not only to legislate for the city and act as magistrates, but also to be generous patrons and to endow the city with public buildings and other amenities. This was an expensive proposition; the urban leadership had to be sure that their resources were equal to the task and that the benefits of municipal status would outweigh the expenditures they would be required to make. It was not completely an economic decision, of course. The buildings they would endow would bear their names, and, as founding fathers, their names would be perpetuated in the annals and traditions of the city. Even if they had the necessary resources and were willing to undertake municipal responsibilities, however, it was still necessary to obtain imperial favor before receiving a coveted municipal charter.

If the town's petition for municipal status were viewed with favor, there were two ways in which it could be implemented. The government might declare the town a *colonia*, move in additional numbers of military retirees, and grant the new city a colonial charter. It was in this fashion that Gloucester in Britain gained municipal status. This procedure offered many advantages to the settlement seeking a charter. The influx of new residents and the increased economic activity that came in their wake made the obligations of patronage by the upper class of the city a lighter burden. It was relatively rare for a settlement to gain municipal status in this fashion, however, since the establishment of a *colonia* was primarily a military consideration and was not undertaken lightly. If was far more common for the administration to receive a petition, assess the resources of the town, and decide whether a grant of municipal status would be of any benefit to the empire. If the findings were positive, the town would receive a charter and become a *municipium*, with all of the rights and obligations that status implied.

Sometimes, of course, the decision was negative, and no charter was granted. Such settlements would often grow and develop municipal institutions without official sanction. Moguntiacum (Mainz), the capital of Upper Germany, for instance, possessed most of the characteristics of a city, but was unable to obtain a municipal charter. It remained, at least in the eyes of the imperial administration, only a aggregation of *vici* until the reign of Diocletian (284–305). Nevertheless, a quasi-municipal corporation, the *conventus civium Romanorum* (Association of Roman Citizens), was active in the city. By the third century, the association was governed by a town council (*ordo*), the members of which were called *decuriones*. In this regard it hardly differed from typical self-governing urban communities such as the *coloniae*, *municipia*, or the tribal towns characteristic of Gaul and Britain.[40]

Urbanization on the Western Frontiers

When we consider the varieties of urban development on the Roman frontier in the West, two factors seem to have been characteristic of the entire process. The first was the dominant role played by the military, and the second was the relative freedom with which urban growth occurred. Both of these factors were reflections of the imperial administration's basic lack of interest in promoting or assisting urbanization in the frontier districts.

The fundamental concern of the government was to establish a fixed and defensible frontier at the least possible cost to the imperial heartland. The first order of business was to move troops into position, have them fortify strategic locations, and provide housing for themselves. Except perhaps in Britain, there appeared to be no inclination to devote any expenditures to establishing urban centers. Even in Britain, urbanization seems to have been more a policy of pacification rather than a planned effort at civilizing the island. Generally speaking, the administration appears to have been disinclined to invest any resources in the social, political, or cultural development of the frontier districts or in the provision of urban amenities for the frontier troops.

Such amenities came, without governmental direction or sanction, with the wives, children, artisans, prostitutes, traders, and shopkeepers who followed the troops to the frontier and built a cluster of huts outside the gates of the fort. It would seem that frontier commanders were generally permissive in allowing their men to have wives, live outside the fort, and even establish private businesses. The *canabae* grew without plan or regulation, and were free to respond to the needs of the local garrison and to evolve along with the local economy.

In its desire to minimize its costs, the imperial administration laid heavy levies of foodstuffs and raw materials on the native residents of the frontier districts to supply the local garrisons. These populations were forced into a period of intensive economic development, in which the natives soon saw that surplus production could be sold to the army for a cash profit. At the same time, the army was directed to build a strategic transport system, utilizing both land and water routes. The long-term purpose of this endeavor was to allow the army to cover more ground with fewer men and thus further decrease costs. The result was that the frontier was provided with an infrastructure that further stimulated economic development. Trade followed the military routes and thus began to concentrate to an even greater extent at the forts that lay at key points within the transport network. Meanwhile, the government had become aware of the potential value of the growing trade with the border tribes of Germany. This trade expanded, and markets, merchants, and manufactories soon began to concentrate at key points.

Under this stimulus, the populations of the *canabae* began to expand with immigrant traders, artisans, agricultural developers, native tribesmen, and others who wished to participate in the economic opportunities that were concentrated at many of the forts of the frontier. The residents of the *canabae* became more civilian in their origins and outlook and less dependent upon providing the local garrison with amenities. In some cases, the populations moved from the immediate vicinity of the fort to form *vici*; in other cases, the *canabae* simply continued to expand. In neither case was there much in the way of central planning or government control. The government was interested in the increasing revenues of the frontier districts, of course, but only passively. Once having conceived of the frontier in a strictly military sense, it was difficult for the imperial administration to view it in any other way. If the government were to have recognized the growing civilian population of the frontier districts, it would have had to take the welfare of these people into account. It would never again have been able to develop policies based on purely military considerations, and the role of the frontier army in protecting the interior of the empire would have been permanently compromised.

The residents of the frontier districts were therefore free from government control to a degree that was almost unprecedented in the Roman Empire. The security provided by the army, coupled with this unofficial exemption from imperial regulation, allowed economic forces to function with unusual freedom. Nevertheless, the growth of urban centers on the frontier was in many ways a by-product of military policy. Military planners usually located their garrisons at vulnerable points where fords, tributary rivers, or old trade routes offered the border tribes access to the interior of the empire.[41] Such sites were also attractive to traders and merchants who moved along these same routes for peaceful purposes, and the market provided by local garrisons encouraged such civilians to settle in the vicinity of the frontier fortresses. These civilian settlements flourished where conditions were favorable, where there were good communications and busy traffic for trade, a source of raw materials for manufacture, and fertile land for agriculture.

Some of these towns were able to outgrow their immediate dependence on a garrison market and develop a more diversified economy.

The test of their vitality often came when the local garrisons were posted elsewhere and the frontier moved on. Many of these settlements failed, or their residents simply followed the troops. Many others succeeded, however, and developed an economic life independent of purely military markets. Some of the great cities of the Rhine–Danube region—Cologne, Coblenz, Mainz, Vienna, Belgrade, Budapest—arose in just such a fashion.

There are few great monuments of Roman civil culture to be found in the region of the old frontier, and urban life there was primitive by Roman standards.[42] One must remember, however, that many of the cities of the interior were artificial creations. They were centers of trade and commerce because the government had decreed that they be so, and they disposed of wealth amassed from slave labor, war booty, and the generally favorable economic conditions created by the government's unequal taxation of the eastern provinces of the empire. The frontier towns enjoyed none of these advantages, but arose purely in response to the economic needs and opportunities of the frontier.[43] They were functioning economic communities of artisans and merchants, and differences in wealth and social standing among their residents were comparatively small and lightly regarded. In this sense, at least, the frontier towns were distinguished by their relative freedom and equality.

Notes

1. It might be better to say that they were ambivalent. Public life was concentrated in cities, and neither labor nor expense was spared in embellishing those cities and providing them with amenities. The Romans seemed to take great pleasure in the crowds, markets, and hustle and bustle of their cities. At the same time, however, these same Romans, particularly the upper classes, longed for the quiet and repose of their country estates. Those whose station in life and resources permitted it alternated their time between city and country, fully content with neither.

2. The Roman city-state was generally about the same area as an American county, and served many of the same functions. There was a great variety in size, wealth, and population among them, however. Some were relatively small towns, and some had populations of several thousands. In cases where a district did not possess a single concentration of population, the Roman government often allowed the villages of a district to confederate and assume the status of a city-state. Such an administrative area was called a *saltus*. Although the city-states differed widely in size and appearance, their local institutions were set by law and were virtually identical throughout the empire.

3. Imperial taxes were collected by independent agencies, however. A tax farming system was used in which consortia of wealthy individuals in Rome would purchase the right to collect the taxes of a given province, usually at a heavy discount. Their agents would then attempt to collect the maximum amount of taxes possible. The system was the source of considerable corruption, and of antagonism between local residents and the tax farmers' agents. The situation grew insupportable during the civil wars of the third century, in the course of which the tax bases of many city-states were virtually destroyed, and during which the frequent debasement of the coinage made any system of financial planning impossible. One of the first reforms of the emperor Diocletian (284–307) was to end tax farming and to make the middle class of the city-states personally responsible for collecting imperial taxes at the local level. The government's assessments were unrealistically high, however, and local tax bases, at least in the western portions of the empire, were shrinking for a variety of reasons. The urban middle class of the Western Empire was ruined by this, the political functions of the city-states steadily decayed, and population, manufacturing, and commerce all declined rapidly. The loss of the city-states as vital centers of Roman life was one of the major contributing factors to the fall of the empire in the West.

4. This can be seen most clearly in Britain, where the distinctions between the southeastern zone of civil administration and the northern and western zones of military administration emerged quite early. As we have seen, the administrators of the southeast used urban life as a means of Romanizing British chieftains, a policy that maintained relative peace within the district for some three centuries, although it failed to extend Roman influences among the village-dwelling mass of the British population.

5. Sheppard Sunderland Frere, *Britannia: A History of Roman Britain*, p. 240; Peter Salway, *The Frontier People of Roman Britain*, p. 39. Tenny Frank, *An Economic History of Rome*, p. 452, states that urbanization of the frontier regions occurred because of natural economic and social factors and not due to official attempts at civilizing the natives by transforming them into city dwellers.

6. The word *canabae* means "huts" or "hovels," which may indicate something of the nature of these settlements. It should be noted, however, that Roman army slang generally put everything in the worst possible light. The existence of *canabae* at frontier fortresses is attested as early as A.D. 70 by a settlement at Vetera (Xanten) substantial enough to be described as a town, and by early inscriptions from the *canabae* at Mainz. It has been noted that the term *canabae* was used only for settlements at legionary fortresses or special stations, not for the settlements outside smaller posts. Given the meaning of the word, this seems like an artificial distinction, and it is unlikely that the common soldier observed such semantic niceties. In this discussion, *canabae* is used for any settlement located in the immediate environs of a fort, regardless of its size, that served primarily the needs of the garrison.

7. See David J. Breeze, *Hadrian's Wall*, p. 179; Salway, *The Frontier People*, pp. 31–32. On the matter of marriage among the military, see Brian Campbell, "The Marriage of Soldiers under the Empire," *Journal of Roman Studies* 68 (1978): 153–166; and Peter Garnsey, "Septimius Severus and the Marriage of Roman Soldiers," *California Studies in Classical Antiquity* 3 (1970): 45.

8. On the subject of women on the western Roman frontiers, see Lindsay

Allason-Jones, *Women in Roman Britain*; and M. M. Roxan, "Women on the Frontiers," in *Roman Frontier Studies: 1989*, ed. V. A. Maxfield and M. J. Dobson, pp. 462–467.

9. Fergus Millar, *The Roman Empire and its Neighbours*, p. 121, states that the Roman soldier of the first and second centuries was allowed to purchase a house in the province in which he served, but not land. The government felt that by attending to cultivation the soldier would neglect his military duties. The troops were able to buy land in other provinces, however.

10. See M. C. Bishop, "Soldiers and Military Equipment in the Towns of Roman Britain," *Roman Frontier Studies: 1989*, ed. V. A. Maxfield and M. J. Dobson (Exeter: University Press), pp. 21–27; and M. C. Bishop, ed., *The Production and Distribution of Roman Military Equipment: Proceedings of the Second Roman Military Equipment Research Seminar* (Oxford: British Archaeological Reports, 1985).

11. *Testa*, or "nut," instead of *caput* for "head"; *caballus*, or "crock," instead of *equus* for "horse," and so forth.

12. Along the Rhine and Danube this process was accentuated by a realization of the growing purchasing power of the border tribes. German imports soon demanded regular marketplaces, and long-distance Roman traders began to use the frontier towns as their bases of operation.

13. Salway, *The Frontier People*, pp. 10–11. The word *vicus* derives from an early Indo-European root and is allied to the English suffixes "-wick" and "-wich." The basic distinction between the *canabae* and the *vicus* was that the latter was the center of a civilian population. As we shall see, it was not necessary that a *vicus* be physically separated from a fortress, and *vici* arose from bases other than the *canabae*. *Vicus* could also mean a neighborhood within a larger unit and, in the Middle Ages, was often used for "village." The term survives in modern Romance languages in various forms. The Spanish word *vecino*, for instance, means "neighbor."

14. Edith Wightman, *Trier and the Treveri*, pp. 128–129, notes the growth of villages, some dating back to pre-Roman times, that had long served as marketplaces for the neighboring countryside as another significant base for the development of frontier *vici*. The existence of abundant raw materials for industry and the presence of navigable rivers proved instrumental in the growth of many frontier towns. See also Frere, *Britannia*, p. 294; and Paul MacKendrick, "Roman Town Planning," *Archaeology* 9 (1956):129.

15. J. Mertens, "The Military Origins of Some Roman Settlements in Belgium," in *Rome and Her Northern Provinces*, ed. Brian Hartley and John Wacher.

16. Ulrich Fischer, "Verulamium and the Towns of Britannia," in *Aufsteig und Niedergang der römischen Welt*, ed. Hildegard Temporini and Wolfgang Haase, 2:290–327. It is probable that the *vicus* at Verulamium eventually gained municipal status. It should be remembered, however, that these particular locations were in the civil zone, rather than the military frontier districts of Britain. The pattern of urban growth here differed markedly from that of the military areas in the North and West.

17. Ulrich Fischer, "Frankfurt–Heddernheim: A Roman Frontier Town beyond the Rhine," *Archaeology* 14 (1961):36–37. A similar case is discussed in Wightman, *Trier and the Treveri*, p. 119.

18. Agricola's troops were called to the continent to meet a threat to the frontier there. His son-in-law Tacitus provides a detailed, although biased, account of that campaign in the *Agricola*. Tacitus's desire to glorify his father-in-law and condemn the emperor led him, for once, to ignore the magnitude and importance of the German tribes beyond the frontier.

19. T. W. Potter, "Romans in North-West England," *Cumberland and Westmorland Antiquarian and Archaeological Society Research Series*, vol. 1 (Kendal: Titus Wilson and Son, 1979), pp. 180, 185, mentions that extramural structures have been found at the Roman fort at Watercrook in northwest Britain situated beyond the northeast side of the fort, and beside the northeast road. A *vicus* also grew up east of the fort. The earliest building dated to the Flavian-Trajanic period, and occupation lasted into the early third century A.D. Salway, *The Frontier People*, p. 165.

20. Such a situation might appear intolerable to a modern society accustomed to urban plans, land-use regulations, regulated developments, neighborhood restrictions, and zoning codes. It should be remembered, however, that such regulation usually impedes individual economic opportunity, carries high hidden costs, and can nevertheless lead to virtually unlivable communities. Traditional Muslim cities, which have few such restrictions, display chaotic street plans that, upon closer examination, are seen to be quite well adapted to the economic pursuits of the residents and to the special character of Muslim family and clan structure.

21. See Salway, *The Frontier People*, pp. 166–167.

22. Generally speaking, the appearance of a building at right angles to its neighbors is an indication, in urban topography, of the existence of a cross street at one time or another.

23. R. G. Collingwood and Ian A. Richmond, *The Archaeology of Roman Britain*, pp. 125–127.

24. Salway, *The Frontier People*, p. 165, would nevertheless suggest that such *vici* were the means by which the native population of the northern frontier was introduced to urban life, no matter how simple its form.

25. Robin Birley, *Vindolanda: A Roman Frontier Post on Hadrian's Wall*, pp. 38–39.

26. Ibid., pp. 123–125. See chapter 4 above, noting that the evidence for this manufacture dates from prior to the construction of the wall in 122–127.

27. Birley, *Vindolanda*, pp. 124–125.

28. It was at this point that the shipping base at York began to lose military importance and the great agricultural project in the Fenlands began to be converted to pasturage.

29. Breeze, *Hadrian's Wall*, pp. 191–192, state that the industrial activity in the *vici* probably satisfied the needs of the local inhabitants. Specialized wares such as bronze *paterea* (soldiers' mess tins), fine footwear, glass, and some mass-produced pottery were imported, but iron was smelted locally at Corbridge, Housesteads, and Chesterholm. Leather was another local product with a wide market. A cobbler's shop has been identified in the *vicus* at Housesteads, and we have already noted the tannery at Vindolanda. Salway, *The Frontier People*, pp. 25–26.

30. Salway, *The Frontier People*, pp. 39–41.

31. See Tacitus, *Annales* 14:27.

32. Collingwood and Richmond, *The Archaeology of Roman Britain*, p. 95; John Wacher, *The Towns of Roman Britain*, p. 17.

33. The name of Cologne (Köln) is itself derived from the Latin *colonia*.

34. Andrés Mócsy, *Pannonia and Upper Moesia: A History of the Middle Danube Provinces of the Roman Empire*, pp. 117–122.

35. H. Hurst, "Gloucester (Glevum): A Colonia in the West Country," in *The Roman West Country*, ed. Keith Branigan and P. J. Fowler, pp. 71–73; Wacher, *The Towns of Roman Britain*, p. 17.

36. See Fischer, "Frankfurt–Heddernheim," pp. 36–37; and Collingwood and Richmond, *The Archaeology of Roman Britain*, pp. 60–63, 67.

37. Even those veterans who returned to their home provinces, which were commonly those along the frontier, often chose to take up residence in the *canabae* and *vici* there.

38. Salway, *The Frontier People*, pp. 27–28.

39. Ibid., pp. 28–29. Ex-service clubs were not normally formed in the auxiliary settlements.

40. Marcel Amand, "Urban Sites of Roman Origin in Belgium," in *European Towns: Their Archaeology and Early History*, ed. M. W. Barley, p. 157, cites Tongres, Tournai, Arlon, and Namur as significant Roman towns in Belgium. These were all located on rivers and date from the beginning of the first century A.D.

41. The establishment of the defensive line at Hadrian's Wall is an obvious exception to this observation.

42. The same cannot be said of cities of the border provinces such as Trier and Sirmium, which, in the days of the soldier emperors, sometimes served as capitals of the empire in the West.

43. The *coloniae* were, of course, governmental foundations and played a significant role on the frontier. They were not characteristic of the region, however, and their importance often depended more upon their own economic vitality than upon imperial sponsorship and subsidies. See Anthony Birley, "The Economic Effects of Roman Frontier Policy," in *The Roman West in the Third Century*, ed. A. King and M. Henig, pp. 39–54; and Lothar Wierschowski, *Heer und Wirtschaft: das römische Heer der Prinzipatäzeit als Wirtschaftsfaktor*.

VII THE GROWTH OF INDUSTRY

Roman industrial development was shaped by a number of factors that were overcome some time ago in the western world. As a consequence, the structure of Roman industry requires some explanation before one can fully appreciate the attraction the frontier exerted upon the manufacturers of the period.

The General Character of Roman Industry

Roman society was based upon slave labor, and a significant portion of the population—the slaves—was therefore almost entirely without purchasing power. Although there were numerous instances of masters allowing their slaves to earn money, this was the rare and urban exception rather than the rural rule. The mass of Roman slaves were agricultural or mining workers who were worked in large gangs, housed in barracks, and fed at a common mess. The Romans had long been accustomed to the constant replenishment of the slave population by the prisoners of successful wars and were not much concerned with the rate at which the physical ability of their laborers declined or whether they reproduced at a rate sufficient to maintain a stable supply of enslaved manpower. Although the Roman slave structure was complex, by and large the Romans appear to have worked their unskilled slaves to death rather rapidly, and secured replacements from conquered peoples.

This meant not only that a significant portion of the population was chronic underconsumers and thus limited the growth of internal markets for manufactured goods, but also that Roman society was generally short of skilled workers. One must add to this the fact that wealth was unevenly distributed among the free population. The greatest purchasing power lay in the hands of a relatively few wealthy men who also owned extensive country estates. It was the pride of these landowners to have their estates managed in such a fashion that they were as self-sufficient as possible. Thus the market for the products of manufacturing concerns was quite limited by modern standards, and the growing prosperity of the empire in the first and second centuries did little to alter that situation.

One would expect that the independent craftsmen would have reacted to these limitations by attempting to expand the scope of their markets. Their ability to do so was restricted by a number of factors, however. The most immediate limitation lay in the high costs of overland transport, an aspect of the Roman economy that we have already discussed at length in connection with the development of commerce on the frontier. The second limitation lay in the fact that conditions were virtually the same throughout the empire. The low purchasing power of local markets precluded any significant expansion by independent manufacturers except for those dealing in luxury wares and export goods.

One must picture the typical Roman manufacturer as operating on a quite small scale, participating in the work himself, with the help of possibly a dozen slaves and salaried employees, and quite possibly living on the premises. Profits were low, and, since there was no stimulus to increase production, the manufacturer had little interest in efficient or labor-saving machinery or equipment. In certain cases, particularly when a clearly superior raw material was desired, a number of such small firms might cluster together to form a manufacturing center, but these were accidental occurrences rather than signs of industrial concentration or integration.

Because of their small scale and their limited investment in fixed assets, Roman manufacturing concerns were able to move to attractive market areas, insofar as the local availability of necessary raw materials allowed them to do so. Although there were certain Roman manufactures that remained in place for many years, a large portion of the manufacturing potential of the empire consisted of highly mobile small concerns, always awaiting the offer of greater opportunity elsewhere.

For the Roman manufacturer, opportunity consisted of a favorable market. If, during the early first century A.D., you had asked such a man what he would consider the perfect market for his products, he might have replied that it would be one that had a relatively high density of population and a low percentage of slaves. He would also have preferred a place where there was a relatively equal distribution of purchasing power among the free population, at least a small guaranteed demand for his product, and few if any self-sufficient villas. Warming to his subject, he might have added that, in his entrepreneur's utopia, there would be good local security, little competition, and perhaps even a chance to produce goods for a long-distance export trade. It would have good transportation routes by both water and land, and yet be so situated that better-established concerns could not reach his potential customers. Last, but not least, he might have added, it should have ample local supplies of cheap raw materials and enough actual cash to keep businessmen from wasting their time in the endless intricacies of bartering.

This imaginary Roman manufacturer would have been describing what the western frontier of the empire would eventually become. This took the army and imperial administrators a considerable time to accomplish, perhaps because this was never their intention, but the frontier in time attracted much industrial potential to the peripheral districts and provinces of the empire, and impoverished and weakened its heartland to a significant degree.

This was a slow process that depended upon the growth of concentrations of population, the building of road networks, the growth of export markets in Germany, and, perhaps most important of all, the development of local sources of raw material.

Frontier Mining

Most ancient manufacture utilized relatively common materials such as sand for glass, clay for pottery, agricultural and animal products for textiles, slate for roofing, and leather for a variety of goods. The need for metals presented a somewhat different problem, since mineral deposits are not evenly distributed throughout the world, and metalworking required not only a nearby source of ore, but massive quantities of ready fuel, normally wood or charcoal.

The Roman Empire was one of the favored regions of the world in this respect. Controlling workable deposits of all the various metals used in the ancient world, the empire was not only self-sufficient, but exported metal goods far beyond imperial frontiers. The Romans sent gold to India and China, silver and copper to the Germanic peoples of the North, and bronzeware in all directions. This was not merely the result of good fortune, but the Romans' intense industry in discovering and developing the mineral resources of their territories.[1] Some relatively rare metals, such as gold, silver, tin, and lead, were avidly sought, and the Romans were quite ready to go to war to acquire control of sources of such metals.[2] Roman interest in mining was not restricted to rare metals, however. Wherever the Romans established their control, the development of local mineral resources was quickly undertaken, and the army often led the way in this activity.

The high point of Roman mining was reached during the first and second centuries A.D., as new provincial and frontier regions were opened to exploitation. The first substantial industrial developments along the frontier, and the bases of later industrial and manufacturing growth, were the mines opened up in the region. The pressing needs of the frontier and the desire of the imperial administration to have the frontier pay its own way had much to do with this rapid expansion of mining. The most important factor, however, was the ease of extraction. The Romans brought new mining techniques and organization to the underdeveloped regions of the frontier and were able to obtain good returns with relatively little labor. This situation was already coming to an end in the third century as diminishing yields and increasing costs signaled the end of an era of easy extraction.[3] During the period with which we are concerned, however, the frontier in the West was the site of a long-term mining boom.

The initial stimulus for mineral exploitation came from the army of the frontier, which not only required great quantities of metal but also treated metal as an expendable material.[4] The Roman soldiers required helmets, armor,[5] weapons, kettles, mess tins, needles, razors, chisels, probes, cleats, meat hooks, hammers, axes, and immense quantities of nails.[6] Gold, silver, and bronze coins were necessary in order to sustain the civilian and military sectors of the economy. Since the army had the most pressing needs and the ranks of the legions included expert engineers, it was only natural that the military should lead the way in exploiting local mineral resources. The provinces of Britain provide an excellent example of Roman development of the mineral resources of the frontier regions.

The Romans were at least partially aware of the potential mineral riches of Britain even before its invasion under the emperor Claudius.[7] They were aware that the island possessed deposits of gold and silver, as well as of relatively rare and extremely useful tin and lead. The desire to control these resources may have been one of the factors that led the imperial administration to undertake a venture that represented a clear departure from the Augustan policy of fixed frontiers. Roman expectations that Britain would supply mineral riches were in large measure fulfilled, although not precisely in the proportions that they had anticipated.

The island proved to be relatively poor in gold, and much of the British gold that had attracted the Romans' attention had in fact been imported from Ireland. Some placers were worked in Wales and Cornwall, but the yield from these sites never contributed significant amounts to imperial gold supplies. Silver was more abundant, and the mines of Britain furnished the interior of the empire with a steady supply of that metal. Tin was plentiful and necessary in the making of bronze. The famous tin mines of Cornwall could have supplied a large native British bronze-working industry, but the Romans were slow to discover and exploit the copper deposits of the province. Copper was initially imported from the continent into southeastern Britain, and even though Welsh mines eventually provided a steady supply of copper until well into the third century, the Romans never exploited these deposits fully.[8]

The Romans were interested primarily in British lead, a metal with a thousand uses in ancient Rome. Lead deposits in the Mendip Hills of southwestern Britain had been worked by native Celts prior to the Roman conquest of the area. These mines were quickly seized, and other sites opened up in Wales and Yorkshire.[9] The legions appear to have taken over the administration of these mining operations. The Second Augustan Legion, based at Caerleon, directed operations in the Mendip Hills, Wales, and perhaps Shropshire, and began shipping lead to the continent no later than the year 68.[10]

Aerial photographs have revealed the street pattern of a Roman town at Charterhouse in the Mendip district, a site from which we can construct a picture of a frontier mining town. The townsite was large, covering some thirty acres. The town center consisted of a row of *insulae*—square, multi-story rooming houses. Less regular blocks of apartments surrounded this core, and the street plan became less symmetrical as one progressed out from the town center. This would suggest that the army had planned the initial settlement, and that later expansion may have been relatively unregulated. A nearby fort housed a garrison of troops from the Second Augustan Legion. The entire town was supervised and security maintained from the garrison's headquarters. The troops directed the entire work force, which seems to have comprised slaves and prisoners of war as well as civilian miners. The fort also probably functioned as a control point at which the lead of the Mendip Hills was assayed, weighed, stamped, and routed to its proper destination.[11] A number of villas were concentrated in the area and apparently supplied the fort and settlement with food and other necessary farm products.[12] The mining settlement at Charterhouse seems to have been an integrated and self-sufficient operation, complete with a fort for protection, a large townsite, and surrounding agricultural areas. The army appears to have been in charge of the mines and the work force, but the villa operators and many of the residents of the town, perhaps shopkeepers and other service personnel, were most probably civilians only lightly regulated by military authority.

In Britain, the army seems to have served primarily to begin the exploitation of important mineral deposits. Except for gold and silver mining, which remained under direct imperial operation, many mines appear to have been turned over to imperial managers and finally, if circumstances permitted, leased to private operators, although they remained under imperial control.[13] The pattern of development varied in other frontier regions. In Noricum, Dalmatia, and Gaul, for instance, large-scale capitalists appear to have controlled major mining enterprises, while in other areas small-scale entrepreneurs or private associations undertook mining operations under imperial supervision. In still other circumstances, as was the case with the Mendip lead mines, mineral deposits were exploited directly by the state, with prisoners and slaves working the mines under the supervision of military detachments.[14]

The wealth of minerals along the frontier and the relative ease of their extraction were so great that all of these systems of exploitation worked well. Noricum, for instance, developed by great capitalists, became one of the great mineral centers of the empire. Although Noricum produced gold, copper, lead, and zinc, iron was the basis of its industrial development. The term *ferrum noricum*, "Norican iron," referred in fact to the high-grade steel produced in Noricum and shipped throughout the empire.[15] Other metalware, such as rings, caul-drons, cups, plates, hoes, hammers, anvils, and axes, were exported from Noricum throughout the empire and free Germany. The Norican mining industries were so extensive that the inscriptions of the region allow us to note a significant change in the work force. Although many slaves and prisoners of war had worked the mines when the frontier was opened, by the middle of the second century slavery had virtually disappeared from central Noricum.

This emphasis upon the great mining centers should not obscure the fact that most of the mining along the frontier probably consisted of small-scale ventures owned and operated by groups or even single individuals. Family-operated tin, copper, and, above all, iron mines produced much of the metal that was used locally along the frontier. The proliferation of such small ventures, coupled with their concomi-tant demand for charcoal, created a large, free work force engaged in metal production. It was on the basis of this cheap, local production of metals and upon the tradition of free labor that frontier manufacturing began to expand.

The ending of the wars of conquest had also ended the steady flow of prisoners of war into the empire, and, as time passed, the number of slaves began to decrease and their price began to rise accordingly. Industries that had relied on slave labor were forced to decrease their production and to increase their prices. Smaller concerns in the interior of the empire could not compete with the larger in securing slave workers, and many were reduced to family-scale production. The na-scent industries of the frontier, by contrast, employed a labor force composed of free men and women. Their labor costs did not increase as the supply of slave labor began to dwindle, and their prices became steadily more competitive with the large-scale enterprises of the inte-rior of the empire. At the same time, the existence of a large salaried class of workers along the frontier created an internal market that increasingly stimulated local production. From a quite early date, man-ufacturers from the interior began to move their operations toward the frontier, seeking cheap materials, favorable local markets, and a free labor force.

Pottery Manufacture

It is possible in some cases to trace the migration of certain industries. The popular red pottery of the early Empire, known as Samian ware, is also called *terra sigillata* by historians because of the potters' practice of stamping their name or mark on each piece. These marks make it possible to date pieces of Samian ware and to determine their place of manufacture relatively precisely. The production of Samian ware was originally restricted to Italy, but during the first century A.D. the major centers of production shifted to Graufenesque, in the Cevennes Mountains of southern France, northwest of Nimes. This movement accelerated during the course of the second century. The main center of production first moved about a hundred miles north along the Alliers River to Lezoux, near the modern city of Clermont-Ferrand. Although Lezoux remained an important center of production for some time, regional centers of production soon appeared at various sites in eastern France, Alsace, and Switzerland. By the end of the second century, however, a main center had again emerged, now on the middle Rhine, dominated by the works at Rheinzabern, near Speyer.[16]

The pottery found at York in Britain provides a more precise chronology of the succession of Samian ware production centers. Between A.D. 30 and 110, most of the pottery found there was manufactured at Graufenesque. From about 125 to 200, most of the pottery came from Lezoux. Some of the material from about 125 on came from centers in eastern Gaul and the Rhine, primarily Rheinzabern. After 200, however, pottery from Rhineland centers became dominant in the district.[17] Additional evidence from Germany and Scandinavia suggests that, during the second century, Samian ware from Lezoux and various Rhenish potteries shared the German export market.[18] In a process that took two centuries to complete, a traditional Italian industry had moved from the heartland of the empire to implant itself firmly in the frontier districts of the West.

Another branch of the pottery industry, that of lamp production, showed the same tendency to migrate to the frontier provinces. The traditional Roman lamp was a small pottery object shaped something like a gravy pitcher. Filled with oil or tallow from the top, its wick protruded from its spout. Although it was smoky and cast little light, it was universally used throughout the empire. At the beginning of the first century A.D., the centers of lamp manufacture were concentrated in Italy, and lamps of Italian shape and ornamentation were widely exported.

This might appear at first to have been a negligible branch of manufacture, but the pottery lamps were easily cracked or broken and generally treated as expendables. Vast numbers had to be produced to meet a constant demand. The military camp at Vindonissa near Basel in modern Switzerland affords an example of the size of this demand as well as illustrating the decline of the Italian manufacture of this commodity. Vindonissa was established under the emperor Tiberius (A.D. 14–37) and was abandoned about the year 100. Archaeologists have uncovered more than 1,600 pottery lamps in the graves and dwellings of the site, and there are probably many more yet undiscovered. A typology of these lamps can be established on the basis of their design and ornamentation. The earliest type lamps are typical of the products of the lampmaking centers of Italy, but very few bear the stamps of Roman potters. The early lamps at Vindonissa were apparently shipped in from Lugdunum, modern Lyon, on the Rhone River in Gaul, where similar imitations of Italian wares have been found. Other lamps at Vindonissa were of a different design. Based upon traditional Gallic and German patterns, these lamps were manufactured in various sites in Gaul and along the German frontier and seem to have been the predominant type at Vindonissa by the end of the first century.[19]

Italian lampmakers were apparently unable to provide the frontier with an assured, or inexpensive, supply of lamps. Whatever the reason, the expanding frontier population quickly came to rely upon its own production of this essential utensil. The troops along the Rhine often used dugouts for winter quarters, and lamps were a necessity for such units. It is not surprising then to find that a lamp factory at Wiesenau, near Mainz, was apparently administered by military authorities.[20] Lamp manufacture on the western frontier and in the border provinces expanded to meet local needs as well as a small but significant demand in Germany and Scandinavia. Few Italian manufacturers continued operations after the end of the second century, and those that did mainly supplied local markets in the interior of the empire.

Glassmaking

Roman glass manufacture displayed the same tendency to move toward the frontier. Gallic glassworks were supplying local markets in the first century A.D. and continued to grow throughout the second and into the third centuries. By the middle of this period of growth, Gallic glass manufacture had outstripped the Italian industry in both quantity and quality.[21] In the course of its growth, Gallic glass manufacture gradually expanded northward into the area of modern Belgium and the Rhine. The rise of centers such as Poitiers and Boulogne, and Autun and Amiens, suggests that the industry may have moved northward along two routes, one along the coast, and the other northward along the Rhone River.[22]

By the end of the first century A.D., a significant glass industry had emerged along the lower Rhine, centered on Cologne.[23] The bluish-green and clear white Rhineland products were highly regarded, and, by the end of the second century, the glassblowers of the Rhenish frontier were producing cut-glass beakers and tumblers on German models. These found favor both within the empire and in the export trade.[24] The products of one Cologne glassworks, that of the maker of the "Lynkeus beaker," appear all over Europe. Wares from this manufactory have been found at Mainz and Strassburg, in England and the Wall area, at Trier and Rheims, east to Fulda and Thuringia, and in the Danube basin.[25] Such frontier glass served as one of the chief exports of the later empire into Germany.[26] As was the case with mining and smelting, the existence of such great works, supplying both the export trade and the interior of the empire, opened the way for smaller establishments to meet the immediate needs of frontier markets. The remains of three small glassworks uncovered in Britain are probably only a token of numerous others scattered throughout the frontier districts and border provinces.[27]

Samian ware, pottery lamps, and glassmaking all demonstrate the same progression. Originally Italian, these industries moved to southern Gaul by the early first century A.D. From these southern Gallic centers, they moved northward and eastward in the course of the century, and were established in the border provinces by the year 100. In the second century, they increased their production in order to meet both local needs and at least a portion of the demand for export wares for Germany. They reached their height by the end of the second century, by which time the major Italian centers of these manufactures had almost disappeared. At the same time, still smaller manufacturing ventures, producing for local markets, began to proliferate throughout the frontier districts.

This process is corroborated by archaeological finds from as far away as Denmark. Up to about A.D. 150, products of Italian manufacture, such as Italian glassware and Capuan bronzes, dominate the

Roman materials discovered. After this time, however, these Italian-made goods are replaced by products from manufacturing centers along the Rhine and Danube.[28] Italian manufacture never recovered even a portion of this market; it had been completely displaced by new frontier industries that were only beginning their period of great expansion.

Wine Production

Although the needs of the army and an expanding civilian population made great demands upon agriculture in the frontier districts, industries based upon agrarian products also came to displace Italian products. This was nowhere more evident than in the production of wine, at one time the most Roman of commodities. The frontier army's need for wine—its ration beverage as well as its favorite recreation—could scarcely have been filled from Italy. The usual difficulty of overland transport was made even greater in the case of wine, since the normal shipping container for wine was the *amphora*, a large pottery jug that was not only fragile, but could weigh one-third of the total load of wine and container. Moreover, many wines, including those of Roman Italy, do not "travel well." They grow sour, develop bitter sediments, and lose some of their alcoholic content. Although the Roman troops relished sour wine, they could not tolerate wine gone bad.

In order to meet the army's needs, vineyards were planted along the Moselle, Rhine, and Danube, and even Britain managed to produce a small amount. The vineyards of Gaul, the Rhineland, and the Danube not only expanded, but came to produce excellent wines, although some fine vintages of the interior, such as the famous Falernian, continued to be favored as luxuries in the frontier districts. The frontier wines, however, quickly dominated the export market. Although few *amphorae* are found in German archaeological sites, the preferred wine container in the North was the wooden barrel, which rarely leaves identifiable remains. A large number of pottery and glass vessels used for mixing and drinking wine have been found throughout Germany and suggest that the export of wine to Germany was carried out on a relatively large scale. The absence of *amphorae* indicates that the wine was shipped in wooden barrels and was therefore the product of the vineyards of Rome's western frontier.[29]

Spinning and Weaving

The growth of the western textile industry offers yet another aspect of the development of frontier manufacture. The two leading textile-producing centers in the Roman world were located at opposite ends of the empire—in northern Gaul and in Syria. The interior of the Roman Empire lagged significantly behind the periphery in textile production.[30] The major reason for this lay in the availability of raw materials of extraordinarily high quality in these regions.[31] In the Middle Ages, the meadows of northern France, Belgium, and eastern Britain would become famous for producing the finest wool in the world. It would appear that the dedication of this remarkable region to sheep raising had begun even before the advent of the Romans. Strabo mentions that the Romans maintained "jacketed" or fine-wooled sheep in Gallia Belgica, a practice that probably dated back to the Belgae.[32] The Belgae may deserve credit for improving the Iron Age breeds of sheep in Britain and for introducing new breeds developed by the Romans. The Roman conquerors possibly improved these flocks still further by importing additional animals from the continent.[33] Gallic and British wool textiles became the most highly desired in the Roman world and found their way into Italy and beyond.

Unfortunately, we know little about this frontier textile industry before its mention in documents of the late empire. Entries in the Edict of Diocletian and the *Notitia Dignitatum* provide significant information regarding the textile industries of Belgium and Germany in the late third and late fourth centuries.[34] The wool of the Ambiani, the Atrebates, the Nervii, and the Treveri was well known, and the location of military textile mills at Rheims, Tournai, and Trier indicates that some of the precious Gallic wool was being used in the fourth century to supply the army.[35]

The great weaving mills of the North produced luxury textiles, which could cost twenty times as much as common cloth. Such prices would easily have returned the substantial cost of transportation. Thus the great textile industry of the frontier produced exports for the wealthy, and these products dominated the imperial markets in woolen cloth. Local consumption, by contrast, depended upon domestic production.[36] Loom weights and the like are among the most common objects found in archaeological sites along the frontier. It must be remembered that ancient agriculture was a highly seasonal occupation, and that the farm population, both men and women, constituted a great underutilized labor force during the winter months. A largely free society, composed primarily of farm families, could manufacture a great quantity of a variety of goods within the household. Small-scale household manufacture probably made the frontier self-sufficient in textiles as well as in many other goods.

The Industrial Pre-eminence of the Frontier

All of those industries that we can trace tell essentially the same story. Italian manufacture withered as new centers arose first in the border provinces and then along the frontier itself. These frontier industrial centers flourished by the second century and came to dominate the important export trade to Germany. Meanwhile, small-scale manufacturing proliferated along the frontier to supply local markets. By the end of the third century, the bulk of the manufacturing potential of the heartland of the empire had migrated to the frontier. The time has come to ask ourselves why this should have occurred.

One of the reasons that immediately comes to mind is that the frontier was rich in underexploited resources. The lead of the Mendip Hills, the meadows of Gallia Belgica and eastern Britain, the iron mines of Noricum, the forests of Germany, the rich soils of the Moselle and Rhine were all ready for easy exploitation and rich yields. Much of the original industry along the frontier was designed to extract the booty that the imperial government expected from conquered lands, and these activities produced little profit that remained in the frontier lands. It may well be that some of the native peoples entered the labor force of these enterprises as salaried workers, but it is also likely that even more were absorbed as prisoners, troublemakers, and tax delinquents.

The movement of frontier industry should probably be seen as a result of markets and available labor, rather than simply as a response to plentiful raw materials, and one should consider the small-scale industrial sites rather than the great manufacturing concentrations. The establishment of large numbers of military units along the frontier created a permanent market for a wide variety of military supplies. The fact that the bulk of these materials were probably levied, rather than being bought, from the local population is beside the point. At the same time that the army created an extraordinarily well developed economic infrastructure, although it was designed purely as a military system, the inhabitants of the border provinces and frontier districts swiftly increased the production and productivity of their local economies.

Population along the frontier grew, countering a trend toward depopulation that had already begun to emerge in the heartland of the empire, and the frontier was able first to meet major military supply needs, then to produce a surplus over and above these needs, and finally to have a surplus of free workers. Although the army of the frontier attempted to absorb as many of these men as possible into the legions and auxiliary troops, there were still enough left over to constitute a sizable labor force. Small-scale manufacturers, who had been drawn to the frontier by the markets fueled by the salaries of over 200,000 soldiers, found themselves not only with these assured markets, but situated within a well-developed transportation network, with abundant local supplies of cheap raw materials and a local work force of free laborers on which to draw.

By the early second century, two factors had emerged that provided a powerful stimulus to the growth of frontier industry and the attraction of still more entrepreneurs from the imperial heartland. The first was the cumulative effect of the empire's loss of slave levies from newly conquered lands. The Roman slave system had not developed with any accommodation for the need to replenish the slave population through simple reproduction. The slave work force thus began to decline with increasing rapidity, and the price of slaves began to rise accordingly. The free population of the empire's heartland was already too small to fill the agricultural and military needs of the empire, much less compensate for the diminution of the enslaved work force. The supply of available laborers began to contract, and small-scale manufacturers were unable to meet the competition of those concerns rich enough to buy slaves and hire laborers or influential enough to obtain from the government the services of criminals. Those manufacturers who were able to stay in business did so by moving to areas where free laborers were more plentiful.

While the manufacturers of the frontier districts, relying on the free labor of the region, were largely unaffected by this crisis in manpower, the entrepreneurs from the interior moved into the border provinces and frontier districts where they found the laborers they needed.[37] The government did little to impede this exodus of small-scale Italian industry, partly because the Roman government had never been overly concerned with the welfare of its middle class, but primarily because imperial administrators saw in the expansion of manufacturing along the frontier yet another means of having the military frontier of the empire pay for itself. The imperial government had to pay its troops, and the army demanded an ever higher salary. It spent much of its pay on the products of frontier manufacturers, who used the income to buy local materials and to pay local workers who in turn bought local wares. Thus, monies paid to the military were kept circulating within the frontier districts and were taxed by the government at every transaction. The greater the economic self-sufficiency of the frontier districts, the closer imperial administrators were to being able to pay the army entirely out of frontier taxes, thus circulating the same money endlessly.

The second new factor contributing to the expansion of frontier industry by the second century was the emergence of a large-scale export trade to Germany. We have already seen how this trade arose from the early inability of the frontier districts to supply all of the needs of the army of the frontier. Various goods, although primarily cattle and leather, had to be imported from Germany. Since the imperial government could not simply levy goods from the free Germans, they were forced to buy them with the silver coins the Germans preferred. With assured Roman markets and a common trade currency, the various German tribes soon coalesced into a vast trade area with a hunger for Roman wares and the silver to pay for these commodities. The reduced Italian manufacturing centers simply could not fill this new and increasing demand, and frontier manufacturers were able to seize the opportunity to pursue these foreign markets.

German imports lessened the pressure upon the local populations of the frontier districts to produce agricultural commodities for the military markets and thus released many of them to fill an increased need for industrial workers. At the same time, a growing portion of frontier manufacture was diverted to the export trade, and the Romans were soon able to recapture through manufactured exports almost all the silver paid to the Germans for commodity imports. The diversion to export markets of many of the products of frontier industry, in turn, opened the way for the proliferation of manufacture throughout the frontier districts and the employment of underutilized labor sources, such as the agricultural population, to meet the local demand for manufactured products. Such part-time and small-scale workers now had wages to spend on manufactured goods themselves, and the increased internal markets created by the improved standard of living on the frontier continued to attract industrial entrepreneurs and to sustain the proliferation of small industries within the frontier regions.

From the point of view of the imperial administration, these developments were all to the good. More industry meant more taxes, which meant that the army could be kept happy with higher wages. The tendency of the emperors to raise military wages and to grant the army regular bonuses is often interpreted as a ruinous financial measure dictated largely by fear of the army. Given the steadily increasing economic wealth and self-sufficiency of the border provinces and frontier districts, this imperial policy may in fact have been designed simply to keep frontier money on the frontier. If the goal of the imperial administration was indeed to see the military frontier pay for itself, then allowing frontier earnings to be diverted to the insatiable needs of the heartland was a precedent to be avoided if at all possible. In addition, the imperial administration had found that at least some of the German tribes had become economically dependent upon their trade with the frontier and had thus become vulnerable to Roman economic pressure. This dependency was a German weakness that the imperial administration could use in keeping the peace along the frontier, but the Roman advantage in this relationship depended upon maintaining a delicate balance between exports and imports. If the frontier could not provide the goods to satisfy the German market, the German dependency upon Roman goods would be lessened, and the imperial administration would not be able to rely upon a regular supply of German imports. The Romans would then have been dependent upon the Germans, rather than the other way around. The economic growth of the frontier was therefore undisturbed by governmental interference, although the flow of goods was carefully monitored and sometimes diverted in response to the needs of imperial foreign policy.

By the middle of the second century, the bulk of Roman industry in the West was concentrated on the frontier, and significant Italian production had substantially diminished. Frontier industry tended to be grouped in small concentrations of diverse enterprises within compact market areas usually centered on legionary or large auxiliary posts. The existence of assured military markets, the availability of cheap and plentiful raw materials, the excellent road system, the common waterway of the North Sea–Rhine–Danube, the uniform reliance upon free and salaried labor, and the general influence of the German export trade produced an economic security and allowed a coordination of activity that would never have been possible in the heartland of the empire. These factors made the dominance of frontier industry in the West an almost inevitable development.

These same factors may also have inhibited Roman industrial and technological development in the long run. The presence of assured local and export markets, strengthened by a general realization of their common interests, reduced competition among frontier industrialists to a minimum. Once the threat from Italian manufactories had ended, there was little impetus for them to improve the quality of their goods or to lower their costs. The fact that labor costs helped to swell internal markets diminished the incentive to invest capital in labor-saving devices or improved techniques of manufacture. It might have been different if the imperial administration had seen fit to drain the frontier of a portion of its currency or if it had forced the residents of the frontier to fill a greater share of the army's need for recruits and done so sooner. The challenge of inflation or that of reduced manpower might have stimulated the frontier manufacturers to develop labor-saving techniques, to rationalize production methods, or to pool their capital in forming large-scale factory systems. The government did not do so, of course, since it could not see any inherent danger in the development of a stable and prosperous frontier industry.

A close observer, however, might have seen some disturbing aspects in the generally stable and prosperous frontier industrial economy. Only in very special cases, such as the textile industry of northern Gaul and some of the glassware of Cologne, did frontier manufacturing penetrate markets in the interior of the empire. The frontier manufacturers did not attempt to sell their wares to a discriminating public, but were content to satisfy the tastes of soldiers, frontier peasants, and German tribesmen. As a consequence, frontier wares broke no new ground in either art or design. On the contrary, once Italian factories could no longer present a competitive challenge, provincial and frontier manufacturers began to abandon their attempts to copy Italian designs. Insofar as they followed any artistic inspiration, it lay in the traditional patterns and designs of the native peoples of the districts in which they were located. Lamps, glassware, pottery, and other wares began to take on a Celtic or German look, while at the same time they became cruder and more primitive in concept and execution. The design of frontier goods was a clear sign not so much that Roman industry on the frontier had ceased to advance, but that it had ceased to be Roman.

Notes

1. Such conditions are, of course, advantageous to any business, regardless of the era.

2. R. J. Forbes, *Studies in Ancient Technology* 7:153.

3. By the third century A.D., complaints surfaced regarding the failure of Rome's mineral resources. Cyrian, "Ad Demitriam," 5:58, says that "to a less extent are slabs of marble dug out of the disembowelled and wearied mountains; to a less extent do the mines already exhausted offer quantities of silver and gold, and the impoverished veins are lessened day by day."

4. Much of the metal required by the army was used for weapons such as javelin heads, arrow points, artillery bolt points, and slingers' pellets—items that were, in short, literally meant to be thrown away. Other items were easily worn out, bent, or broken. A more dramatic example of the army's profligate ways with metal lay in the fact that each retiring legionary by custom kept his own armor. This meant that the army of the western frontier required some 4,000 new suits of armor annually, simply to replace those lost to retirement.

5. H. Russell Robinson, *The Armour of Imperial Rome*, p. 183, states that legionaries depicted on Trajan's Column appear to be wearing body armor made of metal strips and plates. An iron-bound wooden chest was found at Corbridge under the floor of a building close to the headquarters. The chest contained tools, nails, bundles of javelin heads, a sword scabbard, and a quantity of iron armor. See also J. B. Campbell, "Roman Body Armour in the First Century A.D.," *Congress of Roman Frontier Studies: 1969*, p. 82.

6. Robin Birley, *Vindolanda: A Roman Frontier Post on Hadrian's Wall*, p. 130, includes among the iron items found at Vindolanda ballista bolts, a sickle, two heavy stone hammers (one weighing 14.5 pounds), knives, needles, four keys, thirteen stylus pens, a razor, meat hooks, and a multitude of nails, varying from small studs to others considerably longer. N. S. Angus, G. T. Brown, and H. F. Cleere, "The Iron Nails from the Roman Legionary Fortress at Inchtuthil, Perthshire," *Journal of Iron and Steel Industry* 200 (1962):956–968, discuss the three-quarters of a million nails discovered at the first century A.D. legionary fort at Inchtuthil. See also Geza Alföldy, *Noricum*, p. 109.

7. Strabo, *Geographica* 4:5. Tacitus, *Agricola* 12, states that Britain's wealth in gold, silver, and other metals made it worth conquering. See also Pliny, *Naturalis Historia* 24:17.

8. Oliver Davies, *Roman Mines in Europe*, p. 163. See also Sheppard Sunderland Frere, *Britannia: A History of Roman Britain*, p. 283.

9. H. D. H. Elkington, "The Mendip Lead Industry," in *The Roman West Country*, ed. Keith Branigan and P. J. Fowler, pp. 183–184, states that pre-Roman

netsinkers made of lead have been found in the Mendip region. See also Frere, *Britannia*, p. 284; Ian A. Richmond, *Roman Britain*, p. 118.

10. A pig of lead with the inscription "[product] of Nero Augustus, British [lead] the Second Legion [produced this]" was found in 1883 at St. Valery-sur-Somme, near Boulogne. See Elkington, "The Mendip Lead Industry," p. 184. See also Frere, *Britannia*, p. 284. Further evidence of British lead exports derives from Pompeii. Here, samples from a lead cistern, buried in the eruption of Vesuvius in A.D. 79, possess an isotope composition common in Britain. Some of the lead used at Pompeii was probably exported from the Mendip district. Also see Elkington, "The Mendip Lead Industry," pp. 187–188.

11. Elkington, "The Mendip Lead Industry," pp. 184–185. Similar forts acted as control points at other mining centers.

12. Forbes, *Studies in Ancient Technology*, 6:163–164.

13. But Elkington, "The Mendip Lead Industry," pp. 186–187, notes that not one lead pig with the name of a lessee on it has been discovered in the Mendip district and suggests that the workings in the Mendip Hills remained under direct imperial supervision.

14. From the reign of Tiberius, imperial policy was aimed at the acquisition of the mines and quarries, and exploitation by large capitalists was gradually ended. By the time of the emperor Vespasian, the great majority of mining districts belonged to the government and were operated under the direction of state officials. Tenny Frank, *An Economic History of Rome*, p. 198, points to the state's need for precious metals used in the production of coinage as having created a more or less conscious attitude that veins of silver and gold were public property to be regarded as discovered treasure. According to Tacitus, *Annales* 6:19, most of the important gold or silver mines had become state property by the beginning of the second century A.D. See also Forbes, *Studies in Ancient Technology*, 5:159.

15. Geza Alföldy, *Noricum*, p. 113, states that Noricum possessed sizable salt deposits, which were worked even in prehistoric times. Deposits at Hallstatt—where a *vicus* existed in the imperial period—and on the Dürrnberg near Hallein were in production during the imperial era. Copper, lead, and zinc were worked chiefly in East Tirol and Carinthia, while gold washing occurred in the Upper Lavant Valley around Wiesenau. Pliny, *Naturalis Historia* 34:41, mentions the importance of Noricum as a steel-producing region in ancient times.

16. F. W. Walbank, *The Decline of the Roman Empire in the West*, p. 31, states that the original movement of the pottery industry to southern Gaul was due in part to the excellent river communications of Gaul, the availability of labor, and the long-standing trading ties between Gaul and the adjacent territories of Britain and Germany. The frontier demand for pottery, largely to satisfy the needs of the military, encouraged the pottery industry to move further northward and eastward. See also K. D. White, "Technology and Industry in the Roman Empire," *Acta Classica* 2 (1959):83; M. Rostovtzeff, *Social and Economic History of the Roman Empire*, 2d ed., 1:617, n. 39. For Britain see Frere, *Britannia*, p. 289; R. G. Collingwood and Ian A. Richmond, *The Archaeology of Roman Britain*, p. 232.

17. See B. M. Dickinson and K. F. Hartley, "The Evidence of Potters' Stamps on Samian Ware and on Mortaria for the Trading Connections of Roman York," in *Soldier and Civilian in Roman Yorkshire*, ed. R. M. Butler, p. 128.

18. R. M. Wheeler, *Rome beyond the Imperial Frontiers*, p. 87, locates the Rhineland factories at Heiligenberg, Rheinzabern, Buckweiler, Trier, and Westerndorf.

19. W. V. Harris, "Roman Terracotta Lamps: The Organization of an Industry," *Journal of Roman Studies* (hereafter *JRS*) 70 (1980):140–141, provides a discussion of branch workshops for lamps in the frontier regions. Forbes, *Studies in Ancient Technology* 6:159–161, observes a general regression toward cruder designs in the second century A.D. Somewhat later, the frontier manufacturers were producing lamps based upon native Celtic and German types.

20. Harris, "Roman Terracotta Lamps," p. 140. See also Forbes, *Studies in Ancient Technology* 6:158.

21. Forbes, *Studies in Ancient Technology* 5:192.

22. For these early centers of Gallic glass manufacture, see ibid., 5:193.

23. G. Behrens, *Römische Gläser aus den Rheinlanden*, p. 93. Also see Fritz Fremersdorf, *Von Römischen Gläsern Kölns*.

24. Fremersdorf, *Von Römischen Glasern Kölns*, pp. 348–350.

25. Forbes, *Studies in Ancient Technology* 5:194.

26. Olwen Brogan, "Trade between the Roman Empire and the Free Germans," *JRS* 26 (1936):217, mentions that glass drinking horns made at Cologne, which were not only used in the empire but exported outside the Imperial borders, show definite Germanic characteristics.

27. Forbes, *Studies in Ancient Technology* 5:192.

28. Hans Norling-Christensen, "Danish Imports of Roman and Roman Provincial Objects in Bronze and Glass," in *Congress of Roman Frontier Studies: 1949*, p. 77.

29. Brogan, "Trade between the Roman Empire and the Free Germans," p. 218. One should note that although the use of barrels was characteristic of the western frontier manufacturing and commercial districts, they were relatively rarely used, and then primarily for liquid commodities.

30. J. P. Wild, *Textile Manufacture in the Northern Roman Provinces*, p. 185.

31. A. H. M. Jones, "The Cloth Industry under the Roman Empire," *Economic History Review*, 13 (December 1960):185.

32. Strabo, *Geographica* 4:196.

33. Wild, *Textile Manufacture*, p. 10.

34. See the *Edictum Diocletiani et Collegarum de Pretiis Rerum Venalium, Corpus Inscriptionum Latinarum*, ed. Theodor Mommsen (hereafter cited as *Edictum Diocletiani*), 3:19, 25; 9:19; and the *Notitia Dignitatum Occidentis, Notitia Dignitatum et Administrationum Omnium tam Civilium quam Militarium in Partibus Orientis et Occidentis*, ed. E. Böcking, section 12. The date to which the *Notitia* refers is a matter of some dispute. It appears, however, that its various sections derive from different dates, ranging from about 370 to about 440.

35. Wild, *Textile Manufacture*, p. 9.

36. Jones, "The Cloth Industry under the Roman Empire," pp. 186–187.

37. The fact that frontier industry depended upon free laborers is quite apparent. No evidence exists for the employment of slaves in the potteries of Gaul and the Rhine Valley. See Walbank, *The Decline of the Roman Empire in the West*, p. 30; and A. E. R. Boak, *Manpower Shortage and the Fall of the Roman Empire in the West*, p. 17. Hired labor also was commonly employed in the textile industry, at least by the close of the third century, as is indicated by the Diocletian's setting of fixed wages for *lanarii* and *linyphi*. See the *Edictum Diocletiani* 3:22.

VIII THE "ROMANIZATION" OF THE FRONTIER

We have concentrated up to this point upon the economic and urban development of the frontier districts and border provinces, aspects of frontier life in which the Roman imperial civil and military administration interfered very little. Within these limits, Roman administration might appear to have been a somewhat distant and single-minded authority, governing the frontier, as the North American colonies were once said to have been governed by Great Britain, in accordance with a policy of benign neglect. This was true in certain areas of frontier life, but the principles upon which imperial administration operated were hardly benign.

When we turn to a discussion of those areas in which the Roman government did intervene in the life of the peoples of the frontier, we enter an aspect of Roman history that is influenced, perhaps more than any other, by subjective judgment and a certain amount of passion. Just as the study of Roman military history has been the training ground of future generals and would-be conquerors, so too the study of the history of Roman provincial administration has been the training ground of imperial officials. British, French, and even German historians have seen in Rome the model for the governance of subject peoples. As a consequence, this aspect of Roman history has been dominated by admiring analyses of Roman techniques of rule, with little consideration paid to the peoples whom the Romans were ruling except when those peoples proved difficult or even mutinous.

One cannot deny that the Romans brought many aspects of the sophisticated societies of the Mediterranean to the less sophisticated peoples of northwestern Europe, and historians have called this general process of introducing Roman culture to the provinces "Romanization." The benefits of the process of Romanization have been stressed, and it has sometimes been pictured as the manifestation of the civilizing mission of the Roman people. Most such generalizations have little to do with actual history, but were in their day simply expressions of the rhetoric by which the imperial powers of western Europe attempted to justify their conquest and exploitation of non-European peoples. If one is to understand the social and cultural development of the border provinces and frontier districts, it is necessary to view the Romans and the actual policies and goals of their imperial administration more objectively.

We have already seen that the Roman government regarded the frontier almost solely as a military defensive line. The empire was no longer able to afford a mobile field army capable of defending the lands it had already acquired, and the Romans were forced to relinquish their proud tradition of an ever-expanding empire. Many Romans were discontented with this new state of affairs and regarded the military frontier itself as an affront to the dignity and traditions of the empire. Nevertheless, economy was the new and unaccustomed order of the day, and the imperial administration adopted every possible means of shifting the burden of securing the frontier upon the army and residents of that region. Part of this policy lay in demanding as much as possible of the frontier districts and border provinces, and part of it lay in expending on them as little as possible in the way of assistance or rewards. The fact that the frontier populations were exploited posed no difficulty for either the government or those same frontier peoples. Within the limited technologies of the ancient world, wealth could not be accumulated without the exploitation of someone or another, and most of the population of the empire was exploited to a greater or lesser degree. The nature of the responsibilities thrust upon them, however, led to an ambivalence in the attitudes of the peoples of the frontier. They were expected to strive and sacrifice on behalf of Romans who neither recognized nor rewarded their efforts and held them in general contempt.

Roman Bigotry

There were many things that the Romans disliked about the native residents of the border provinces and frontier districts. In the first place, the Germans, Celts, and Britons were taller and more robust than the Romans,[1] who felt uncomfortable about having barbarians loom over them.[2] The average height difference between Gallic and German soldiers on the one hand and Roman troops on the other was probably two to three inches, while the Britons were even taller than the Gauls and half a foot taller than the average Roman.[3] This was not, of course, the fault of the Celts, but it was something that the Romans held against them.

The Romans were also annoyed with the Celts and Germans for wearing trousers.[4] The traditional garb of upper-class Romans was the toga worn over a tunic, and they marked their entry into manhood by donning the toga, which distinguished an adult Roman. There were correct and incorrect ways of draping the toga; social classes within Roman society were distinguished by the color and breadth of the stripes along the borders of their toga; and it was considered poor form to show the bare arm above the elbow from under the toga. A Roman pulled a fold of his toga over his head when he wished to be alone, and other Romans respected this fragile privacy. Perhaps just as important, the toga was an extremely inconvenient article of clothing in which to do any productive labor, and thus marked the wearer as a man who did not have to work. It was virtually impossible to run in one, and so Romans walked with a dignified gait. In short, the toga was an important aspect of Roman society and culture. As a consequence, Romans viewed the Celtic *braca* with mixed amusement and suspicion, as a symbol of both barbarism and a lack of a sense of social propriety. Pliny comments that southern Gaul was formerly called *Gallia bracata*, or "trousered Gaul," but was later called *Gallia Narbonensis*, after the chief city of the region.[5] Even after the Romans had accepted trousers as occasional garb themselves, their prejudice against the "trousered barbarians" continued.

It was the Roman custom to keep hair short and faces clean-shaven, and Romans were both fascinated and repelled by the long hair and beards worn by many of the Celtic and German tribes. They familiarly referred to northern Gaul as *Gallia comata*, or "long-haired Gaul."[6] Tacitus describes, with mixed admiration and distaste, the hirsute customs of the Germanic tribe of the Chatti. On reaching maturity, Chatti men would cease cutting their hair and beard until they had killed a man.

> Standing over the bloody corpse they have despoiled, they reveal their faces to the world once more, and proclaim that they have at last repaid

the debt they owe for having been brought into the world and have proved themselves worthy of their native land and parents. The coward who will not fight must stay unshorn.[7]

Eventually the Romans adopted long hair and beards also, but it was a result of eastern influences rather than Celtic and Germanic custom, and the Romans were still disturbed by the outlandish hairdressing of the barbarians beyond the frontier.

Such attitudes might strike one merely as amusing quirks in the noble Roman character, but it should be realized that it is exactly such attitudes that are the stuff of racism, and that the Romans were both racists and bigots. They reserved their greatest contempt for Greeks and Syrians, but had more than enough left over for others.[8] At best, they simply ignored other peoples; at worst, they tried to exterminate them. This same strain of bigotry ran through social relations within the empire itself. Social and economic distinctions were great, a tendency of every society based upon a slave economy, and each class tended to look upon the ones below it with disdain.

This stratification makes it difficult to assess general Roman attitudes, since the middle and lower classes of Roman society left little record of their thoughts and values. What we have said up to now about Roman bigotry has been based largely upon the views expressed by representatives of the upper classes and writers catering to their tastes. It is unfortunate that the most prominent of the classical writers to discuss the Celts and Germans were in many ways poor examples of the outlook of the Roman public.

Roman Views of Themselves and Others

Strabo

The geographer Strabo (born c. 63 B.C.) devoted three books of his *Geographica* to a discussion of Celtic and German lands and peoples. Strabo found these barbarians repulsive, yet suggested that their defects were not innate, but a result of the economic and physical conditions under which they lived.[9] In general, Strabo claimed that agriculture and an urban environment provided the only conditions under which humans could lead a civilized life, and that the majority of the barbarian peoples lacked both agriculture and urban centers. The point of this argument was that barbarians could be civilized.[10] The security and peace that Roman domination brought to these people promoted agriculture, this agriculture fostered civic life, and civic life provided the conditions under which the barbarians could become civilized and acceptable to the Romans. Strabo suggested the tribe of the Allobroges as an example of the civilizing influences of agriculture and urban life. Their chief settlement, Vienna, had become a real city, all of their nobles lived there, and the influence of their new urban life was transforming their tribe's institutions and conduct.[11]

Strabo's point is that although barbarians are loathsome, they are capable of becoming civilized under the proper conditions. The implication was that the Romans should provide those conditions and assimilate the tribesmen once they had become civilized. This is a remarkably liberal view, but it is one that should be expected of a scholar of Strabo's background. Strabo was not a Roman, nor even a Greek. He was born in the city of Amasia, in Pontus on the Black Sea. The city had been greatly influenced by Greek traditions, but, as far as "true" Greeks were concerned, was still a semi-wilderness inhabited by near-savages. Strabo followed in the train of Roman officials, but was aware that to them he would never be anything more than "another one of those clever Greek chaps." His view was not that of a Roman or a Greek proposing humane and liberal relations with the "people on the outside," as the Romans called foreigners, but that of one those people on the outside pleading that he and his fellows be allowed in.

Seneca

Writing in the time of Nero, Seneca expressed a desire for the fusion of Romans and conquered natives based upon the exercise of clemency.[12] He suggested a policy of benevolent rule rather than harsh oppression; obedience to Rome should be secured through the provision of benefits rather than by force of arms.[13] Even apart from the fact that his Stoic philosophy taught the importance of humane conduct in human affairs, Seneca had ample reason to advocate a policy of benevolence as the best means of capturing the loyalty of subject peoples. A native of Corduba (Córdoba) in Spain, Seneca had had ample opportunity to view Roman provincial administration at work. The history of the rebellions and resistance of the peoples of the Hispanic provinces to Roman rule was an object lesson in the long-term costs of authoritarian rule. In addition, Seneca advocated benevolence primarily because he believed that it would be cheaper and more effective in the long run. His combination of general philosophical principles and *Realpolitik* did not really address the human values involved in the relationship between the Romans and other peoples, but was rather an essay in techniques of imperial administration. The fact that Seneca advocated the adoption of benevolent rule suggests that he did not consider that benevolence had played any significant role in imperial administration up to then.

Tiberius

In A.D. 48, some of the leading men of *Gallia comata* appeared before the Senate to ask for admission to that august and select body. There was a great deal of opposition by various senators to this threat to their exclusivity. They claimed that rule by true Romans was good enough for the empire and that the ancestors of these Gauls had been the fierce enemies of Rome, but what they actually feared was that the wealthy Gauls would soon occupy the posts and monopolize the privileges that had previously been reserved for them. The emperor Claudius answered their arguments by reminding the Senate that it had been the Roman tradition, from the time of Rome's founding, to absorb other peoples. He noted that the founder of his own family had been a Sabine, and that the present Senate admitted men from throughout Italy. He pointed out that Athens and Sparta had fallen through their inability to accept foreigners into their societies, and concluded by declaring that he would continue traditional Roman policies by recognizing and accepting excellence from whatever source it might come.[14] The Senate accepted his decision, although one might question whether they had accepted his reasoning.

The emperor's statement was remarkable not only for its clarity of vision and the station of the speaker, but also for the fact that the emperor was prepared to act upon his principles. The Gallic chieftains were admitted to the Senate, grants of citizenship to worthy individuals were increased, and a system was instituted whereby auxiliary troops were granted Roman citizenship for themselves and their sons upon retirement.[15]

Claudius remains an enigmatic figure, and it is difficult to discern the full extent of his plans. Not a warlike leader, he nevertheless de-

parted from Augustus's warnings against new conquests by ordering
the invasion of Britain. Various motives have been suggested for this
act: that he wanted a military triumph to increase his personal popularity, that he wished to gain control of the sources of British gold and
pearls,[16] or that he wished to eliminate free Britain as a stimulus to
discontent and unrest among the Celtic tribes of the continent. There is
another possible reason. All of the Celtic peoples of western Europe
except those of the British Isles had by now been brought under the
control of the Romans. It is possible that the emperor saw his mission
as that of uniting the entire Celtic world with that of the Mediterranean
Romans and together standing against the constant pressure of the
Germans. With the Germans to the north and the Persians to the east, it
cannot have escaped the notice of any thoughtful observer that the
Romans were a minority even within their own empire and were not
particularly beloved. A Romano-Celtic union in the West would have
restored the cultural balance of the empire and provided a western bloc
of peoples capable of successfully facing the empire's adversaries.

This is merely conjecture, however. Whatever principle lay behind
Claudius's transcendent vision of the past and future of Rome and the
Romans, it was discarded in the years that followed. The tyranny and
mismanagement of the emperor Nero (A.D. 54–68) alienated both the
armies and the subject peoples of the West, while his antic aping of the
ways of Greek aesthetes aroused the contempt of many Romans.[17] A
period of revolt and civil war followed, in which dreams of unity and
peace were laid aside, and Roman attitudes toward both foreigners and
each other grew harder and more suspicious.

Tacitus

The historian Tacitus (c. 56–post-115) provides an excellent example
of this mentality. Although born in a province of Gaul, he rose to the
highest levels of Roman political and intellectual life. He was a member of the preeminent order of Roman society and, because of his
personal experiences, he held a dim view even of his own class. Tacitus had been a senator under the tyrannical emperor Domitian (81–96).
Domitian had held the Senate in contempt and, when he had decided to
execute some of their number because of a suspected conspiracy
against him, he required the Senate to vote the execution decrees. The
cowed senators, Tacitus among them, acquiesced in voting the death of

their friends and relatives. Tacitus's disillusionment and bitterness provide underlying themes to his literary works.

Although born in the provinces himself, he ridiculed natives who attempted to adopt Roman ways and viewed non-Romanized provincial peoples with lofty disdain. His view of the Romanized peoples of the settled provinces, the old "people of the toga," was tempered by the fact that the emperor Trajan (98–117) had been born in Spain and was the first emperor from the provinces. Tacitus left us his view of the provincials who moved to the frontier in his statement that all the riff-raff and scum of Gaul had flocked to the newly conquered region beyond the headwaters of the Rhine and Danube at the chance of grabbing some free land.[18] Although he admired military bravery, he also rejoiced at the manner in which Roman legions were held back to watch as auxiliary cohorts were sent in to bear the brunt of battle and take the bulk of casualties.[19]

Despite his general bitterness, Tacitus was a man of considerable insight and breadth of vision. His *Germania* was completed in 98, during which time the emperor Trajan was in the Rhine provinces, and it reads almost like a lecture to the emperor. Tacitus warned that the free Germans were a greater threat to the security of the empire than were the subjects of the Persian Empire. His description of the relations between Rome and the Germans contained a mixture of admiration and fear. He noted that the Germans and Romans had now been fighting for 210 years.

> Such is the time it is taking to conquer Germany. In this long period much punishment has been given and taken. Neither by the Samnites, nor by the Carthaginians, not by Spain or Gaul, or even by the Parthians, have we had more lessons taught us.[20]

Tacitus's concerns reveal something of the attitudes of the time. The attention of the Romans was fixed on the Arsacid Persian threat in the East, and they failed to appreciate that the Germans represented a far greater danger. The government was concerned with maintaining a cheap defensive frontier in the West, rather than considering how to end the German menace once and for all. And yet, in his overview of the varieties and numbers of the peoples of free Germany, Tacitus presented no plan as to how they might be conquered except to hope that their love of warfare might afford the Romans the delight of seeing them slaughter each other. For Tacitus, the affairs of the empire were now beyond the control of men; the empire was hurrying down a path set for it by Destiny.

Meanwhile, his fear of the Germans had produced in him something very much like respect, and it would appear that a similar respect was generally accorded the German peoples in the border provinces and along the frontier. This was so much the case that some people in the frontier districts of the Rhine publicly congratulated themselves upon their German descent.[21]

This should not be too surprising. The residents of the border provinces and frontier districts found themselves under the control of a Roman people who were certain of their own racial and cultural superiority and of the innate inferiority of other peoples and cultures. Insofar as they concerned themselves about their subject peoples, the Romans busied themselves in establishing Roman institutions among them and encouraging the natives to despise their traditional patterns of life and to adopt these Roman models of conduct. The fact that institutions such as Roman law, the Roman villa system, the Roman town, and the Roman army all proclaimed the glory of the Roman way of life while at the same time consolidating the power of the Romans in general and of the imperial government in particular cannot have escaped the notice of any thoughtful resident of the frontier. Tacitus reports a speech of the German leader, Arminius:

> Germany will never tolerate Roman rods, axes, and robes between the Rhine and the Elbe! Other countries, unacquainted with Roman rule, have not known its impositions and its punishments. We have known them and got rid of them![22]

The Instruments of Cultural Control

Most historians, however, have not regarded Romanization as a process of cultural imperialism or a tool of imperial administrators, but rather as an expression of the civilizing mission of the Roman Empire. Discussions of the social and economic context of the frontier, for this reason, are usually cast in terms of the progress of Romanization in the area. We have seen that the Romans normally had little real interest in the welfare of other peoples, and that their particular concern in the frontier was that it perform its functions as effectively and as economically as possible. Beyond this, the Romans do not appear to have bothered themselves to any great degree with the welfare of the natives of these districts. The most important single thing that one must understand about the Roman frontier in the West is that it was established, developed, and administered for the benefit of the Romans, for which one may read, "Italians." Lawyers and historians often approach the analysis of complex situations by asking the basic question, *qui bono?*—"who benefits?" Such a test can provide a guide to understanding some of the more complex manifestations of Roman traditions and culture that appeared on the frontier. Romanization was, at all times, designed to benefit the Romans, not the inhabitants of the frontier, and it only remains to determine the nature of these benefits and how they worked to the Romans' advantage.[23]

Romanization of Tribal Leaders

The most prominent method used to secure the loyalty and support of the provincial and frontier populations of the empire was the inexpensive expedient of awarding Roman citizenship in recognition of meritorious service to the state. In 49 B.C., Julius Caesar made a blanket grant of citizenship to the Venetian and Insubrian tribes of northern Gaul as a reward for their assistance. In early imperial times, such blanket grants were extremely rare, and individual grants were used primarily for specific political purposes. Tribal chiefs were offered Roman citizenship when their territories were taken over by the Romans. Given their subject state, they could hardly refuse such an offer, but their acceptance of Roman citizenship weakened the bonds that united them with their peoples. In such instances, the effect of the extension of citizenship was not so much to promote Romanization as it was to compromise the tribal leaders and diminish the natives' capacity to resist Roman rule. At other times, citizenship could be granted by the emperor rather capriciously.[24]

Nevertheless, the Romans generally prided themselves on their liberal policy of offering Roman citizenship to the most meritorious of their subject peoples and on opening to them access to high office within the imperial administration. The Romans flattered themselves that merit was the sole criterion on which they made such grants of citizenship, and liked to hear themselves praised for this policy. In the middle of the second century, the Sophist Aristides produced one of

those orations in praise of Rome and the Romans that the Romans
tended to regard as constituting the highest expression of Greek literature. Aristides declared that Rome governed the Earthly Globe and
represented the "common city" of the finest elements on it. He claimed
that in Rome, "No one is a foreigner who is meritorious,"[25] and
summed up the matter for the Romans by stating,

> You have made Roman status the name not only of a city but of a
> general species or race, not one of many races, but a race that balances
> all the rest.[26]

Much of Roman pride was simple self-deception, however. It is true
that some individuals from the provinces eventually made their way
into the inner circles of the imperial administration. We have already
considered Tacitus's account of introduction of the Gauls into the Senate. We should remember, however, that these men were nobles from
one of the most highly Romanized provinces of the West and that their
admission into the Senate was hotly opposed by the Italian members of
that body. They succeeded only because the emperor Claudius ordered
their admittance. The truth of the matter was that provincials, even if
they were Roman citizens, could not hope for full acceptance by the
Romans.[27]

It was important for inhabitants of the provinces to believe otherwise, however, and to know that provincial citizens had attained high
places at Rome, since grants of Roman citizenship were an important
tool in the imperial administration of the peoples of the frontier.
Roman provincial administrators used Romanization and Roman citizenship much as the British administrators of India would use British
education and the status of imperial subject, and British policy in India
provides an excellent model by which to understand what the Romans
were doing in their empire.

The British administration of India maintained a traditional policy
of recognizing Indians of merit and ability, as well as the traditional
leaders and wealthy families of the land. Every effort was made to
encourage such people to gain a typically British education, and elite
public schools and universities in both Britain and India welcomed
them. They were formed by this education into an anglicized class that
was more or less under the domination of the British overlords whom
they were emulating. Titles and decorations were given with a lavish

hand to those who had been of service to the empire, and leaders who visited Britain were received graciously. Moreover, the British ensured that these facts should be widely known throughout India. In this fashion, potential leaders of the Indian people were cut off from the masses they might have led. Those who resisted such anglicization were known as troublemakers, and their ability to lead was limited by frequent jail terms for minor offenses or simply on general principles.[28]

Lower-class Indians who ventured into those portions of the empire outside the subcontinent were segregated, discriminated against, and effectively excluded on racial grounds from political and economic power. Their status as subjects of the British Empire did not win them equality with white subjects of the crown. Interestingly enough, despite the fact that this was well known among anglicized Indian leaders, it was not until after Mohandas Gandhi had preached the fact for a considerable time that some anglicized Indians actually realized that their "privileged" status was in fact a sham, designed to keep them quiet and nullify whatever leadership qualities they might have had. Meanwhile, the British people congratulated themselves on the success of their civilizing mission in the world and the generous manner in which they recognized and embraced worth and merit in whatever dress or color it might appear.

British India provides a picture of how Roman administrators operated on the frontier, using Romanization and Roman citizenship as means of controlling and dominating native populations. By and large, the policy worked as well in classical Europe as during the reign of Queen Victoria. The provinces quickly accepted many of the outer trappings of Roman civilization, and many prominent provincials came to consider themselves as being just as Roman as the Romans.

Urbanization

The establishment of urban centers and the concentration of political and economic activities in them was an important part of the Roman program for controlling its border provinces. Such towns were carefully graduated in terms of municipal privileges, government support, and social prestige.[29] The most prestigious were the *coloniae*, urban settlements well-endowed with lands and other amenities intended to serve as residences for soldiers retired from the legions. The *coloniae* served to demonstrate the excellence of Roman urban life, and over the course of time attracted leading members of the local native population.[30] Below the *coloniae* were the *municipia*, a rank that included many pre-existing urban centers, among them native settlements. The rank was conferred by the imperial administration upon settlements considered to have achieved a certain degree of Romanization, or to have rendered important services to the empire. The receipt of such a municipal charter automatically conferred Roman citizenship upon all the residents of a town and was eagerly sought after for this reason.[31] Communities with "Latin Status" (*latium maius*) formed the lowest rank of officially recognized communities. In such towns, magistrates and town councilors were granted Roman citizenship by virtue of holding civic office.[32] The number of families enjoying Roman citizenship gradually increased in such communities, leading to a possible future recognition as a *municipium*.[33]

The urbanization of the frontier was a powerful administrative device, particularly when combined with grants of Roman citizenship. The traditional organization of the native population was tribal and rural, which made it difficult to control. Tribesmen who could be induced to reside in Roman cities and towns were in some measure cut off from their people, and more easily watched and controlled. The same ends were served on the American frontier by restricting tribesmen to reservations by a combination of force and the distribution of needed supplies. The extension of Roman citizenship, particularly to leading figures among the native population, was particularly effective in weakening tribal society. This aspect of Roman generosity merits some explanation.

Rights and responsibilities among the native peoples of the frontier derived primarily from kinship. The guilt of an individual who had committed a crime was borne by his or her entire kindred, and the entire kindred took vengeance upon the kindred of anyone who injured one of its members. Property was considered to belong to the kindred, and elaborate rules governed marriages to balance the loss incurred by the kindred who had given up a woman. Within the kindred, relationships and obligations were well understood by everyone, and the tribal society functioned relatively well.

When a tribesman accepted Roman citizenship, however, he received a whole new set of rights and responsibilities that conflicted with, and often superseded, the kinship ties of tribal society. His identity was no longer defined in terms of his family, clan, and tribe, and he could not be depended upon to observe the responsibilities and loyalties normally expected of him. Such men were, in fact, lost to their tribes.[34] The constant presence of an alternative way of life and the steady drain of potential leaders weakened, and in some areas destroyed, traditional tribal societies.

Despite its effectiveness elsewhere in the empire, the policy of urban settlement and Roman citizenship met with only limited success in the western districts of the frontier. Relatively few urban centers were established in the two Germanies, northern Gaul, and the north-western provinces generally. As a consequence, relatively few of the inhabitants of these regions entered the ranks of the legions, much less the imperial administration.[35] There were a number of reasons for this apparent failure of Roman policy.

There were few secure areas along the frontier where the Romans could establish civilian towns that would adequately reflect the material and cultural benefits of Roman society, and there was therefore less incentive for the native inhabitants to adopt Roman ways.[36] Population centers were generally military establishments that could not attract the native aristocracy or offer them the normal civil avenues to gain citizenship. Moreover, these districts were relatively lightly populated, and the imperial administration was content that their inhabitants should remain rural and engaged in the necessary work of filling the army's needs for agricultural and animal products. In addition, the life of local tribes had been so thoroughly disrupted by the militarization of their land, and the amount of Roman military power concentrated in the frontier districts was so overwhelming, that there was little need for the imperial administration to be concerned about any serious local challenge to Roman rule.

The Extension of Citizenship

The extension of Roman citizenship among the residents of the frontier districts sprang primarily from military needs, rather than civil policy, and it proceeded through military mechanisms. As recruitment for the legions declined in Italy, the army was forced to seek new sources of manpower. Since the legions were by law and tradition composed of Roman citizens, it was clear that the army had to create new reserves of Roman citizens among the provincial and frontier populations. If it could accomplish this in such a manner as to gain greater support among the native populations, so much the better, but popularity was never the main goal of this form of frontier Romanization.

The largest group of new citizens was composed of retired auxiliary troops. Such grants of citizenship were originally given in recognition of services rendered by non-Romans in times of war,[37] and eventually were extended to all auxiliary troops to reward and recognize the completion of their twenty-five year term of service. The recipients of such grants were given lead tablets, or "diplomas," as proof of their citizenship. The earliest such tablet found to date was issued in the year A.D. 54 and granted citizenship to a Pannonian who had served in a Spanish auxiliary cohort. Many such certificates have been found dating from later years, but all adhere to the same format as that of the year 54. This is a good indication that the system was instituted in the reign of the emperor Claudius (41–54).[38] Historians have considered the establishment of this system as highly important in the Romanization of the border provinces and in securing the loyalty of the non-Roman contingents of frontier troops. The fact that there is no written record of the beginning of the practice, however, suggests that the Romans of the period regarded it as being of little or no importance. There is something to be said for this view. One must consider the purpose of the practice and its actual extent before assessing its significance for frontier society.

Although individual soldiers were sometimes given Roman citizenship before they had fulfilled their term of service, presumably for an act of conspicuous bravery,[39] they were exceptions to the general rule. The rule was that, upon retirement after twenty-five years of service, auxiliary troops were awarded Roman citizenship. They would then settle into civilian life, usually in the area where they had served, where they enjoyed a relatively high standing in their local communities.[40] If they had established a relationship with a woman during their service, that relationship was recognized as legal, although not equal in dignity to a Roman marriage. The retiree's wife was not regarded as a citizen, although their children were recognized as legitimate issue. This was an important point, since the citizenship of the father passed on to his sons by hereditary right.

The reason that such complex arrangements were made for ensuring that the veteran's sons would be Roman citizens, while no such consideration was given to his wife, was to increase the pool of local Roman citizens eligible for recruitment into the frontier legions. This conclusion is corroborated by the fact that the system was modified in 139 so that the sons of retired auxiliaries received Roman citizenship only if they, too, entered military service.[41] The extension of citizenship to retired auxiliaries was neither a generous recognition of meritorious service nor a progressive policy of welcoming worthy candidates into the ranks of the Roman citizenry. It was merely another means by which the government attempted to shift the burden of defense of the entire Western Empire onto the residents of its frontier.

The men and women of the frontier cannot help but have been aware of the real reasons for granting citizenship to auxiliary veterans, but seem to have made no complaint. Whatever the government's motives, Roman citizenship brought the recipient significant benefits. Moreover, even though Romans like Tacitus may have denied that the system was based on merit, the residents of the frontier, who recognized what twenty-five years of military service entailed, knew better. Such grants of Roman citizenship were therefore marks of distinction, and were highly valued. However, the overall effect of the policy on changing frontier demography would appear to have been limited.

An estimate of the average number of annual grants of citizenship is enlightening in this regard. There were about 18,000 auxiliaries in Britain,[42] 24,000 along the Rhine, and, after the wars of Trajan, approximately 60,000 on the Danube frontier. Thus there were approximately 102,000 auxiliaries in service in the West. These troops probably did not enter service until about the age of twenty, and would have been about forty-five at the time of their retirement. One should consider that the life expectancy of the time was not much more than forty-five, that the conditions of service along the frontier were harsh, that clothing and food were deficient in many respects, and that death in battle and from wounds and disease was all too common.[43] Any estimate of mortality among the auxiliaries can only be a guess, but it is difficult to believe that more than one-quarter to one-third lived to enjoy retirement. Assuming the more generous figure, only 34,000 members of the total auxiliary force would have completed their full term of service. This means that some 1,360 such troops would have been awarded Roman citizenship each year.

This is not an insignificant number, but it must be placed within its context. The number of Roman citizens increased rapidly during the first century; a census in the time of Augustus recorded some four million, a number that grew to six million in the census conducted in

A.D. 48.[44] During the first half of the first century, therefore, the ranks of the Roman citizenry were increasing by some 40,000 persons annually. Compared to this massive growth, the 1,360 auxiliary veterans annually enfranchised was a relatively minor number.

Such a number could mount up over time, of course, but these men did not have much time. Having reached the age of forty-five, they had proven themselves sturdy, but had also probably accumulated a series of weaknesses and infirmities. Extremely few would have lived past sixty-five, and well over half would have died before reaching fifty-five. Making the liberal assumption that the death rate would be 5 percent annually between the ages of forty-five and sixty-five, the total number of auxiliaries having received Roman citizenship alive at any one time would have been only about 13,000. During the same twenty years that a veteran might hope to enjoy his retirement, the total number of citizens might have risen by as much as 800,000. The increase of Roman citizens was an important feature of the imperial period, but the extension of citizenship to auxiliary veterans cannot have played a significant role in that increase.[45] Most of the increase was no doubt a reflection of the population growth that was part of the Roman recovery from the civil wars of the late Republic. Much of the remaining increase appears to have been the result of bloc and individual grants to the Romanized inhabitants of the interior of the empire.

Even within the restricted context of the frontier districts, where citizenship was rare, it seems unlikely that the retired auxiliaries would have contributed much to the Romanization of society. Assuming that about one-third of such men returned to their home provinces, there would have been only about 10,000 enfranchised auxiliaries along the entire frontier at any one time. In terms of numbers alone, legionary retirees were far more significant, and the military *coloniae* were much more important as centers of Roman culture.

The general practice appears to have been for the government to maintain at least one *colonia* for each legion stationed in a given province. Retirees were given grants of land to encourage them to settle in such colonies, and the community of old comrades-in-arms also exerted a strong attraction. It is likely that most legionary veterans concentrated in these settlements. Moreover, their numbers would have been significantly greater than those of the auxiliary veterans. The legions were the favored branch of service and received the best equipment, shelter, food, clothing, and care. Roman commanders were also quicker to order auxiliaries into actions that threatened to involve heavy casualties, and were more ready to desert auxiliary units when it became necessary to abandon the field.

In any event, it is likely that mortality was much lower among the ranks of the legionaries than among the auxiliaries, and that perhaps more than half of the former reached retirement. About 3,400 legionaries retired annually from the units in the West.[46] Moreover, their life expectancy after retirement was somewhat greater than that of the auxiliaries. The age of enlistment was about eighteen and the average age of retirees would have been forty-three. If we assume a uniform death rate between forty-three and sixty-five, there would have been 37,400 retired legionaries alive at any one time, compared to about 13,000 retired auxiliaries. Moreover, the legionaries were more likely to possess special skills, to be wealthier, and to enjoy greater prestige as having been members of the elite units of the Roman army.

The army thus had about 50,000 military families on the frontier from which to recruit almost 7,000 men annually, and this was clearly an inadequate base. The army of the frontier quickly turned to the recruitment of additional units, known as *numeri*, from among the least Romanized tribes along and beyond the frontier.[47] No attempt was made to Romanize these units. They were allowed to operate in tribal or regional contingents and also to retain their native weapons and speech, and, where it was practical, their native customs. They were less well equipped and trained than regular and auxiliary troops, but were also much cheaper. By the second century, the *numeri* had been upgraded and garrisoned frontier districts under the command of Roman officers.[48] Citizenship was gradually extended to the *numeri*, and the sons of these men served to increase the pool of legionary recruits, if only slightly.[49]

As far as the effect of the granting of Roman citizenship upon frontier morale goes, there were a number of factors that cannot have escaped the notice of frontier residents. Romans were far more likely to survive their terms of service than non-Romans, their conditions of retirement were far more generous, and their retirement cities were more populous and well appointed. The auxiliary troops received grants of citizenship, which cost the empire nothing and were being granted to thousands of inhabitants of the interior of the empire for no better reason than that they had done an acceptable job of learning to act like Romans. The knowledge that the Romans themselves regarded such grants of citizenship as unrelated to merit must have been particularly galling. From the point of view of the individual auxiliary veteran, however, it was a great accomplishment to secure the benefits of Roman citizenship for his sons and to gain for them the privileges and prestige he had himself never enjoyed. Even this sense of accomplishment came to an end in 139, however, when the government determined not to grant citizenship to the sons of auxiliary veterans unless they themselves entered the military. At this point, the motivation for the policy of auxiliary enfranchisement became unavoidably clear, and the residents of the frontier districts were again reminded that the underlying goal of government policy was to exploit them as much as possible.

Replenishing the legions grew steadily more difficult as it became increasingly rare for Italians to serve.[50] Finally, the levy of troops from Italy was completely banned by the emperor Trajan.[51] This act transferred the responsibility for the defense of the empire entirely to the peoples of the provinces and the frontier, and was followed in 212 by the universal grant of citizenship to all the inhabitants of the empire. This ended the army's difficulties; recruitment for the legions no longer depended upon the promotion of Romanization and the extension of Roman citizenship.

The Effectiveness of Roman Policy

The universal extension of Roman citizenship may have served the greater political needs of the empire and simplified the matter of military recruitment, but it also eliminated the Roman administrators' most effective tool in managing provincial and frontier affairs. In many areas this resulted in the restoration of leadership to local aristocracies. Along the frontier, it had the effect of passing an increasing share of the burden of defense on to the local population. The residents of the frontier now had the task of manning the fortresses as well as that of supplying them, and it was perhaps inevitable that these two functions should become joined. The capacity of the army of the frontier declined as its units became increasingly bound to their posts. Since the government was no longer able to guarantee the supply of army units on the move, these units became fixed in place and dependent upon local economies lacking in manpower. As time passed, many of the once-proud units of the army of the frontier degenerated into peasant militias capable of defending only their immediate environs.

This was in many ways the logical conclusion of Roman administrative policy along the frontier. Romanization was never really a policy of raising native peoples to the level of Roman culture, but an administrative device with which to control the inhabitants of the provinces. Nor was Roman citizenship really a recognition of merit and service so much as a means of detaching native aristocracies from their peoples and creating a source of recruits to fill the ranks of the legions. Since the time of Augustus, the goal of Roman policy had been to establish a fixed frontier on which as much of the cost as possible would be borne by the native inhabitants. By the third century, this goal had, for all intents and purposes, been reached. The burden of defense had been placed entirely on the shoulders of the inhabitants of the frontier districts.

They met this challenge far better than one might have expected. Although the frontier defenses were occasionally breached, and the imperial government had to invest vast sums in maintaining a mounted field force composed of German mercenaries, the empire's defenses in the West held for some two centuries longer. Even then, much of the responsibility for the final defeat was due to the insistence of the imperial high command on stripping the western frontiers of troops in order to defend an Italy that had many years before ceased to carry its own weight in the empire.

Notes

1. Tacitus, *Annales* 1:64, states that the stature of the Caledonians reminded him of the Germans. Tacitus, *Germania* 4:2.

2. The barbarians are often pictured, particularly by Tacitus, as unrefined and unpredictable, as likely as not to start shoving polite people around or grabbing them with rough paws. The Romans consoled themselves with the belief that the Germans and Celts, as large and powerful as they were, were psychologically and physically incapable of sustained effort. Roman military actions against the Germans and Celts often featured extended campaigns, long marches, sieges, and attrition. Whatever the reason, such tactics were generally successful.

3. For the height of soldiers, see J. P. V. D. Balsdon, *Romans and Aliens*, p. 214. Strabo, *Geographica* 4:5; 7:1, discusses the height of the Britons.

4. Tacitus portrays the Germans clad in cloaks without any undergarments, and Roman statuary sometimes corroborates this picture. Enough archaeological material has been discovered in Germany, however, to suggest that trousers were a common article of German dress. The lack of undergarments was repelling to the Romans, who usually wore a tunic beneath the toga.

5. Pliny, *Naturalis Historia* 3:31. See also A. N. Sherwin-White, *Racial Prejudice in Imperial Rome*, pp. 58–59. For Strabo, Romanization and the wearing of the toga were necessary concomitants; he alludes to the Romanized natives of

Spain and southern Gaul as "people of the toga"; *Geographica* 6:4; 3:2.

6. Pliny, *Naturalis Historia* 6:4. Strabo connected long hair and trousers in his description of Celtic characteristics. Tacitus refers to the Gallic nobles who petitioned the emperor Claudius for senatorial status as "the leaders of long-haired Gaul"; *Annales* 11:23.

7. Tacitus, *Germania* 31. Tacitus, *The Agricola and the Germania*, trans. by H. Mattingly, revised by S. A. Handford (New York: Penguin Books, c. 1970), pp. 127–128. Some of the Chatti seem to have gone unshorn because they were not warriors, and others because it was the custom of a Chatti warrior cult. In *Germania* 38, Tacitus describes the distinctive hairstyle by which members of the Suebic tribes distinguished themselves from other Germans.

8. Even so, it should be noted that such an attitude was not unique to the Romans. The Greeks were even more bigoted, viewing all the non-Greek-speaking world as "barbarians." The word is in fact, Greek for "babblers." While the Romans steadily extended Roman citizenship to other peoples throughout their history, the citizens of a Greek city-state rarely offered a similar recognition even to other Greeks. The imperial heritage left to the Greeks by Alexander the Great was lost through this parochialism.

9. Strabo, *Geographica* 4:4, attributed the Celts' propensity for violence partly to their physical size and partly to their great numbers. He also noted that the conditions under which they lived were barbaric; the Celts of northern Gaul still slept on the ground and ate their meals sitting on mattresses of straw. In *Geographica* 4:5, he called the customs of the Britons simpler and more barbaric than those of the Celts, and emphasized their lack of urban centers. The Britons' only towns, he said, were woodland places of refuge walled with hedges.

10. Strabo, *Geographica* 4:4. Strabo states that northern Gauls are able to listen to rational arguments and are capable of being educated. In *Geographica* 4:1, he also mentions that the Celts gave up their old, militant ways and changed to an agricultural life as a result of the Roman conquest.

11. Ibid., 4:1.

12. Seneca, *Epistolae* no. 87, section 41; Seneca, *De Clementia*, vol. 2, letter no. 34, section 4.

13. Seneca, *Epistolae* letter no. 95, section 52. Seneca's plea for a benevolent empire was founded upon Roman self-interest. He never felt the need to justify Roman rule or to advocate a method of attaining a worldwide state. See Miriam T. Griffin, *Seneca: A Philosopher in Politics*, pp. 238, 249.

14. Claudius's speech is reported in Tacitus, *Annales* 11:23–24.

15. As we will note below, the extension of citizenship to auxiliary veterans was in fact a cheap way to secure a new source of recruits for the legions. This does not mean, however, that Claudius intended it to be so when he instituted the practice.

16. What little gold the British possessed came primarily from Ireland, and although Colchester oysters are excellent to eat, their pearls are few, small, and poor in quality. It is unlikely that the Romans would have embarked upon war for wealth without first being certain that such wealth actually existed.

17. It should noted, however, that the lower classes were not alienated by Nero's actions. Quite to the contrary, the emperor enjoyed the support of the masses until his death. It was his misfortune that the populace of Rome lacked any real military or political power.

18. Tacitus, *Germania* 29. It is interesting to note that two characteristics of the American frontier—the lure of free land and the "escape valve" for those without opportunity in the heartland—both appear to have been at work here. Even taking Tacitus's prejudices into account, it is clear that the frontier would have held no attractions for well-to-do, propertied, and privileged citizens. Many who went to the frontier were those without standing or opportunity at home.

19. Tacitus was probably born in *Gallia Narbonnensis*, and rose to become a member of the Roman Senate, a consul, and governor of Asia. He married the daughter of Agricola, onetime governor of Britain, and part of his hatred of Domitian may have been due to the fact that the emperor recalled troops from Britain at a critical point in Agricola's campaign in Scotland and then permanently reduced the British garrison. This ended Agricola's chance to gain a great triumph, and halted the empire's expansion in this area. Tacitus believed that it was the empire's destiny to conquer and rule, and so this frustration of Agricola's plans was doubly painful for him.

He also believed that the Germans, and not the Persians, constituted the greatest danger to the empire. Although he makes no great point of the matter, he may have been influenced by the fact that three legions and an equal number of auxiliary cohorts were permanently garrisoned in Britain, whereas these troops could have been shifted to the Rhine frontier had Agricola been permitted to complete the pacification of the island.

20. Tacitus, *Germania*, translation by H. Mattingly (Baltimore, MD: Penguin Books, 1969), p. 132.

21. Tacitus, *Germania* 28. In much the same way, some whites in the American Southwest are proud of having "Indian blood."

22. Tacitus, *Annales* 1:58; translation from *Latin Literature: An Anthology*, edited and translated by Michael Grant (New York: Penguin Books, 1978), p. 66. The rods symbolized the Roman magistrate's power to inflict beatings, and the axes represented his ability to order executions. Taken together, the rods and axes were the symbol of Roman *imperium*, or rule. The robes were, of course, the Roman togas.

23. This is a provocative approach with which many excellent historians may profoundly disagree, but it is also a valid formulation. One may search historical records in vain for another empire based upon predominately altruistic motives, so there is no reason to believe that "Romanization" was any less of a rationalization than "la mission civilatrice," "manifest destiny," "the white man's burden," or "the Asiatic sphere of economic co-prosperity" were in their own times.

24. For instance, Tacitus, *Annales* 12:54, recounts how two Batavian emissaries to Rome created a scene in the theater of Pompey. They declared that the Batavians were the bravest people in the world. The crowd was amused at this "old-fashioned patriotism," and Nero granted citizenship to the visitors.

25. Aristides, *Orationes, Opera Quae Exstant Omnia*, p. 60.

26. Ibid.

27. D. B. Saddington, "Race Relations in the Early Roman Empire," *Aufsteig und Niedergang der römischen Welt* (hereafter *ANRW*), pp. 118–119. Tacitus, *Annales* 14:53. Balsdon, *Romans and Aliens*. In time, of course, provincials even attained the emperorship, but such men were usually descendants of Roman provincial administrators, military commanders advanced by their troops, or usurpers.

28. The similarities between the Roman and British imperial administrations were

not mere accidents. A classical education was the foundation of the British upper-class educational system, and the British administrators of India possessed a wide knowledge of Greek and Roman history. It was natural for them to turn to Roman precedents, and there is ample evidence that they consciously modeled British imperial policy in India upon that of the Romans in the provinces of the Roman empire.

The British governing class easily equated the Roman Empire with their own, and classical scholars frequently wrote on British imperial topics. Much the same was true of the French and their empire. This is, of course, one of the reasons why the Roman empire has traditionally been regarded so sympathetically by scholars.

29. We have discussed the lack of any deliberate policy of urbanization in the frontier districts; the matter was quite different in the civilian-administered border provinces that lay behind that frontier.

30. Saddington, "Race Relations in the Early Roman Empire," pp. 125–126; A. N. Sherwin-White, *The Roman Citizenship*, p. 185. See also Eric Birley, *Research on Hadrian's Wall*, p. 55; Sheppard Sunderland Frere, *Britannia: A History of Roman Britain*, p. 305.

31. Saddington, "Race Relations in the Early Roman Empire," p. 126.

32. Gellius, *Noctes Atticae* 16:13. See also Sherwin-White, *The Roman Citizenship*, pp. 198–199.

33. Saddington, "Race Relations in the Early Roman Empire," p. 126.

34. It has been suggested that the basic function of law is to make social life possible by making individual actions predictable within a given range. If this is indeed the case, then the individual who accepted another set of social norms, even if he attempted to retain his ties with his kindred, was nevertheless lost to tribal society in the sense that his actions were no longer predictable.

35. Saddington, "Race Relations in the Early Roman Empire," p. 133.

36. See Sherwin-White, *The Roman Citizenship*, p. 200. The civil districts of Britain were something of an exception to this rule, and, as we have seen, the Roman administrators made full use of urban centers to win the adherence of the native British aristocracy.

37. Tacitus, *Annales* 3:40, mentions that Julius Florus of the tribe of the Treveri and Julius of the Aedui were nobles whose ancestors had obtained grants of Roman citizenship. Interestingly enough, these two were leading a rebellion against Rome in A.D. 21.

38. Such *diplomata* may be found in *Corpus Inscriptionum Latinorum* (hereafter *CIL*) 16. See also Saddington, "The Development of the Roman Auxiliary Forces from Augustus to Trajan," *ANRW* 2(3):181–190.

39. Saddington, "Race Relations in the Early Roman Empire," p. 128. *CIL* 16:10, 17, 25, 60, 68, 114, 132. Saddington, "The Development of the Roman Auxiliary System from Augustus to Trajan," p. 192, states that the auxiliary system reached its peak in the concluding decades of the first and early part of the second centuries A.D. Probably the most important development to affect the auxiliaries of the later Flavian and the Trajanic periods was the emergence of the *limes* concept in Roman defense. This resulted in more and more units being assigned to virtually permanent occupation of a particular fort.

40. Grace Simpson, *Britons and the Roman Army: A Study of Wales and the Southern Pennines in the 1st–3rd Centuries*, p. 117.

41. Sherwin-White, *The Roman Citizenship*, p. 215, mentions that in A.D. 139

the emperors ceased to grant citizenship automatically to the offspring of soldiers begotten during service. Such children, in order to gain citizenship, had to serve as did their fathers. For an example of this new type of diploma see *CIL* 16:93.

42. Frere, *Britannia*, pp. 207–208, states that the army swelled the ranks of citizens in Britain by 45,000 per century. In the second century A.D., at least nineteen auxiliary units were recruited in Britain alone, amounting to approximately 14,000 soldiers. Figuring that half of these troops survived to retirement and half settled elsewhere than in Britain, then 3,500 every quarter century, or 14,000 native Britons each century, received citizenship through auxiliary service. The increased recruitment of Britons into other auxiliary units probably added to the number of Britons obtaining citizenship in this manner. The 45,000 auxiliaries stationed in Britain, might, on the same assumptions, have provided 45,000 citizen settlers each century.

43. It is important to remember that there was relatively little actual fighting along the frontier. In that which did take place, however, the auxiliaries usually suffered more than their share of the casualties.

44. The figures are generally taken to represent the total number of men, women, and children in families enjoying Roman citizenship.

45. This is perhaps the reason why Claudius's establishment of the system went unremarked. Although their historians rarely expressed an interest in demography, Roman leaders generally seemed keenly aware of population factors. Much of the Romans' fear of the barbarians was due to their apprehension of their enemies' numbers and population growth. It was commonly believed that the name of Germania was derived from the rapidity with which its inhabitants germinated. Tacitus makes numerous implied comparisons of the customs of the Germans and the Romans to suggest the virtue of the former in not restricting their population. For examples, see *Germania*, 19 and 20. The Romans were probably well aware of the expansion of the citizen population, but did not regard the system of enfranchisement of auxiliary veterans as affecting that movement to any significant degree.

46. The total number of legionary troops was about 170,000, of whom we assume that 85,000 completed their term of twenty-five years.

47. For *diplomata* granting citizenship to *numeri* see *CIL* 16:10, 17, 25, 60, 68, 114, 132, 3191, 3216, 3234, 3255, 3259, 3308, 3311. See also H. T. Rowell, *Paulu-wissowa* (hereafter *PW*), *Real-Encyclopädic*, 17:1329ff.; Michael Speidel, "The Rise of Ethnic Units in the Roman Imperial Army," *ANRW* 2(3):202–203. R. E. Smith, "The Army Reforms of Septimius Severus," *Historia* 21 (1972):481.

48. *CIL* 16:5, 54, 107, 3191, 3216. See also J. C. Mann, "A Note on the Numeri," *Hermes* 82 (1954):501–504; Speidel, "The Rise of Ethnic Units," p. 203. Arrian, *Tactica. Flavii Arriani Quae Exstant Omnia*, p. 44.

49. Several *diplomata* that made special grants to various kinds of units are *CIL* 16:10, 17, 25, 60, 68, 114, 132. *CIL* 16:10, 17 are two instances in which citizenship and discharge were granted before it was due. Rowell, *PW* 17:1329ff., argues that the *numeri* received different privileges on discharge from those of the auxiliaries. See also *CIL* 11:393 for *Numerus Equitum Electronum ex Illyrico*, and *CIL* 3:1197 for *Numerus Illyricorum*.

50. Saddington, "Race Relations in the Early Roman Empire," p. 129.

51. *Scriptores Historiae Augustae*, "Marcus," 11:7; *Dionis Cassii Cocceiani Historia romana* 74:2.

IX THE GODS AND GODDESSES OF THE FRONTIER

The experience of the imperial government after the army revolts of A.D. 69 convinced it that maintaining the Roman character of the legions and fostering loyalty among their ranks was particularly important. This importance was not considered so great, however, as to convince the Italians to continue manning the legions themselves. The inculcation of Roman values within the legions became an even more pressing task as the legionary recruits came increasingly to be drawn from the provinces and the frontier districts themselves. The prominence given to religious ritual within the legions has led many to believe that religious observances were among the chosen vehicles for impressing the men of the legions with government-approved attitudes and values.[1] We will examine two aspects of this feature of army life on the frontier: whether the rituals were such as to inculcate Roman values among an increasingly Celtic and German military force, and whether the goal of military religious ritual was in fact political.

It must be remembered that the troops of the Roman army of the frontier were drawn from subject peoples whose traditions were under attack by various forms of Roman cultural imperialism, and whose dignity was constantly wounded by the general contempt shown them by their Roman rulers. Historians have found that subject peoples in such circumstances often adopt the forms and symbols of the dominant culture but translate them into their own traditional terms. Many slave owners of the American South heard their slaves singing about a chariot coming to carry them home and indulgently believed that "home" was a Caucasian-dominated heaven. On the Roman frontier, the Romans were generally content with the outward appearance of things, and seldom inquired what their subject peoples really thought or believed. For this reason, Roman accounts of the "Romanization" of subject peoples must always be viewed with skepticism. The program of worship established for the Roman army thus tells us more about the concerns of the imperial government than about the attitudes of the troops. In order even to guess what the rank and file and common people of the frontier may have felt and believed, it is necessary to attempt to view Roman customs and institutions within the context of native traditions.

The Military Cycle of Ritual

The military year was filled with religious ceremonies of various types, many of which are recorded in a list of festivals that was discovered in the ruins of the eastern military post of Dura Europos.[2] The striking thing about this religious schedule is the multiplicity of observances and the general lack of focus in the program of events as a whole. The official rites of the Roman army attempted to achieve so many different ends that it is unlikely that any were really well served.

Generally speaking, the religious events of the military year appear to have been designed to require the troops to affirm their loyalty to the gods of Rome, of the state, of the emperor, and of the unit in which they served, and also to the abstract virtues of military life.[3]

The cycle of festivals fell into three groups, those devoted to the imperial family being the most numerous and accorded the most prominent positions. The legions' year began on January 3, when the men of units all over the empire assembled before their banners and standards to take a sacred oath to the emperor and to the imperial government.[4] This event was of the utmost importance to the government; the oath was a particularly solemn one, and was therefore a test of the army's loyalty.[5] News of the oath-taking by the various units of the army was conveyed to the emperor immediately upon conclusion of the ceremony, and its arrival was anxiously anticipated by the ruler.[6] Given the importance of the event to the government, it is not surprising that the first of the units' three annual paydays came four days later, on January 7. Other festivals dedicated to past emperors followed throughout the year.[7]

The imperial administration required that the troops observe these traditional festivals, yet appears to have been unconcerned with how

the rank and file of the army regarded them. The solemn oath of
loyalty to the emperor offers a good example of how the attitude of the
troops may have been far different from what the Roman command
supposed it to be. The oath paralleled, at least in external form, those
taken by members of the traditional German and Celtic war bands.[8]
These war bands comprised warriors who had taken oaths of personal
allegiance to a war chief, promising to fight under his leadership. Both
Germans and Celts regarded this relationship as a sacred bond and the
band itself as a brotherhood; no member of a war band would willingly
leave the battlefield before his chief had retired, and a warrior who
abandoned the body of his dead chief could expect a life of shame that
would be remembered in song and story long after his death. In return
for this loyalty and service, the chief fed and clothed his followers,
gave them the opportunity to gain glory in his service, and honored
them with gifts.

The oath to the Roman emperor, followed a few days later by the
distribution of money, may have seemed to the imperial administration
a solemn and proper symbol of the relationship between the leader and
the led. Whatever the value of the tradition may have been for the
Romans, it was probably quite different for the native trooper who
played out this ritual within the context of his own Celtic or Germanic
customs and values. A comparison between the Roman imperial oath
and the oath of the traditional native war bands would have been
inevitable and would have influenced the trooper's attitude toward the
ritual he was being required to perform.

There were great differences between Roman and native institutions. The warrior oaths of Celtic and Germanic tradition established
personal, not collective, ties, and native warriors expected to follow
their chief, not his deputies, into battle. Moreover, the chieftain honored
his warriors by giving them gifts, not pay. German and Celtic troops
may have considered the official practice a rather offensive parody of
an honorable tradition. In any event, the Celtic and German troops
would not have considered themselves bound by their oath to the emperor, since his officers required them to perform physical labor. No
native chieftain would have made such a demand on his warriors since
such work was considered demeaning. If a trooper cared to look at it in
such a fashion, the required oath to the emperor was only another
example of Roman contempt for native sensibilities. Imperial officials
felt reassured by the annual oath, however, and so it was continued.

Goddesses representing the abstract qualities of Victory, Peace, and Harmony were also included in the army's program of religious ritual. Although one might consider the veneration of these concepts to be particularly fitting for army units, the legions were not intended as the beneficiaries of these observances. Dedications of statues and altars at army posts and the symbolism of imperial coinage make it clear that the goddess Victoria was the goddess not of the troops but of the emperor, and all units were required to make annual vows to Victoria for the emperor's welfare.[9] From the point of view of the imperial administration, this was yet another test of a unit's loyalty; an army that contemplated rebellion would find it difficult to pray to a deity who brought victory to the cause of the imperial government. Much the same was true of Discipline; it was the goddess Disciplina Augustorum who was worshipped.[10] Finally, although some dedications to Harmony seem to have been aimed at maintaining peace between various detachments occupying the same post, imperial coins demonstrate that Concordia was primarily intended to represent the harmony among the imperial family, the state, and the army.[11] At least, this was what the imperial administration understood by Harmony.

The actual attitude of the troops may have been far different. Although the form of this worship was dictated by Roman leadership, its content may in fact have been basically Celtic. The Celts worshipped many goddesses, but reserved a particular veneration for the Three Mothers, who appeared with various attributes and names throughout the Celtic and much of the Germanic world. It is not unlikely that, in their veneration of Peace, Harmony, and Victory, the rank and file of the Roman army of the frontier were simply continuing the traditional Celtic reverence for the Three Mothers. Again, however, the imperial administration was content if the rituals were performed, and seemed to have had little interest in whether or not they were inculcating Roman values.

A final and perhaps even more striking aspect of the imperial cult lay in the fact that the statues of the emperors were housed together with the unit standards in the *principia*, or headquarters building, of every fort on the frontier.[12] It is difficult to say what effect this institutionalized loyalty to the emperor may have had on the average frontier soldier. A rudimentary knowledge of history would have informed him that the emperor was in fact dependent upon the loyalty of the army to maintain his position. More of the army's energy as a fighting force was expended in fighting in various civil wars than in battle against the enemies of the empire. It would have been a dull trooper who did not realize that loyalty to the persons of the emperor and the imperial family was not quite the sacred duty that the religious observances instituted and required by the imperial government were supposed to imply.

It should also be noted that the housing of the statues of the emperors in the headquarters building may have given the average soldier a somewhat mixed message. Although the Celts in pre-Roman times had had holy places housing statues of their gods, they were also headhunters and kept the trophies of their victories in a similar fashion. The cult of the human head was widespread and of great antiquity in Celtic lands. A Celtic trooper venerating the bust of a deified emperor could have either one of two quite different concepts in mind. The Roman high command does not appear to have taken this possibility into account.

It is clear that many of the religious observances of the units of the frontier army were intended by the imperial administration to exalt the imperial concept in general and the person of the emperor in particular. It is particularly interesting to note that the selection of deified emperors and empresses to be venerated included only one, Septimius Severus, who had been advanced to the *imperium* by the army. It would appear that the government was reluctant to remind the army that one aspect of the relationship between the emperor and the military lay in the fact that the army had traditionally made and unmade emperors.[13] It may be that the government was generally aware of the difficulty of convincing the frontier troops that the emperor was sacrosanct and that the welfare of the military was mystically connected with the fortunes of the ruling dynasty. In any event, concurrent with the various imperial observances there was a schedule of festivals that seem to have been designed to inculcate in the troops a sense of the glory and traditions of Rome. A few of these festivals, such as the *Quinquatrus* of March 18 and the *Armilustrium* of October 19, had been observed in the armies of the Roman Republic and were perhaps intended to symbolize for the troops the unbroken tradition of military service to Rome.[14] Others, such as the *Saturnalia, Neptunalia,* and *Vestalia,* were probably observed because their carnival character allowed the troops to take a respite from the rigors of military life and to express their resentment of their officers in acceptable fashion.[15]

The festival of the birth of the city of Rome lay at the heart of this attempt to inculcate a love of the city and ideal of Rome in the hearts of the frontier troops. The cult of the Eternal City of Rome *(Urbs Roma Aeterna)* was established in the reign of the emperor Hadrian.[16] As Roman power had extended, many subject peoples began the veneration of the goddess Roma. Hadrian took this provincial goddess and placed her in the official pantheon, and by so doing supposedly united the peoples of Italy and the provinces in the worship of a single deity and a single ideal.[17]

It should be noted that the cult of Roma and that of the deified emperors both first began in the provinces, and both were capable of varied interpretations. The traditional form of worship in the classical world was propitiatory. The worshiper paid the deity something in the form of self-abasement, ritual, sacrifice, or the like. When the worship was conducted properly, at worst the deity would refrain from harming the worshiper, and at best would actually help him. This meant that, by knowing the nature of the deity, the kind of payment required, and the ritual forms to be observed, the worshiper could control the deity and guide his or her actions. The people of the provinces had adapted this religious principle to their relations with Rome itself. The Romans and their imperial families could be fed with flattery and adulation, and the cults of Roma and the deified emperors did just that. We cannot know how the ancient worshiper actually viewed his or her gods and goddesses, but it would be surprising if the worshiper did not feel an inward sense of power from his or her ability to control the deity.

In the same way, the provincial cults of the deified emperors and the goddess Roma may have been genuine religious expressions and at the same time have been regarded by the peoples of the provinces as means by which they could exert a certain degree of control over their masters. From this perspective, Hadrian's policy of making the cult of the Eternal City of Rome official and universal deprived the provinces of their ability to use it as a means of influencing the Romans. From the Roman point of view, however, inclusion of these and other observances within the religious schedule of the army served an obvious need. Imperial military resources were shifted increasingly to the frontier during the second and third centuries. Roman military units were becoming progressively localized with the permanent attachment of legions to their frontier fortresses. This tendency was strengthened first by Septimius Severus's concessions allowing troops to contract marriages while on active service,[18] and by granting them lands near the frontiers. Such land grants were originally given to the troops upon their retirement, but the policy was eventually extended to include soldiers still under arms.[19] The imperial army in the West was now composed of big, brutish, long-haired, trouser-wearing barbarians, lacking any sense of propriety, whose ancestors had done their level best to conquer Rome and had very nearly succeeded in doing so. Many Italians no doubt saw the situation in exactly this manner, and were apprehensive about their safety. The fact that there was a mandatory official program of military religious observances, stressing reverence toward the concept of an eternal Rome and loyalty toward the imperial family, perhaps helped allay this apprehension. If the official religious functions of the Roman military did have a political purpose, it was as likely to have been that of reassuring the inhabitants of the heartland of the empire as that of inculcating Roman values among the frontier troops.[20]

There was another aspect to the issue, however. Historians often forget that people of the past may actually have believed in their gods and instead treat religion merely as a means by which a ruling class attempted to achieve certain social, political, and economic ends. It is clear that the schedule of religious observances drawn up for the Roman army was intended to express the military's loyalty to the empire, but there was more to it than that. We have noted that Roman religion was propitiatory and that the Romans believed that the proper sacrifices to the gods and goddesses could avert misfortune and secure benefits. It was not necessary for the person desiring these benefits to perform the sacrifices himself; as a matter of fact, professional priests were generally employed to ensure that the business would be conducted properly. By its insistence upon regular military rituals on behalf of the empire and the emperor, the imperial administration was using the army as a vast, disciplined priesthood to conduct regular and massive ceremonies to gain the favor of the gods for the state and its leaders. The army of the frontier was organized to defend the empire not only in a physical sense, but also in a supernatural one.

In pursuit of this aim, Roman military religion stressed not only the proper relationship between the military units and the state but also the proper relationship between the individual soldier and his unit. Each trooper was to feel himself subsumed within the greater whole of his unit and to allow his actions and identity to be defined by his corps.

This policy not only encouraged a high degree of military discipline, but also made each unit of the army a priestly corporation charged with religious functions that were served by the entire garrison. The limits of the Roman military camp were considered a sacred boundary, and the camp itself was a temple housing a military unit that also acted as a religious brotherhood. It made little difference in the long run whether or not the troops believed in what they were doing, so long as they were well trained and performed their rituals with regularity and care.

This is not to say that a sense of pride in unit and of brotherhood in arms was forced upon the Roman troops. Given their long terms of service, the wide variety of tasks they were expected to accomplish, and their constant state of readiness for conflict, it is only to be expected that the Roman troops developed a deep affection for one another and for the unit in which they served. This affection was demonstrated in ceremonies that were apparently conducted throughout the army and were recognized, although not required, by the imperial government.

The symbol of each unit and the focus of its religious observances was its standard.[21] Standards consisted of poles upon which various adornments such as eagles, capricorns, acorns, crescents, and disks were affixed.[22] Standards were kept in the headquarters building, at the very center of the camp, and taken out for parades, reviews, and other ceremonies. Each unit had a man called the *signifer*, or standard-bearer, to carry its standard in the field, and the standard served as a rallying point in battle. A unit that lost its standard in battle was dishonored, and the entire army felt itself shamed by the fact that an enemy possessed a Roman standard.

Perhaps the gayest festival in the Roman military year occurred on May 9. On that day, the *Rosaliae Signorum*, the troops of all of the units of the Roman army would assemble in front of the headquarters building of their camp.[23] The unit's standards would be paraded out one by one, placed upon the central altar of the camp, and there would be decorated with roses.[24] In addition, each unit possessed its own tutelary god, or *genius*, and the worship of its *genius* formed an important part of the religious life of every unit of the army. There is no evidence that the unit gods were either assigned or defined by the imperial administration, or that they were considered as playing any function in protecting the state or inculcating desirable virtues in the troops. On the other hand, large numbers of dedications to such gods have been found. All types of units seem to have had them, and the dedications range from official memorials to private offerings. All this suggests that the worship of the unit *genius* was spontaneous, and reflected an actual devotion on the part of the troops. In this area, at least, the rank and file of the army appeared to have experienced a transcendent sense of unity that was free from imperial control or direction.[25]

The official military religion was limited in a number of ways. It was propitiatory, and the troops acted corporately in performing rituals that did not require any deep belief or emotional involvement on their part. Moreover, these rituals were expected to gain benefits for Rome, the emperor, the state, or the unit. The welfare of the individual soldier was forgotten in all of this corporate activity. The worship was public, not only open to all but required of all, and logic would have told the individual that the simple continuation of traditional practices devoid of new insights had little chance of making the world any better a place than it had been in the past. Roman religion as a whole had little place for the individual, placed little emphasis upon moral conduct, and offered little hope that there would ever be anything better. The dead descended indiscriminately into an underworld in which there was no love, no joy, no happiness, and no hope.

The Mystery Cults: Jupiter Dolichenus and Mithras

This situation prevailed throughout the empire and accounts for the rapid spread of so-called "mystery cults" during the late republic and early years of the empire.[26] Although widely differing in the details of their worship, mystery cults shared many characteristics. Most were native to the eastern portions of the empire and claimed to have been founded by a god or goddess who had triumphed over death and was willing to share the secret of that triumph with humankind. The individual went through rites of initiation in which he or she acquired power over death, and then heard the story and learned the meaning of the symbols by which the founder had first gained this power and passed the secret on to his or her followers.

Among the most popular of these cults were those of the Persian Mithras, the Egyptian Isis, the Greek Orpheus, the Syrian Adonis, and the Jewish Jesus, all of which borrowed various trappings from each other and from the traditions of the near eastern culture from which they had all sprung.[27] Each called upon its followers to begin a new and moral life, although none possessed the powerful ethical message that Christianity had derived from its Jewish origins, and all promised true believers everlasting life in an afterworld of peace and joy.

Some of these cults spread swiftly along the frontier for various reasons. The Black Sea, Danube, Rhine, and North Sea formed an almost continuous route along which goods and ideas could spread swiftly from the East to the West, and Syrian traders were active along the entire route carrying eastern ideas as well as eastern wares. Many of the frontier units were manned with recruits from the eastern provinces, troops who had brought the beliefs and practices of their native lands with them. The population of the frontier districts was dominated by military units in which little room was left for individual concerns, and manned by troops for whom the promise of a triumph over death had a particular fascination. The traditional Roman and Italian character of these units was breaking down, and the units were becoming increasingly heterogenous. The offensive function of the military was ending, permanent posts were being fixed far from the interior of the empire, and massive new demands were being placed upon the physical capacities of the army. The frontier was an area of rapid change for its civilian residents as well. The traditional life of the native population was under assault by intrusive Roman institutions and the undisguised contempt of their masters; heavy taxes and military procurements were forcing a rapid transformation of local economies; and Roman administrators were adept at luring tribal leaders away from their people and leaving the natives without leadership at a critical point in their history.

It is not unusual for people to be particularly susceptible to new religions, especially those that promise the believer a special status and security in the next world, if not in this one. The people of the Roman frontier were no different in this respect, and eastern cults spread swiftly and widely along the frontier. There were a variety of such cults from among which the residents of the frontier might have chosen, but only two, those of Mithras and Jupiter Dolichenus, gained extensive popularity.

Historians generally pay more attention to the cult of Mithras than to that of Jupiter Dolichenus, perhaps because more is known of Mithraism, and also perhaps because Mithraism shared many features with Christianity and was Christianity's last and most dangerous rival.[28] It was the cult of Jupiter Dolichenus, however, that was characteristic of the frontier. Although clusters of Mithraic temples existed along Hadrian's Wall, the middle and lower Rhine, Illyria, and Dacia, temples of Jupiter Dolichenus were found along the entire extent of the frontier. The cult was a curious hybrid of the thunderbolt-wielding Roman god, Jupiter, and the trappings of a typical eastern mystery cult. Originating in the district of Doliche in Asia Minor, the cult spread swiftly along the frontiers. Except for a few sites in Italy, and along military routes to the frontier, the worship of Jupiter Dolichenus never achieved much popularity in the interior of the empire.

Its popularity within the army of the frontier was great, however, and there were numerous reasons for this popularity. Jupiter Dolichenus was a powerful war god who offered protection to the soldier in battle.[29] He also embodied the might of the Roman Empire, being the greatest of the traditional Roman gods and bearing the thunderbolt that was the symbol of both sovereignty and power. Interestingly enough, this same cult was also popular among the Germans along the frontier. The image of the thunderbolt-bearing Jupiter was close enough to that of their own war god, Thor, that an identification of the two was natural. The fifth day of the Roman week was named after Jupiter, *Joves*, and the Germans came to name their fifth day Thursday, after Thor. The Celts could make much the same type of identification with their own traditional deities. The cult of Jupiter Dolichenus thus served as a symbol of the Empire peculiarly adapted to the needs of a soldier, and provided the ritual, emotion, and hope of an eastern mystery cult that could nevertheless be easily identified by each of the ethnic groups inhabiting the frontier with its own traditional divinities.

Much more is known of the cult of Mithras, and its attraction for the Roman soldier is much more easily appreciated. Mithras was originally a Persian deity, an angel of light in the service of the god of light, Ormazd, but always pictured as a soldier.[30] The symbolism, organization, and ritual of Mithras was perhaps the most elaborate of the many cults that spread from the East in the late stages of the Roman Republic.[31] Mithraism was restricted to males, and its rites were conducted in caves, or temples constructed to resemble grottos. There were seven stages of initiation, each more complex than the last, and each admitting the initiate to a greater role in the complex rituals that characterized the cult. The fellowship of believers was emphasized by communal meals of bread and water, or sometimes wine. The congregations were allowed to form legal corporations, capable of owning property and receiving endowments.

The very complexity of the ritual may have had its own attractions for the military. The soldiers were trained to perform complex and coordinated actions, and were expected to engage in a series of religious observances on behalf of the emperor, state, and unit. Participants may have taken a particular pleasure in performing flawlessly even more complex rituals on their own behalf. Moreover, having been trained to consider themselves a priestly brotherhood, soldiers would have found the hierarchical and corporate organization of the cult of Mithras both familiar and satisfying. Even more important, however, was the imperial support given the cult by the end of the second century. The cult of Mithras embodied certain Persian beliefs that the Roman emperors found attractive and worthy of favor. The Persians believed in the principle of divine monarchy, that the sun carried the grace of Ormazd to the ruler, and that the ruler governed by right of this grace. Since Mithras had become identified with the Immortal Sun, *Sol Invictus*, he had also become identified as the means by which *imperium*, the right to rule, was transmitted by Heaven to the emperor.

The official military attitude was curiously mixed toward the worship of Mithras and Jupiter Dolichenus.[32] Despite their corporate organization, the cults both promised individual salvation, and individualism was not allowed within the sacred precincts of the military post. It may also have been that the soldiers' religious functions within the camp were clearly defined, and that the administration had no intention of allowing unnecessary innovations, especially innovations that offered no benefits to the empire, to disturb the regular process of the army's priestly functions. Finally, the imperial administration no doubt felt that there was no reason to permit the army to become any more foreign than it already was. At any rate, the status of the cults was clearly circumscribed by military regulation.

The eastern cult gods, including the semi-Roman Jupiter Dolichenus, were banned from the official pantheon. Their shrines, temples, votive offerings, and veneration were forbidden within the limits of the camp. In order to participate in cult worship, the soldiers were required to go outside the walls.[33] Not a single statue, votive relief, or dedication relating to an eastern cult has ever been found in the *praetorium* of a Roman military camp. This indicates that the policy of keeping the official military religious observances free from cult influences was rigid, inflexible, and very successful. This strict prohibition kept the eastern cults outside the Roman forts.[34]

Beyond this, the official policy was one of toleration, although the army command would probably have found it difficult to forbid such worship even if it had wanted to. As long as the troops performed their duties in the official military religious observances, they were permitted to participate in their own cults, but only so long as cult worship did not threaten even the appearance of military order and loyalty to Rome.

Despite the fact that the imperial administration and army command excluded the cults from military posts and appear to have viewed them with some distrust, they also provided these same cults with considerable official support and encouragement.[35] Numerous temples were built on the land around the camp, over which the military commander had jurisdiction, and must have been constructed with his approval. There are also records of temples of Mithras or Jupiter Dolichenus that were founded or rebuilt by local commanders.[36] On the other hand, such temples were often constructed in local civilian settlements, sometimes at a considerable distance from the post. Despite official toleration and occasional active support, the cults of Mithras and Jupiter Dolichenus were, in reality, the cults of the *canabae* and *vici*, and their congregations usually comprised a mingling of soldiers and civilians.[37]

Imperial Intents and Local Perceptions

Religion along the Roman frontier presents a number of interesting aspects. Ignoring popular religion, for which there is little coherent archaeological or literary evidence, frontier religion was essentially bipartite, consisting of the propitiatory, corporate rituals of the military camp and the redemptory, individualistic cults of the settlements outside the camp. The imperial administration was concerned almost exclusively with the former. The camps and forts of the frontier were sacred precincts in which an annual cycle of festivals, rituals, oaths, sacrifices, and offerings of diverse origins were observed. The troops who inhabited the forts were trained to conduct these rites accurately and regularly. Although historians generally hold that this policy was intended to inculcate loyalty to Rome and the emperor among the increasingly non-Italian Roman army, there is little evidence that the government really cared what the soldiers believed about these rituals as long as they performed them as ordered.[38] The rites of the official military schedule of religious observances were propitiatory rituals intended to gain the favor of the gods for the emperor, the imperial family, and the Roman state; and each unit of the army acted as a priestly corporation in performing those rituals. The army of the frontier thus defended the emperor and state both physically and spiritually, and the emperor and state were largely unconcerned about how the rank and file of the army felt about their duties.

This lack of concern may have permitted the survival of Germanic and Celtic religions within the camp, even though the high command seemed determined to keep the camp free from foreign religious influences. Many of the devotions required of the troops were similar to aspects of Germanic and Celtic traditional beliefs, and so the troops could adhere to the Roman forms demanded of them by their commanders even while continuing to think in traditional terms. Minerva played a role in official observances as the guardian of stores and arms, but the Celts had worshipped a war goddess strikingly similar to Minerva for centuries.[39] It is impossible to cast back and discover what might have been in the mind of a Celtic soldier sacrificing to Minerva, but it is quite likely that he was thinking less of the Roman Minerva than of his own deity. All we know of official religion is its form, and that form was Roman. The content of worship was another matter, however, and the probability is that that content was heavily influenced by native tradition.

This leads us directly to the consideration of yet another aspect of religion on the frontier. German, Celts, and Romans were brought together in the frontier districts and were easily able to see similarities, even if only superficial, among their various traditions and customs. Thus the Germans saw in Jupiter Dolichenus the figure of Thor, the Romans saw in him the father of the state wielding the *imperium*, and the Celts saw in him a redemptory figure guarding them in battle and sharing with them a secret knowledge of life and death that their Roman masters did not possess. It was inevitable that these various understandings would affect each other, and so Minerva, the Roman goddess of the domestic arts, developed along the frontier a consuming interest in the fabrication and storage of weapons and armor, while Mithras, the Persian angel of light, busied himself in carrying sovereignty from Heaven to a Roman emperor.

This was only one aspect of the fluid state of affairs along the frontier. If the Romans were attempting to practice cultural imperialism in the frontier districts, they also found their own beliefs challenged both by the peoples native to the area and by the exigencies of building and maintaining a defensive line with inadequate resources in the face of an overwhelmingly powerful enemy. The traditional patterns of life of the residents of the districts were thoroughly disrupted by the new economic organization demanded of them, the various peoples and goods now flowing through their districts, the intrusions of foreign social institutions such as the villa and town, and foreign political forms such as the rods and axes of Roman law. The coalescence of a great German trading area created much the same sort of disruption of traditional patterns of life on the other side of the frontier.

Thus the inhabitants of both sides of the Roman frontier, like the inhabitants of the American frontier, were open to new forms of worship, particularly messianic, emotional, and salvationist faiths that provided a firm moral basis for the individual. They found them in the mystery cults of the East. The imperial administration viewed these cults with some suspicion and ensured that they would not interfere with the army's spiritual duties. Beyond this, however, they found that the cults of Mithras and Jupiter Dolichenus could actually be used to support the political philosophy of the imperial government. They encouraged these particular cults only in a limited and tentative way, but it is clear that it was along the frontier that the imperial administration first realized that the mystic and individualistic cults of the East could be harnessed to the needs of the empire. The first step toward abandoning the traditional, propitiatory state religion in favor of the redemptory eastern cult of Christianity may, curiously enough, have been taken on the Roman frontier in the West.

The Frontier Religions and Christianity

Religion along the Roman frontier was a reflection of individual needs and the particular circumstances of frontier life. One of these particular circumstances was that virtually all aspects of life along the frontier were dominated by the needs of the army. The two eastern cults that gained popularity along the frontier were those of battle gods, and their moral and ethical codes were based upon the military virtues of loyalty and discipline. These religions left little room for other gentler faiths.

Although there were a few scattered temples of Isis in Britain and the lower Rhine, these had probably reached the North from Spain and the Rhone Valley rather than through the military districts along the Danube and Rhine. There were no significant sites dedicated to Isis along the upper Rhine, Hadrian's barrier, or along the entire length of the Danube except in the immediate vicinity of the Black Sea. The official state religion of the frontier was concentrated in the camps and forts of the region; the cult of Mithras was restricted to men; and cults open to women, such as those of Isis and Cybele, found little favor along the frontier. Formal religion was male-dominated, and there is little evidence that any recognized religious role existed for women.

It was perhaps the male domination, military orientation, and emphasis upon power characteristic of the frontier faiths that made the region so resistant to the influence of Christianity. Christianity had a particular appeal to the urban, artisan and commercial classes and preached an ethical code based upon humility, pacifism, and acceptance of suffering. None of these qualities particularly recommended it to the troops of the frontier. The Danube and Rhine were thus closed as a route for the expansion of Christianity, which was generally restricted to following the commercial and shipping routes of the Mediterranean. Thus, Christianity reached the northwestern provinces of the empire quite late.

Nevertheless, frontier religious traditions may have helped to strengthen Christianity at a critical time in its history. When Benedict of Nursia came to write his *Rule* in the late fifth century and lay the foundations of western monasticism, military organization, virtues, and nomenclature came easily to his mind. He conceived of his monastic community as a *schola*, a crack military unit, and his monks as *milites Christi*, Christ's troops. The monks were to be bound together by discipline and obedience, and, like the Roman legions in the early days of the frontier, were to work to clothe, house, and feed themselves insofar as possible. They were to live together in the sacred precincts of the monastery, and be trained to offer up prayers to God in the proper form and with clocklike regularity. By these prayers, they were to appeal to God to defend and show mercy to those faithful to Him. Their years were endless cycles of religious observances, each with its own ritual and meaning.

The parallels with the Roman army of the frontier were obvious. If the units of the army of the frontier had been composed of soldiers bound together in priestly brotherhoods, the Benedictine monks conceived of themselves as priests bound together in military brotherhoods.[40] In this sense, the medieval monks were the legitimate heirs of the traditions of the army of the frontier, and it was they who were able to achieve what the army of the frontier had been unable to accomplish: the conquest of the Germans.

Notes

1. Certainly religious ritual within the legions was an ancient practice, with many of the traditions apparently dating back to republican days. It is questionable, however, when these rituals were systematized for the permanent army and what the function of these activities were. Arthur D. Nock, "The Roman Army and the Religious Year," *Harvard Theological Review* 45 (October 1952): 194–195, considers the assumption that it was Augustus who established the military calendar of religious observances as being totally consistent with his entire policy of creating a decent Roman order in which every segment of society had its function, status, and duty. Augustus was convinced that the old virtues, one of which was piety, had to be restored.

2. Robert O. Fink, Allan S. Hoey, and Walter F. Snyder, "The Feriale Duranum," *Yale Classical Studies*, vol. 7: pp. 11, 28, describe the *Feriale Duranum* as one of the Latin papyri from the archives of the Roman garrison at Dura that were discovered in 1931–1932. It represents the only surviving military festival list, and its place of discovery and contents substantiate its military connection. Although derived from an eastern post, it is most likely that the festivals and observances listed in the *Feriale Duranum* were standard throughout the army (see Fink et al., p. 31). The *Feriale* contains forty-one entries, covering more than nine months of the year, not one of which bears any relationship to the religions of the region in which the unit at Dura was stationed.

The festival list is somewhat late. The editors date it with certainty to the years from 224 to 235 and with some probability to the period from 225 to 227 (pp. 23–24).

3. Eric Birley, "Religion of the Roman Army," *Aufstieg und Niedergang der römischen Welt* (hereafter cited as *ANRW*), ed. Hildegard Temporini and Wolfgang Haase, 2:16.2, p. 1509.

4. Pliny, *Epistolae. Epistolae ad Trianum Epistolarum Libri Decem* 10:100, mentions a ceremony in which both the troops and the provincials joined.

5. The oath bound the individual soldier in loyalty to the emperor by both legal and sacred sanctions. Anyone breaking the oath was cursed, and liable to punishment by men and gods.

6. Pliny, *Epistolae* 68:2–4. Michael Grant, *The Army of the Caesars*, p. 79, notes coins of the late first and early second centuries A.D. that commemorate the oath-swearing scene. The emperor, clad in a toga, is shown clasping hands over an altar with an officer in military uniform. A soldier in the background appears holding a standard while another is armed with a spear and shield.

7. Grant, *The Army of the Caesars*, pp. 165–167. Among the celebrations were those of the birthdays of Julius Caesar, Germanicus, and various deified

emperors and empresses; the anniversaries of the accessions of Trajan, Antoninus Pius, Marcus Aurelius and Verus, Septimius Severus and Caracalla; and a group of days connected with Alexander Severus and his family.

8. The German war band was referred to by the Romans as a *comitatus*, while the Celtic war band was called a *teulu*. Similar organizations have arisen in warlike societies around the world.

9. Dedications at Benwell *(Corpus Inscriptionum Latinarium* [hereafter cited as *CIL*] 7, no. 726), Greatchesters *(CIL* 7, no. 891), and Castlesteads *(CIL* 11, no. 3780) in Britain refer to *Victoria Augusti*, and other such dedications have been found at Maryport among a group of altars to *Iuppiter Optimus Maximus* and *Mars Militaris (CIL* 7, nos. 386, 390, 391). See also Ian A. Richmond, "The Roman Legionaries at Corbridge," *Archaeologia Aeliana* 21 (1943):158. Numismatic evidence also emphasizes the close association between the emperor and Victoria. Some of the coins of Nero, for example, bear the legend *Victoria Augusti*. See C. H. V. Sutherland and R. A. G. Carson, *Roman Imperial Coinage* 1:165, no. 304. See also Laura Breglia, *Roman Imperial Coins*, p. 23.

10. Richmond, "The Roman Legionaries at Corbridge," 21:165–166. At Castlesteads *(CIL* 7, no. 896) a dedication from A.D. 209–211 appears within the fort. Other dedications in the same area also date from the period of the Antonines and the Severi, and corroborate Severus's reputation as a stern disciplinarian. Richmond notes that the cult of Disciplina rarely appeared in other provinces of the empire. It was prominent only in Britain, Africa, and Mauretania, and was important in these regions for both legionary and auxiliary troops (pp. 166–167). It is difficult to determine why this should have been the case unless it was related to opposition to the accession of Septimius Severus. If this were the case, however, one should have expected it also to have been prominent among the units stationed in Gaul.

11. A mural tablet inscribed *Concordiae Leg VI Vi(c) pf Leg XX* found at Corbridge was obviously an attempt to lessen friction between the men of the two legions posted there. For imperial coinage picturing Concordia, see Harold Mattlingly, *Roman Coins from the Earliest Times to the Fall of the Western Empire*, p. 65.

12. John Helgeland, "Roman Army Religion," in *ANRW* 2:16.2, pp. 1488, 1491.

13. Lily Ross Taylor, *The Divinity of the Roman Emperor*, p. 207, suggests that the military program was unplanned, and that the precise notation for festivals of the imperial cult is merely that established by Augustus united with that of the *genius* of the reigning emperor.

14. See Fink et al., "The Feriale Duranum," pp. 94, 163, 287. The Quinquatrus had special importance as the festival of Minerva, who along with Jupiter and Mars was one of the three great deities of the Roman state religion. Her association with these dates may be reflected in the Christian celebration of the Annunciation, "Lady Day," on March 21. She was celebrated in the Roman army as the guardian of records and quartermasters' stores. There are relatively few votive offerings to the Roman deities along Hadrian's Wall, but one to Minerva was found by archaeologists at the remains of the fort at Corbridge; it was dedicated by an accountant.

15. Fink et al., "The Feriale Duranum," p. 167, 170.

16. Jean Gàge, *Recherches sur les Jeux séculaires*, pp. 94–97.

214 THE WESTERN FRONTIERS OF IMPERIAL ROME

17. Fink et al., "The Feriale Duranum," pp. 103–104.

18. A. N. Sherwin-White, *The Roman Citizenship*, p. 215.

19. Fink et al., "The Feriale Duranum," p. 206.

20. Helgeland, "Roman Army Religion," p. 1477, claims that although barbarization of the army did occur, the military program of worship did not represent a conscious invention aimed at a single purpose. He contends that the calendar was probably an accumulation of festivals reflecting a desire that religion and piety be cultivated throughout the empire.

21. Tacitus, *Annales* 2:17, states that the standards functioned as the special gods of the army and were greatly venerated. For examples of dedications to standards in Britain see *CIL* 7:1030, 1031.

22. Many depictions of such standards have been preserved, and Trajan's column is a particularly rich source for their study. We know little about the symbolism of the devices shown on military standards, but one might suppose that some of them were battle honors, and that others honored the founder of the unit, its origins, and the like.

23. Fink et al., "The Feriale Duranum," p. 115, claim that the Rosaliae Signorum were the military form of a civilian festival, attached to the standards primarily to make them an integral part of the army's religion.

24. Richmond, "The Roman Legionaries at Corbridge," p. 160.

25. For examples of dedications to the *genii* of various units, see *CIL* 7:440, 1030, 1031. See also Richmond, "The Roman Legionaries at Corbridge," p. 162.

26. The "mystery" does not refer to hidden knowledge, but to the fact that worship was restricted to those who had undergone an initiation ritual.

27. It seems relatively clear, for instance, that Christianity borrowed its holiday of December 25 and its calling baptismal water "the blood of the Lamb" from the cult of Mithras; its early veneration of Mary and the infant Jesus from the cult of Isis; and perhaps the picture of the presentation of the head of John the Baptist from that of Orpheus. The power of Christianity during this period did not lie so much in the purity of its practice as in its ability to distinguish between its message and the symbolic trappings in which that message was packaged.

28. Although the triumph of Christianity within the empire was complete by 396, pockets of Mithras worship persisted in the Alps well into the fifth century. It may well be that one-time worshipers of Mithras also contributed to the popularity of Manichaeanism in the fourth and fifth centuries. For the relationship of Mithraism and the Roman army, see C. M. Daniels, "The Role of the Roman Army in the Spread and Practice of Mithraism," in *Mithraic Studies: Proceedings of the First International Congress of Mithraic Studies*, vol. 2; Michael Speidel, *Mithras-Orion: Greek Hero and Roman Army God*; and Gunter Ristow, *Mithras im römischen Köln*.

29. Michael Speidel, *The Religion of Jupiter Dolichenus in the Roman Army*, pp. 5–10. Also see Alexaru Popa, *Le culte de Jupiter Dolichenus dans la Dacie romaine*.

30. Perhaps it was his military character that made Mithras, like Jupiter Dolichenus, attractive to the Germanic peoples of the frontier.

31. Mithraism was introduced to the Roman world by Cilician pirates captured by Pompey the Great.

32. The same is true of the official treatment of some other mystery cults, such as those of Cybele and Isis, that had attracted a few followers on the frontier.

33. See Ian A. Richmond, "Roman Army and Roman Religion," *Bulletin of the John Rylands Library* 45 (September 1962):196.

34. Allen S. Hoey, "Official Policy towards Oriental Cults in the Roman Army," *Transactions of the American Philological Association* 70 (1939):463–464.

35. Ibid., pp. 456–458; Hoey maintains that the large amount of epigraphical and archaeological evidence pertaining to the Oriental religions proves that the official policy toward worship of Oriental cults by the soldiers was one of tolerance. Further verification of a policy of tolerance is found at the British site of Corbridge, where part of the initial planning of the site included setting aside space for temples and shrines outside the military precinct. See Richmond, "The Roman Legionaries at Corbridge," pp. 144–147.

36. Hoey, "Official Policy towards Oriental Cults in the Roman Army," pp. 463–464.

37. Ibid., p. 466.

38. Although much is written about the concern of the government in Romanizing its troops and subject peoples, the readiness with which the government recruited barbarian *numeri* and settled foreigners within the empire suggests that the imperial commitment to a civilizing mission was not as great as is commonly supposed. The Romans appear to have pursued Romanization only when it offered them some immediate advantages.

39. Julius Caesar, *War Commentaries: De bello gallico and De bello civili* 6:17.

40. The Benedictine monks were not priests in the technical sense, but their functions of offering prayers and maintaining ritual observances were priestly in the traditional sense of the term.

X FINAL THOUGHTS

Almost from its very inception, the Roman imperial administration realized that its economic and human resources were insufficient to support continued Roman expansion and barely adequate to defend the frontiers of those lands that had already been acquired. Moreover, the Italian heartland of the empire had been exhausted by civil wars that had accompanied the fall of the republic and never recovered its earlier vigor and vitality. The traditional Roman sources of manpower, money, and material continued to dwindle during the early imperial period. One last effort at expansion was conducted under the emperor Augustus and had to be abandoned in the face of determined resistance. It was clear to Augustus and most of his immediate successors that the empire no longer possessed the power to conquer and subdue more hostile territory. The immediate task became that of finding and manning defensible boundaries. By the middle of the first century A.D., Roman legions had taken up positions in Britain and along the Rhine and Danube rivers, and were industriously constructing a fortified and fixed defensive frontier. Except for some relatively minor and temporary adjustments, this line was held until the final crumbling of the Roman Empire in the West during the course of the fifth century.

The Frontier Process

The conquest and occupation of these border provinces and frontier districts caused dramatic changes, altering the physical aspect of the land and transforming the economic, social, and political structure of

216

its native inhabitants. It was clear from the beginning that the imperial administration, both civil and military, intended that as much of the cost of this defensive line as possible would be borne by the frontier itself. The legions were expected to build the roads, bridges, canals, signal-stations, harbors, and ports that would make a limited garrison as mobile as possible, as well as to construct the walls, ditches, palisades, forts, and fortresses that would compensate in fortifications for an inadequate number of men at any given point. Meanwhile, the women, children, sutlers, pawnbrokers, and other civilians who followed the legions threw together shacks outside the main gates of the legionary fortresses.

The imperial administrators were not dedicated to the tasks of either civilizing the natives of the frontier regions or gaining their affection. They were concerned with establishing the most secure lines their limited resources would allow. They spared little time in putting the residents to the task of supplying the legions with urgently needed food and raw materials. Forced levies of goods, backed up by Roman military might and the threat of enslavement should natives fail to meet the demands placed upon them, soon became the driving forces of native life. Traditional ways of life were swept aside by these imperative demands. Pastoral peoples soon began opening up vast tracts of agricultural lands; agricultural peoples somehow found ways to increase their production; and indolent peoples were soon felling timber, quarrying stone, and digging for iron, copper, lead, zinc, tin, gold, silver, and whatever other mineral wealth their district might hold. The Roman military demanded tens of thousands of cattle, and somehow the frontier managed to produce them.

The peoples of the frontier were also expected to supplement and conserve the manpower of the legions. Native units, *auxilia* and *numeri*, were raised and equipped. Roman commanders led these units in onerous patrol duties and in numerous petty skirmishes that have gone largely unrecorded. When major confrontations were unavoidable, the Roman sent in the native auxiliaries to bear the brunt of the casualties and soften the enemy up for the legions' advance. When it was necessary to withdraw, the auxiliaries were thrown into hopeless rearguard actions in order to save legionary lives. Within a short time, fully half the Roman army of the frontier was composed of such native troops. This was not enough, however. As the number of Italians available for service in the legions continued to decline, it became apparent that the frontier population would eventually have to man these units also.

The imperial administrators established Roman institutions throughout the frontier. Model Roman cities were constructed and native settlements encouraged to imitate their pattern. Private citizens from the interior established villa estates and introduced Roman modes of life and production, while entrepreneurs introduced Roman industries and offered the natives jobs paid in Roman silver. Elaborate systems were established to induce the natives to adopt Roman ways, and compliance was rewarded with Roman citizenship. Native villa owners, native municipal officials, retirees from auxiliary units, residents of Romanized towns, members of loyal tribes, and other individuals and groups received this coveted distinction, which steadily grew more and more common. As the number of Roman citizens along the frontier increased, so too did the pool from which the legions could draw recruits. By the end of the second century, the Roman army of the West, both legionary and auxiliary units, was manned almost entirely by non-Italians.

The establishment of the Roman frontier in the West was a triumph of human will and indicates what can be accomplished by an administration lacking in any consideration for its subject peoples or respect for their traditional patterns of life. And yet, the enterprise was a success. Not only did the frontier districts become self-sufficient, they eventually bore the entire burden, both economic and physical, of defending Rome's German frontier. Moreover, that defense was effective; border tribes broke through from time to time, but their force was soon spent and the breaches quickly repaired. It was not until the eastern emperor Valens had permitted the Visigoths to cross the Danube as Roman guests, and Stilicho, the western commander in chief, had stripped the frontier of its garrisons to defend Italy against those same Visigoths, that the frontier was no longer able to perform its defensive function. By 407, German tribes were passing through the deserted frontier works without opposition. Nevertheless, the Roman frontier in the West, depending almost entirely upon its own resources, had protected Rome against greatly superior numbers for almost four centuries.

If this is the history of the western frontier from the point of view of the imperial administration, the residents of the frontier itself might have seen it differently. During those four centuries, a dynamic, productive, and relatively free frontier society had emerged that was neither completely Roman nor entirely barbarian, but an amalgamation of both and adapted to the peculiar circumstances of the frontier. This amalgamation of cultures and traditions, as well as some of the unique characteristics of frontier society, derived in large measure from the dynamics of the frontier experience.

When the Roman legions entered the frontier, they were a catalyst for change. That change may have been painful, but it wrenched the native peoples out of their traditional patterns of life into the economic life of a much larger world. They had to learn how to produce greater quantities and a larger variety of commodities than had been their practice, but their time was no longer absorbed in cattle raids, clan feuds, petty squabbles, and head-hunting. Their quarrelsome tribal chiefs retired to villas and cities to practice Latin and refine their Roman manners, and the tribesmen were left to their pursuits. They soon found that the army provided a ready market for almost anything that they could produce over and above government demands and their own needs. What is more, the army paid for their purchases in silver. The traditional barter economies of the frontier districts were replaced by more sophisticated and flexible money economies. At the same time, the military roads and waterways provided the transportation infrastructure to support new economic activities. The imperial administration was not interested in regulating this economic growth, but was generally satisfied if military needs were met promptly. If anything, more trade meant more taxes.

The presence of the army loomed over this entire process. In defending the frontier for the Romans, it also provided the frontier peoples with a greater degree of security than they had ever known before. This same security helped to draw developers, entrepreneurs, and settlers from the interior to the undeveloped resources and untapped markets of the frontier. In the beginning, this development, exploitation, and settlement tended to concentrate around individual legions. The legion offered protection, an assured market, and an assortment of expert artisans to assist in the development of native skills. Semi-independent local economies emerged around each legionary fortress and some of the larger auxiliary forts.

The individual was valued on the frontier in a way that was not true in the interior of the empire. As the number of slaves began to diminish in the interior, whatever slaves inhabited the frontier were either sold into the heartland, or freed, or they escaped over into free Germany. The labor force on the frontier had to be paid and well treated. This factor led to a still more dynamic frontier economy and society. The Roman entrepreneurs who settled on the frontier employed local residents in their ventures, treated them with respect, and paid them in cash. It was at this level and under these conditions that local and Roman traditions began to merge in an unforced and gradual manner. At the same time, the growth of a wage-earning class created a scale of consumer market for local production that was rare in the ancient world.

In contrast to the depopulation of the interior of the empire, the population of the frontier districts slowly increased. The elevated status of the individual remained unchanged, however, for there were never enough men to meet the frontier's needs. The army had an insatiable appetite for recruits, and offered heady inducements: a regular cash salary, the prestige that came with being a soldier, relatively good and plentiful food, shelter, comradeship, adventure, and, at the end of twenty-five years' service, Roman citizenship. It also consumed men at a prodigious rate. Disease, wounds, injuries, and death on the battlefield all contributed to keep the army's need for men relatively constant. At the same time, the normal military policy was to forbid or at least discourage marriage during active service. Although this policy was often honored only in the breach, it generally acted to slow down the rate of population increase along the frontier.

Meanwhile, the frontier economy kept growing, always pressing at the limits of the manpower available to sustain it. In the early stages of the establishment of the frontier, the Romans had been forced to buy necessary commodities from the tribes beyond the frontier. They had paid with silver coin, and this money provided the means of exchange that allowed the tribes of free Germany and Scandinavia to regularize their economic interrelations and form a great trading area with an appetite for Roman manufactured goods. The local manufacturers of the frontier districts and the border provinces quickly undertook the task of supplying the German market, and large-scale industries arose all along the frontier. These industrial concentrations spawned numerous local centers that supplied local, internal markets. By the close of the second century, western Roman industrial capacity was concentrated on the frontier, and industrial centers of the interior had decayed beyond repair.

The first and second centuries along the Roman frontier in the West had been a golden age. Although driven, and often despised, by their Roman masters, the residents of the frontier had managed not only to shoulder the burden of frontier defense, but to achieve a remarkable standard of living and economic growth. The catalyst for this growth had been the security, markets, and infrastructure provided by the Roman army of the frontier, and the growth had been sustained by the abundance of easily exploited and extracted resources of the frontier, coupled with the proximity of the great market area of free Germany. These were not the only reasons, however. Much of the credit for frontier achievements must be given to the nature of frontier society itself.

The societies of the frontier districts of the Roman West were, by and large, comparatively free, and the economic growth of the region was perhaps the first in civilized history that had not been based upon the exploitation of an enslaved mass. The traditional ways of the frontier peoples had been shaken by the first shock of the economic demands their new Roman masters had placed upon them. They were ready for change, but their Roman rulers were not particularly interested in thrusting cultural and social changes upon them. Well aware that tampering with native beliefs and traditions was an invitation to resistance and revolt, the Romans practiced as much tolerance as was consonant with their own security. And so cultural change was a relatively slow and mutual process.

In social as well as economic status, the Roman and native residents of the frontier were relatively equal. We might consider the differences in wealth and status among these people to have been substantial, but they were minor compared to the immense inequalities that characterized the society of the heartland of the empire. In addition, there was far greater social mobility on the frontier. Opportunities were numerous, businesses could be established with minimal capital, and there was relatively little competition within a steadily growing economy. Roman frontier society, although springing from roots far different from those of the American experience, nevertheless displayed many of the same characteristics: personal freedom, lack of economic regulation, relative equality, a sense of individual worth, and a high degree of social and economic mobility.

And yet the Roman frontier was fundamentally different from the frontier of the American West. There was little doubt in the minds of the Americans of their ability to continue expanding, conquering whatever native peoples lay in their path. American resources in population, material, and technological advantage were so great by the middle of the nineteenth century that the potential opponents to expansion were negligible factors. The Americans thought of the West as "empty land." Affairs were quite different for the Romans. By the early years of the first century A.D., they had come to realize that they lacked sufficient resources ever to defeat the Germans, and that the resources that they did possess were dwindling. Why, then, did they launch themselves forward to the frontiers of the Rhine and the Danube, investing much of their meager resources and all of their available manpower in establishing an advanced line of defense within German territory?

Viewed with a dispassionate eye, the entire policy represented a great gamble. What if the Germans had united in the face of this new Roman presence and attacked before the frontier fortifications were in place? What if the frontier had proven incapable of supplying the troops concentrated along its length? Finally, and most important, if the effort to establish the frontier had been so great, how could the Romans expect to maintain it for any length of time? The answer to this last question lies in a traditional aspect of Roman military policy— the use of client-states.[1]

The Celtic Character of the Imperial Frontiers

The Romans usually attempted to avoid defending themselves. It was their custom to establish their ascendancy over states along the frontiers and then to furnish them with the equipment and training to defend themselves from their neighbors. With Roman assistance, such client-states were usually able to dominate their regions, and, by defending themselves, they protected the Roman lands that lay behind them. Only when there was a clear danger that a client-state might be defeated and conquered would the Romans commit their own troops to change the balance of power. The Romans attempted to surround their empire with such buffer states, but the policy did not work everywhere. It was possible to do so in the East, where the multiplicity of independent states lying between the Romans and the Persian Empire favored such tactics. It was less simple in the tribal West, where no stable kingdoms were left after the Gallic conquests of the late republic and where the genocidal wars of Julius Caesar had left a residue of resentment and hostility.

The Romans seized upon a common element among the Celtic peoples. At one time, the Celts had occupied most of Europe, but they had slowly been pushed westward by the more numerous and warlike Germans. At the beginning of the first century, the German advance had reached the Rhine and Danube and had even penetrated a short distance beyond in some places. In leaping forward to establish their armies along this line, the Romans bypassed those Celts who still remembered their defeats and humiliations at the hands of Roman legions a generation earlier, and placed themselves among Celtic peoples whose primary hostility was directed at the German bands that were slowly forcing them westward.

Once having reached that line, the Romans initiated a policy that was directed with single-minded purposiveness toward raising the economic and military capacities of the border provinces and frontier districts to a point where they could defend the frontier without a permanent Roman presence or continued Roman subsidies. In short, the Romans never intended to undertake the responsibility of defending the Rhine and Danube frontier, but instead to force the frontier districts to evolve to the level of client-states, undertake their own defense, and allow the Romans to withdraw. Roman frontier policy in both East and West was essentially the same, although expressed in necessarily different terms.

This explains many of the peculiarities of the Roman frontier in the West. Why did neither Romans nor native auxiliaries find it strange that native troops should be sent into battle to die while Roman legionaries simply looked on? Perhaps because the auxiliaries were protecting their own farms and towns that lay immediately behind the frontier they were defending. Why should the Romans expend vast quantities of money and labor to build a barrier against the Germans and then allow the local inhabitants to develop close economic ties with those same Germans? Perhaps because a buffer state at peace with its neighbors was even more effective a defense for the empire than one constantly at war. Finally, why should the Romans build their defensive frontier so far from their areas of vital interest and the strategic routes to the heartland of the empire? Perhaps because it was not the Roman frontier at all, but the Celtic frontier.

The Romans failed to anticipate either the strength and vitality that frontier society would develop or the degree to which the heartland of the empire would decline. They were unable to withdraw their forces from the Celtic frontier that they had created because those forces had themselves become Celtic, even though grants of Roman citizenship obscured that fact from the more idealistic Romans. The Roman heartland lacked the capacity to man and maintain a native army in the interior to aid the western frontier in case of need. The Celtic frontier became the Roman frontier, because the Romans of the heartland had neither the strength nor the will to defend themselves and simply relied upon the frontier Celts to do the job for them. The universal extension of citizenship throughout the empire in 212 may have been intended in part to eliminate that anomaly. If the frontier Celts were Roman citizens, why should the inhabitants of the interior not expect them to defend the empire that was the common possession of all?

This was more rhetoric than reality, however, for the Romans of the interior continued to regard all peoples outside of Italy with greater or lesser degrees of disdain. In the opening years of the fifth century, the imperial high command began stripping the frontier of its troops to fight in a series of bloody and fruitless efforts to bar the passes into Italy to Alaric and his Visigoths.[2] The frontier that had been established to defend Celtic lands was denuded to defend Italy. Protests, delegations, and army mutinies directed against this policy were to no avail. The military and economic resources of the western frontier were systematically plundered to save Italy. The policy succeeded; a Roman emperor continued to rule for another seventy years. Meanwhile, the Celtic lands of Gaul, Spain, and Britain were inundated by the German invaders.

Notes

1. See David Braund, *Rome and the Friendly King: The Character of the Client Kingship.*

2. A series of emperors beginning with Septimius Severus and culminating with Diocletian had drawn upon the resources of the frontier and the manpower provided by barbarian immigration into the empire to establish a mobile field army in the interior. The Severan force was virtually destroyed in the civil wars of the third century. Having been restored by Diocletian in the period after 285, the western imperial field army was quickly depleted in the struggles against Alaric beginning in 406. The imperial high command quickly turned to the frontier in order to continue the fight. Remnants of the field army were posted into Italy, where, at the end of the century, they were influential in forcing the abdication of Romulus Augustulus, the last Roman emperor in the West (476).

CHRONOLOGY OF THE ROMAN FRONTIER

27 B.C.–A.D. 14   CAESAR AUGUSTUS

16–12 B.C.   Sugambri raid across the Rhine into Gaul.

16–15 B.C.   A German victory over Roman troops leads to an extension of the frontier. The provinces of Rhaetia, Noricum, and Vindelecia are added to the empire. Roman authority thus reaches the upper Danube.

12 B.C.–A.D. 9   Revolt in Pannonia and continued struggles against the Germans tax Roman resources.

A.D. 6   Augustus establishes the Military Treasury to pay bonuses to retiring veterans.
Thrace is made a client-state and Moesia made a province, fixing the Roman frontier on the lower Danube.
Great revolt in Illyria.

9   Varus and a force of three legions are annihilated by the German Arminius in the battle of the Teutoberg Forest. Augustus abandons plans to fix the frontier on the Elbe.

14   At the death of Augustus, the Roman army is re-

duced from as many as eighty legions to twenty-eight. The army probably numbered a total of about 300,000 men.

The legions in Pannonia and on the Rhine revolt.

14–37   TIBERIUS

14–16   Drusus Germanicus suppresses the Pannonian and Rhine revolts. Invading Germany, he defeats Arminius, and the German kingdom disintegrates.

21   Revolt of the Treveri and Aedui, native tribes of Gaul, demonstrates that some areas behind the military frontier are not yet secure. One of the causes of the revolt is the rumor that men are to be drafted into the *auxilia* and posted to various units in distant provinces.

Completion of the *Geographica* of Strabo.

37–41   CALIGULA

39   Caligula attempts to invade Germany, but is frustrated by his own officials.

40   Caligula, mentally unbalanced, assembles troops to invade Britain. According to later report, has them instead gather seashells as proof of his conquest of the sea.

41–54   CLAUDIUS

43–51   Britain is invaded; after initial successes, pacification proceeds slowly until the capture of Caractacus, the leader of the British, in 51.

54–68   NERO

c. 56   Birth of the historian Tacitus, who died sometime after 115.

61   British revolt under Queen Boudicca devastates much of Roman-held Britain. Boudicca is defeated and killed by legate Paulinus.

65   The philosopher Seneca is forced to commit suicide by order of Nero.

67   Nero has the popular general Corbulo and two ex-legates of the army of the Rhine executed.

68   The legate of the Rhine troops revolts; the revolt is suppressed by troops from the upper Rhine. The troops of Spain revolt and acclaim their commander, Galba, as emperor. The Praetorian Guard supports Galba and forces Nero's suicide.

68–69   GALBA

69   "The Year of the Four Emperors." The eight Rhine legions revolt, declaring their own commander, Vitellius, emperor. Otho, legate of Lusitania, has Galba murdered and assumes the emperorship himself.

69   OTHO

69   Vitellius invades Italy and defeats Otho, who commits suicide.
A Sarmatian tribe (Rhoxolani) raids Moesia, but is defeated while returning with booty.

69   VITELLIUS
Vespasian, legate in Judaea, is proclaimed emperor and supported by the Danube legions, who invade Italy and defeat and kill Vitellius.
Dacians cross Danube and are beaten off in an attack on Moesia.

69–79   VESPASIAN

69–71   Revolt of Batavian *auxilia* on the lower Rhine is joined by some of the Rhine legions and by the Treveri with the goal of seceding from the Roman empire and establishing an independent state. After the revolt is suppressed, auxiliary troops are no longer allowed to serve in the same area from which they were recruited. The legions come to be recruited from veterans' colonies and the provinces, and become more provincial in their sympathies. The emperor disbands four disloyal Rhine legions; five new legions have been raised during the civil war. There are now twenty-nine legions.

73–74   The Danube is frontier reorganized. Vespasian begins conquest of German lands between the Rhine and Danube.

75–76   Julius Frontinus, governor of Britain, pacifies the Silures and consolidates military control of Wales.

77–84   Julius Agricola, governor of Britain, invades Scotland.

79–81   TITUS

81–96   DOMITIAN

83   Domitian invades Germany to battle the Chatti. Calls levies from Britain, ending Agricola's attempt to conquer Scotland. Agricola abandons fort at Inchtuthil. Domitian fortifies the region beyond the Rhine and Danube, and builds road throughout the districts.

84   Army pay is increased from 225 to 300 *denarii* per year.

85   Dacians cross the Danube into Moesia. Defeated by Domitian.

86   Roman invasion of Dacia ends in defeat.

88   Revolt of Saturninus, legate of Upper Germany, soon collapses. Victorious troops invading Dacia are nevertheless recalled.

89   Romans are defeated by the Quadi and Marcomanni, who had hitherto defended the upper Danube in alliance with Rome. Domitian is forced to make peace with the Dacians. The Danube frontier is threatened along its length. Quartering of more than one legion in a single camp is forbidden. Legions begin to lose mobility.

90   By about this year, the British garrison is reduced to three legions. Old legionary bases are converted; Lincoln and Gloucester become *coloniae*, Exeter and Wroxeter are turned over to civil population as new capitals.

96–98   NERVA

98–117   TRAJAN

98   Born in Seville, Spain, Trajan is the first provincial emperor. Continues the construction of the German palisade begun by Domitian. Throughout his reign, there is a general program of replacing timber forts with stone.

98   Completion of Tacitus's *Agricola* and *Germania*.

101–107   The Dacian Wars (101–102, 105–107), in which the Dacians are defeated. Dacia is annexed as a province and peopled with Roman settlers. The Dacian Wars are pictured on Trajan's column in Rome.

107   Four legions are posted to the upper Danube opposite the Marcomanni and Quadi. With two le-

gions in Dacia and three on the lower Danube, the Danube line now has a total of nine legions.

107–270   The annexation of Dacia leads to general prosperity in the area of the lower Danube, the Black Sea, and Thrace.

117–138   HADRIAN

117   Hadrian's reign is characterized by extensive efforts to strengthen the frontier through the building of massive fixed fortifications. *Numeri*, units of native troops fighting in their own style, are taken into the army and posted with the *auxilia*. The emperor stimulates increased urban growth in frontier regions. Veterans are probably encouraged to buy land in their frontier districts on which to settle.

122–127   Construction of Hadrian's Wall in Britain.

138–162   ANTONINUS PIUS

142–143   Revolt of the Brigantes in Britain (modern Yorkshire) is suppressed. Construction of the Antonine Wall from the Clyde River to the Forth; this fortification is soon abandoned.

161–180   MARCUS AURELIUS

166–175   In the wake of a great plague in the empire, the Marcomanni and allied tribes cross the Danube. A treaty with the Marcomanni allows large numbers of them to settle in the empire. The Sarmatians attack the lower Danube frontier.

178–180   Marcomanni again attack the empire.

180–192   COMMODUS

193   PERTINAX

193   After the murder of Pertinax, the emperorship is sold to the highest bidder by the Praetorian Guard. The army in Britain rebels, naming legate Septimius Albinus emperor; the army in Pannonia chooses Septimius Severus, and Syrian troops choose Niger.

193–211   SEPTIMIUS SEVERUS

193–197   Severus defeats Albinus and Niger. In the defeat of Albinus, the region of the Rhone is devastated and never fully recovers.

197   Severus recruits three more legions, stationing them in Italy. He adopts the policy of placing members of the equestrian order in military positions hitherto reserved for the senatorial class. Military marriages are recognized as valid. Legionary pay is raised; auxiliary troops are given public lands in exchange for military service and begin to become peasant soldiers. Devaluation of currency.

211   Severus goes to Britain to fight the Scots; abandons the Antonine Wall; dies at York.

211–217   CARACALLA

211   Caracalla raises army pay to such a level that state revenues are exhausted. Devaluation of currency.

212   Edict of Caracalla: Roman citizenship extended throughout the empire.

213   Alamanni threaten Rhine frontier and are thwarted by Caracalla.

214   Goths threaten lower Danube; they, too, are stopped by Caracalla.

217–218   MACRINUS

217   Macrinus attempts to reduce army pay.

218–222   ELAGABULUS

222–235   ALEXANDER SEVERUS

234–235   Alexander buys peace with the Alamanni and is murdered by troops of the Rhine. The beginning of military anarchy.

235–238   MAXIMINUS

235   The Rhine troops acclaim Maximinus emperor; African troops acclaim Gordian.

238   Maximinus invades Italy, murdered by his own troops.

238–244   GORDIAN
Grandson of Gordian is murdered by Philip.

244–249   PHILIP

249   Decius, legate of the Danube, revolts; invades Italy and defeats and kills Philip.

249–251   DECIUS

251   Because of the treachery of Gallus, a legate in Moesia, Decius is killed by Goths in Dacia.

251–253   GALLUS

253   Gallus's successor as legate in Moesia rebels. Gallus marches against him, but is murdered by his own troops.

| 252–269 | Plague throughout the empire. |

| 253–259 | VALERIAN |

| 254 | Valerian is unsuccessful in stopping the Franks from crossing the Rhine. |

| 256 | The Alamanni invade Italy as far as Milan. |

| 257 | Valerian is unsuccessful in battle against the Goths. |

| 258 | Cities throughout the empire begin to fortify themselves. |

| 259–268 | GALLIENUS
Although there are numerous claimants to power in this period of "the thirty tyrants," Gallienus continues to rule. Goths reach Black Sea and raid into the Aegean by ship. |

| 268 | Galienus is killed by his own troops in Italy. |

| 268–270 | CLAUDIUS II |

| 269 | Claudius defeats the Goths in the Balkans, settles large numbers of them on vacant land. |

| 270–275 | AURELIAN
Called *restitutor orbis*, "Restorer of the World," Aurelian was acclaimed emperor by the legions of the Danube. |

| 270 | Dacia is abandoned, and Roman settlers are reestablished in Moesia. |

| 271 | Alamanni is driven from Italy. |

| 274 | Aurelian recovers Gaul from the usurper Tetricus. |

275   Aurelian is murdered by his own officers when preparing to invade Persia.

275–276   TACITUS
Tacitus is appointed by the Senate with the army's permission. Defeats the Goths and Alans in Asia Minor, but is killed by his own troops.

276–281   PROBUS
Probus is elevated by the eastern army.

276–277   Probus drives the Franks and Alamanni from Gaul.

278   Probus strengthens Danube frontier.

281   Probus orders troops to rebuild and repair public works, and is murdered by them.

281–283   CARUS

283   A former Praetorian prefect, Carus dies of unknown causes.

284–285   Carus's sons try to hold the West, but one dies and the other is defeated by Diocletian and killed by his own troops.

284–305   DIOCLETIAN

GLOSSARY

Aachen: A city in Germany. Originally a rest camp shared by two Rhine legions, it became the capital of Charlemagne, king of the Franks (A.D. 768–814).

Adonis: A cult figure whose worship centered on the ancient city of Byblus. Adonis seems to have represented the spirit of vegetation, the annual regeneration of which was regarded as a symbol of his worshippers' rebirth and immortality.

Adrianople: Modern Edirne, a city of European Turkey. The site of the battle in A.D. 378 in which the Visigoths defeated the army of the Eastern Roman Empire.

Ala: The basic unit of auxiliary cavalry troops.

Alans: A Sarmatian tribe that drifted into Central Europe in the second and third centuries A.D. In company with Vandals and Sueves, the Alans crossed the Rhine in 407 and began the "barbarian" invasions of the Western Roman Empire.

Alaric: King of the Germanic Visigoths, who sacked the city of Rome in A.D. 410. Alaric died shortly afterward, and his plans for establishing a Visigothic state in Sicily were ended.

Amber Coast: The southern shore of the Baltic Sea, modern Germany and Poland, where large quantities of amber could be found washed up on the beach.

Ambiani: A Celtic tribe that inhabited what is now northern France and Belgium.

Amphora: A large two-handled pottery jug, often with a pointed bottom, long used in Mediterranean lands for the shipping and storing of a wide variety of commodities.

Ampsivarii: A Germanic tribe of the lower Rhine. Refused land west of the Rhine by their German allies, they were eventually destroyed while trying to gain lands at the expense of the Germanic neighbors.

Aquincum: A major fortress on the Danube, on the site of the modern Hungarian city of Budapest.

Armenia: A mountainous territory in what is now Turkey, much disputed between the Romans and Persians.

Armilustrium: A traditional Roman military festival dating from republican times, held each year on October 19.

Arsacid: The ruling dynasty of the Persian Empire, 171 B.C.–A.D. 226.

Asciburgium: A legionary fortress on the Rhine opposite the mouth of the Ruhr River, on the site of the modern city of Moers-Asberg.

Atrebates: A Celtic tribe that inhabited what is now the district of Artois in northern France.

Augusta Vindelicorum: A Roman city in Upper Germany, on the site of the modern city of Augsburg.

Aurochs: Large European ruminants, related to the buffalo and now extinct.

Auxilia: "Helpers," units of provincial and allied troops under Roman command that formed a large part of the Roman army. *Auxilia* correspond in some measure to the sepoys under British rule in India.

Basilica: A large, rectangular building located by the forum of most Roman cities, in which public affairs were conducted. The form and floor plan of the basilica were used for many villas and most early Christian churches.

Beckfoot: A fort on Hadrian's Wall in Britain.

Belgae: A Celtic tribe that inhabited most of what is modern Belgium.

Binchester: A fort on Hadrian's Wall in Britain.

Bohemia: A region in central Europe, the land of the modern Czechs. Inhabited by the Marcomanni in Roman times.

Bonna: A bridgehead camp on the right bank of the Rhine, on the site of the modern city of Bonn. Numerous Roman artifacts have been uncovered here and placed in the excellent Rheinische Landesmuseum.

Braca: The trousers that formed part of the traditional garb of the Celts and were viewed by the Romans as a sign of barbarism.

Brigetio: A Roman fortress on the Danube, on the site of the modern city of Szny, Hungary.

Brougham: A fort on Hadrian's Wall in Britain.

Burgundians: A Germanic tribe that eventually settled in eastern Gaul, leaving its name to the region of Burgundy.

Caerleon: A town near Newport in southeastern Wales. The name of the place is a form of *Castrum legionis*, or "camp of the legion." The Second Augustan Legion was garrisoned here for over 300 years.

Camulodunum: A Roman city in Britain, on the site of the modern city of Colchester. Camulodunum was the first Roman settlement in Britain and the headquarters of the civil administration of the province.

Canabae: Small settlements alongside army forts that provided amenities for the forts' garrisons. Often located opposite the main gate.

Cappadocia: A Roman province in what is now Turkey.

Car Dyke Canal Zone: A network of canals in eastern England, stretching from Cambridgeshire northward to the Humber Estuary.

Carnuntum: A legionary fortress on the Danube opposite both the mouth of the Marus River and the site of the modern city of Deutsch-Altenburg.

Castra Vetera: An early legionary fortress on the Rhine, near the site of the modern city of Xanten.

Catuvellauni: A Celtic tribe of Britain, with its capital at Verulamium.

Centurion: A senior noncommissioned officer in the Roman legion, commander of a century of about eighty men. The legion's centurions directed the training, supply, and operations of the legion, while the commanders concerned themselves with tactics and strategy.

Century: The "company"-sized unit of the Roman legion. Usually numbering about eighty men and commanded by a centurion. A legion normally comprised sixty centuries.

Charterhouse: A fort on Hadrian's Wall in Britain.

Chatti: A German tribe that inhabited the region east of Mainz.

Chesterholm: A fort on Hadrian's Wall in Britain.

Chesters: A fort on Hadrian's Wall in Britain.

Civitas: A city, the fundamental unit of Roman local government. A *civitas* consisted of the city and its surrounding countryside, or *pagus*. Most *civitates* were about the size of an American county, but some were as large as a small state such as Delaware.

Classis: A fleet, the standard unit of the Roman navy. Most of the Roman fleets in the West were stationed on rivers.

Classis Britannica: The main naval force for Britain, based at Bononia, the modern city of Boulogne in France.

Client-States: Independent states along the imperial frontiers allied with and subsidized by Rome. Especially in the east, they functioned as buffers separating the Roman and Persian empires.

Cohors: A cohort. A Roman military unit numbering 400 to 600 men. A legion consisted of ten cohorts. The cohort was the largest formation of auxiliary troops.

Cohors Equitatus: A mixed infantry–cavalry cohort of auxiliary troops.

Cohors Peditatus: An infantry cohort of auxiliary troops.

Colonia: A settlement provided for retired veterans as a reward for their service and as an attraction to keep them in the neighborhood of the frontier.

Colonia Agrippina: The major veterans' settlement in Lower Germany, located on the site of the modern city of Cologne. A legionary fortress, it became a civilian settlement with the reposting of the legions in A.D. 35, and was elevated to the rank of colony in A.D. 50.

Colonia Nervia Glevensium: A veterans' colony in southwestern England on the site of the modern city of Gloucester.

Colonia Ulpia Traiana: A veterans' settlement on the lower Rhine, on the site of the modern city of Xanten.

Concordia: The goddess Harmony; along with Discipline and Victory, the object of official military ritual devotion.

Corbridge: A fort on Hadrian's Wall in Britain.

Curiales: Members of the Roman middle class. The *curiales* provided the councilors and other public officials of the Roman municipality and were expected to provide public amenities from their private funds.

Cybele: An ancient cult figure, known by the Romans as The Great Mother of All the Gods, *Magna Mater*.

Dacia: A region north of the Danube, corresponding to modern Rumania.

Dalmatia: Roman province on the Adriatic Sea, corresponding to modern Bosnia and portions of Croatia.

Decuriones: Members of the town council of a self-governing municipality.

Denarius: A Roman coin usually made of bronze, of lesser value than the silver *solidus*. Often considered as corresponding to the modern penny, but of considerably greater value.

Deva: A Roman legionary fortress on the site of the modern city of Chester, on the border between England and Wales.

Diplomas: Lead tablets presented to soldiers as proof of their service and retirement.

Disciplina Augustorum: The goddess Discipline; along with Harmony and Victory, the object of official military ritual devotion.

Dura Europos: An eastern legionary fortress, the excavation of which yielded important information on the cycle of religious festivals observed by the Roman army.

Eburacum: The modern city of York in northern England. Eburacum was garrisoned by two Roman legions for a considerable time, and was the headquarters of a military command that extended some hundred miles northward to Hadrian's Wall.

Edict of Diocletian: An attempt made by the Roman emperor to set wages and prices throughout the empire (A.D. 285).

Emona: Roman city on the Save River.

Etruscans: A people that inhabited the lands north of early Rome. The Etruscans were probably immigrants from Asia Minor, and they had a more sophisticated culture than that of the Romans. The Romans traced the origins of many of their ceremonies and rituals to Etruscan influence.

Falernian: A famous wine of Italy, prized throughout the empire.

Fenlands: A marshy lowlands lying south of the Wash in southeastern England, including part of East Anglia and most of Cambridgeshire.

Ferrum Noricum: "Norican Iron," a fine-quality iron, mined and smelted in the province of Noricum (modern Austria).

First Cohort: The first cohort of a Roman legion was usually twice as strong as the others, and the centurion of the first cohort was the senior noncommissioned officer of the legion.

Flevum: A fortress of Frisia, beyond the Rhine, in what is now the Netherlands.

Franks: A Germanic tribe that inhabited the lower Rhine by the fourth century A.D. The Franks expanded from the region around Tournai, Belgium, to control all Gaul.

Frisians: A Germanic tribe that inhabited the region that is now the Netherlands.

Gallia Belgica: A Roman province corresponding to modern Belgium.

Gallia Bracata: A less Romanized portion of Gaul; called "Trousered Gaul" because of the Celtic inhabitants' custom of wearing trousers (*braca*).

Gallia Comata: A less Romanized portion of Gaul, called "long-haired Gaul" becuase of its inhabitants' custom of wearing their hair long.

Gallia Narbonensis: A Roman province on the Mediterranean, named after its capital of Narbonne. Sometimes called "Gallia Togata," or "Civilized Gaul."

Gaul: The Roman name for the regions corresponding to modern France.

Gavelkind: The Germanic inheritance pattern of dividing an estate equally among one's children or their heirs.

Genius: A deity peculiar to a given individual or group, perhaps corresponding to the Christian concept of the guardian angel. Each Roman military unit revered its own *genius*.

Geographica: "The Geography," the best-known work of Strabo.

Germania: "The Description of Germany," a work by Tacitus that provides valuable information on the early Germans.

Goths: A Germanic people consisting of two main tribal groups, the Ostrogoths and the Visigoths.

Greatchesters: A fort on Hadrian's Wall in Britain.

Hadrian's Wall: A stone fortification extending across Britain from Carlisle to Newcastle on the Tyne.

Hermundiri: A German tribe inhabiting an area between the Weser and Elbe rivers.

Housesteads: A fort on Hadrian's Wall in Britain.

Illyria: The region containing the Roman provinces of Pannonia and Dalmatia.

Imperium: Sovereignty; the power possessed by the ruler over the ruled.

Inchtuthil: A fortress intended by Agricola as a base for his abortive subjugation of Northern Britain.

Isis: A cult figure derived from Egypt, particularly popular among Roman women.

Janus: The Roman god of the doorway—of comings and goings, beginnings and endings.

Judaea: A Roman province corresponding to modern Israel.

Jugera: A Roman measurement of land area, roughly equal to two-thirds of an acre.

Jupiter Dolichenus: A cult figure derived from Syria, popular along the Rhine–Danube frontier, who combined attributes of Roman, Celtic, and German deities.

Latium Maius: "Latin status," the type of charter possessed by self-governing communities below the rank of colonia and municipum.

Legate: The commander of a legion.

Legion: The primary unit of the Roman army, consisting of some 5,000 infantry and a full range of supporting services.

Lex Coloniae: The municipal rights accorded to an officially established veterans' colony.

Liles: An ancient form of fortification. Holes of about two feet in diameter, sometimes fitted with sharpened stakes and hidden by a sod cover, "lilies" could be effective in breaking up both cavalry and infantry attacks.

Limes: A general term for the complex of forts, camps, colonies, roads, and canals that formed the defensive network of the frontier.

Lindum Colonia: A veterans' colony in England on the site of the modern city of Lincoln.

Lugdunum: The major city of Gaul, located on the Rhone River on the site of the modern city of Lyon. Lugdunum was the headquarters for the pacification of Gaul after its conquest by Julius Caesar.

Marcomanni: A Germanic tribe that inhabited Bohemia. The Marcomanni fought a series of wars against the Romans during the period A.D. 166–180. The name means "frontiersmen."

Maryport: A fort on Hadrian's Wall in Britain.

Minerva: The Roman goddess of household arts, corresponding to the Greek Athena. Among the Roman frontier troops, Minerva was particularly revered by quartermasters, accountants, and stores-keepers.

Mithras: A cult figure of Persian origin. The "Angel of Light," Mithras was always pictured in military garb and was the most popular of the redemptory deities among Roman troops. Mithras's connection with the divine origin of sovereignty gained for his cult a measure of official support.

Moesia: Upper and Lower Moesia were two provinces on the Danube, corresponding to Serbia and northern Bulgaria, respectively.

Moguntiacum: A Roman legionary fortress on the Rhine opposite the confluence of the Main River, on the site of the modern city of Mainz. The headquarters of the army of Upper Germany.

Moravian Gate: A mountain pass between the upper Oder and the Vistula rivers.

Municipium: Except for the *colonia*, the highest rank of self-governing municipality.

Mursa: A Roman city situated on the Drave River near its confluence with the Danube, in what is now southern Hungary.

Mystery Cult: One of a number of redemptory religions that penetrated the Roman world from the East, beginning in republican times. The word "mystery" refers to the sacred initiation through which newcomers became members of the cult. The cults of Mithras, Isis, Orpheus, and Jupiter Dolichenus were among the more popular of these religions. Christianity must be counted as having been one of the mystery cults.

Neptunalia: A festival and games in honor of Neptune, god of the sea, earthquake, and storm.

Nervii: A Celtic tribe, inhabiting the lands along the Scheldt River, in northern France and Belgium.

Nida: A Roman cavalry base east of the Rhine on the site of the modern town of Heddernheim.

Noricum: A Roman Danubian province, corresponding to modern Austria.

Notitia Dignitatum: Preserved in later copies, a document listing the offices and military units of the later Roman Empire, together with their locations. The date of this information is a matter of debate, but probably applies to the period A.D. 375–445.

Novaesium: A legionary fortress on the Rhine at the confluence of the Erft River and on the site of the modern city of Neuss.

Noviomagus: A legionary fortress on the Waal River, on the site of the modern Dutch city of Nijmegen.

Numeri: Units of barbarian troops allowed to retain their native dress and weapons, and to fight under their own commanders.

Ordo: The town council of a self-governing municipality.

Ormazd: The God of Light in Persian religion, opposed by Ahriman, the God of Darkness. Mithras was considered a servant of Ormazd.

Orpheus: A mystery cult figure popular in Asia Minor, related to the progression of the seasons. The regular return of spring was seen as the result of Orpheus's victory over the power of death.

Pagus: The rural lands lying within the jurisdiction of and attached to a *civitas*.

Pannonia: A Roman Danubian province, corresponding to southern Hungary.

Pecuarius: A Roman soldier assigned to caring for military livestock. The term is the direct ancestor of the modern *vaquero*.

Pellionarius: A military furrier, someone who prepared skins for military use.

Picts: A tribe that inhabited Scotland along with the Scots. Hadrian's Wall was built as a barrier against Pictish and Scottish raids.

Piercebridge: A fort on Hadrian's Wall in Britain.

Poetovio: A Roman city on the Drave River in modern Hungary.

Pompey's Theater: A theater that was a major landmark in early imperial Rome. A bust of Pompey stood at the entrance, and it was under this statue that Julius Caesar was assassinated in 44 B.C.

Praetorium: The complex of headquarters buildings located in the center of the Roman camp or fort, facing a parade ground.

Prata: Meadows used for the feeding of stock. Technically, the *prata* were used for the mowing of grass for winter feed, and the *pascua* were lands utilized for grazing.

Principia: The center of a Roman fort or camp, site of the review grounds, *praetorium*, and other command buildings.

Quadi: A Germanic tribe that inhabited the area of modern Moravia and Slovenia.

Quinquatrus of March 18: A traditional military festival, dating from republican times.

Raetia: A Roman province corresponding to modern Switzerland.

Ratiaria: A Roman fortress on the Danube, on the site of the modern city of Arcer, Bulgaria.

Roma: The embodiment of the city of Rome, revered as a deity.

Romanization: The process of the adoption of Roman customs, culture, and institutions by subject peoples.

Rosaliae Signorum: A Roman military festival in which the unit standards were paraded and then decorated with roses.

Sala Magna: Latin for "large room," signifying the main room of a Roman villa. The term *sala magna* is found in many modern European names of places.

Saltus: A rural district administered as if it were a *civitas*.

Samian Ware: A common red pottery also known as *terra sigillata* from the fact that pieces were often stamped with the name of the manufacturer. Samian ware is very useful to the archaeologist in determining the dates of sites, probable routes of trade, and shifts in centers of production.

Saturnalia: A traditional Roman festival with a carnival air, often characterized by licentious and riotous behavior.

Save River: A river rising in modern Croatia and flowing into the Danube at Belgrade in Serbia.

Scots: A Celtic tribe inhabiting the region north of Hadrian's Wall in Britain.

Signifer: A Roman military duty office. The *signifer* carried the unit's standard, and was distinguished by wearing the skin of a wild animal.

Singidunum: A Roman fortress on the Danube, on the site of the modern city of Belgrade in Serbia.

Sirmium: A Roman fort on the Drave River near its confluence with the Danube in modern Serbia.

Siscia: A camp and later a city on the Drave River in modern Serbia.

Sol Invictus: The "Invincible Sun," a cult commemorating the sun's recurrent recovery from its "death" at winter and later associated with the cult of Mithras. The great festival of Sol Invictus was December 25.

Standards: The Roman equivalent of the flags and banners of modern military units. The standards were poles to which various emblems, such as acorns, crescents, and lightning bolts were affixed. Legion standards often bore the effigy of an eagle.

Stonea: An archaeological site in the Cambridgeshire Fenlands, perhaps the location of the agricultural station managing the great imperial estate composed by the Fenlands.

Sueves or Suebi: A German tribe that lived between the Elbe and Oder rivers. The Sueves are recalled in the place-name of Swabia.

Sumelocenna: A Roman camp in Germany, on the site of the modern town of Rottenburg.

Terra Sigillata: Widely used Roman pottery that often bore the name of its maker.

Territoria: A term used for the pastureland maintained by Roman military units.

Thor: The Germanic sky god. Wielding the battle hammer of lightning and sometimes called "Donner," meaning "thunder," Thor was regarded as equivalent to the Roman Jupiter.

Thrace: A Roman province corresponding to what is now southern Bulgaria and European Turkey.

Three Mothers: The *Tria Matronae*, subjects of Celtic worship. A group of three women held in veneration, under various guises, by most of the peoples of ancient Europe. They could be the Roman goddesses Juno, Minerva, and Venus; Peace, Harmony, and Victory; or the Germanic Norns. Macbeth's three witches were a survival of this ancient assemblage.

Toga: A woolen cloth used by the Romans as an outer garment. Donned upon reaching maturity, the toga was worn by Roman men on all public occasions and was regarded by them as the symbol of a civilized society.

Treveri: A Celtic tribe inhabiting what is now the region of Trier in eastern France.

Urbs Roma Aeterna: "The Eternal City of Rome," venerated as a goddess in one of the Roman army's prescribed religious festivals.

Vandals: A Germanic tribe that inhabited the region between Vienna and Budapest in the fourth century A.D. Along with the Sueves and Alans, the Vandals crossed the Rhine in 406 and began the "barbarian" invasions of the Western Roman Empire.

Varangian Route: The eastern route along the rivers of Russia uniting the Baltic and Black seas. Opened by the Swedes in the ninth century, the Varangian was a major trade route between the Byzantine Empire and the North until the beginning of the eleventh century.

Venator: A Roman military duty office. The *venator* was charged with supplying his unit with meat.

Verulamium: A Roman city of England, on the site of the modern city of St. Albans.

Vestalia: The festival of Vesta, a deity representing the Roman family.

Vetera: A legionary fortress on the Rhine opposite the confluence of the Lippe River, on the site of the modern city of Xanten.

Vicus: A small civilian settlement below the rank of city or municipality.

Victoria: The goddess Victory; along with Concordia and Disciplina, the object of official military ritual devotion.

Villa: A Roman country estate; a traditional Roman institution for agricultural exploitation.

Vindobona: A Roman fortress on the Danube, on the site of the modern city of Vienna.

Vindolanda: A fort on Hadrian's Wall in Britain. The site of extensive excavations, Vindolanda has yielded printed material that provides invaluable information on Roman army life.

Vindonissa: A legionary fortress on the site of the modern town of Windisch, near Basel in Switzerland. The fort's rubbish heap has yielded a great amount of archaeological materials.

Visigoths: A Germanic tribe that was allowed to enter the eastern empire and settle lands on the Danube in A.D. 376. Rebelling against Roman authority, they defeated the eastern Roman army at Adrianople in 378.

SELECTED BIBLIOGRAPHY

Primary Sources

Aristides. *Orationes. Opera Quae Exstant Omnia.* Edited by F. W. Lenz and C. A. Behr. Lyon: E. J. Brill, 1976.

Arrian. *Tactica. Flavii Arriani Quae Exstant Omnia.* 2 vols. Edited by A. G. Ross. Leipzig: B. G. Teubner, 1976–1968. Vol. 2.

Caesar, Julius. *War Commentaries: De bello gallico and De bello civili.* Edited and translated by John Warrington. London, Dent; New York, Dutton 1953, 1969 printing.

Corpus Inscriptionum Latinarum. 16 vols. Edited by Theodor Mommsen. Berlin: Walter de Gruyter, 1873.

Cyrian. "Ad Demetriam." In *The Ante-Nicene Fathers. Translations of the Writings of the Fathers Down to A.D. 325.* Edited and translated by Alexander Roberts and James M. Donelson. 6 vols. Grand Rapids: William B. Eerdman's Publishing Company, 1957.

Dionis Cassii Cocceiani Historia romana. 2 vols. Edited by Ludwig Dindorf. Leipsig: B. G. Teubner, 1890–1894. Vol. 2.

Edictum Diocletiani et Collegarum de Pretiis Rerum Venalium. Corpus Inscriptionum Latinarum. 16 vols. Edited by Theodor Mommsen. Berlin: Walter de Gruyter, 1873. Vol. 3.

Gellius. *Noctes Atticae.* Edited by P. K. Marshall. Oxford: Clarendon Press, 1968.

Marcellinus, Ammianus. *Rerum Gestarum Libri Qui Supersunt.* 2 vols. Edited by Wolfgang Seyforth. Leipzig: B. G. Teubner, 1978. Vol. 2.

Notitia Dignitatum Occidentis, Notitia Dignitatum et Administrationum Omnium tam Civilium Quae Militarium in Partibus Orientis et Occidentis. Edited by E. Böcking. Bonn: Adolphi Marci, 1839–1853.

Pliny. *Naturalis Historia.* Edited by H. Rackham. Cambridge, MA: Harvard University Press, 1938.

———. *Epistolae. Epistolae ad Trianum Epistularum Libri Decem.* Edited by R. A. B. Mynoir. Oxford: Clarendon Press, 1963.

Ptolemy. *Geographia. Opera Quae Exstant Omnia.* Edited by J. L. Heilberg. Leipzig: B. G. Teubner, 1998–1919.

Scriptores Historiae Augustae. Edited by E. Hohl. Leipzig: B. G. Teubner, 1965–1971.

Seneca. *De Clementia*. Edited by F. Prechac. Paris: Les Belles Lettres, 1961.

———. *Epistolae*. Edited by L. D. Reynolds. Oxford: Clarendon Press, 1965.

Strabo. *Geographica*. 3 vols. Edited by A. Meineke. Leipzig: B. G. Teubner, 1877–1898. Vol. 1.

Suetonius. *De Vita Caesarum*. Edited by Evelyn S. Schuckburg. New Hork: Arno Press, 1979.

Tacitus. *Germania*. Edited by D. R. Stuart. New York: Macmillan, 1916.

———. *Annales*. Edited by Henry Furneaux. Oxford: Clarendon Press, 1965.

———. *De Vita Agricolae*. Edited by R. M. Ogilvie. Oxford: Clarendon Press, 1967.

———. *Historiae*. Edited by H. Heubner. Stuttgart: B. G. Teubner, 1978.

Secondary Sources

Agache, Roger. *La Somme pre-romaine et romaine: d'après les prospections aeriennes à basse altitude*. Amiens: Société des Antiquaires de Picardie, 1978.

Alföldi, Andràs. "The Moral Barrier on the Rhine and Danube." In *Congress of Roman Frontier Studies. 1949*, edited by Eric Birley. Durham: University of North Carolina Press, 1952.

Alföldy, Geza. *Noricum*. Translated by Anthony Birley. London: Routledge and Kegan Paul, 1974.

Allason-Jones, Lindsay. *Women in Roman Britain*. London: British Museum Publications, 1989.

———. "Roman and Native Interaction in Northumberland." In *Roman Frontier Studies: 1989*, edited by V. A. Maxfield and M. J. Dobson, pp. 1–5. Exeter: University Press, 1991.

Amand, Marcel. "Urban Sites of Roman Origin in Belgium." In *European Towns. Their Archaeology and Early History*, edited by M. W. Barley. New York: Academic Press, 1977.

Ambrus, Victor G. *Horses in Battle*. New York: Oxford: University Press, 1975.

Angus, N. S.; Brown, G. T.; and Cleere, H. F. "The Iron Nails from the Roman Legionary Fortress in Inchtuthil, Perthshire." *Journal of Iron and Steel Industry* 200 (1962):956–968.

Applebaum, S. "Roman Britain." In *The Agrarian History of England and Wales*, edited by H. R. R. Finberg. Cambridge: University Press, 1972.

Aricescu, Andrei. *Armata in Dobrogea Romana*. Translated by Nubar Hampartumian. British Archaeological Reports International Series, 86. Oxford: British Archaeological Reports, 1980.

Arnold, C. J. *Roman Britain to Saxon England*. Bloomington: Indiana University Press, 1984.

Baaty, D. "Research on the Limes of Germania Superior and Raetia 1983–1989." In *Roman Frontier Studies: 1989*, edited by V. A. Maxfield and M. J. Dobson, pp. 175–178. Exeter: University Press, 1991.

Balsdon, John P. V. D. *Romans and Aliens*. Chapel Hill: University of North Carolina Press, 1980.

Barbarians and Romans in Northwest Europe from the Late Republic to Late Antiquity. Edited by John C. Barrett, Andrew Fitzpatrick, and Lesley Macinnes. Oxford: British Archaeological Reports International Series, 471, 1989.

Barnes, T. D. "Who Were the Nobility of the Roman Empire?" *Phoenix* 28 (1974):444–449.

Barrow, R. H. *Slavery in the Roman Empire.* London: Meuthen, 1928.

Baumann, Victor Henrich. *Ferma Romana din Dobrogea.* Tulcea: Muzeul "Deltei Dunarii," 1983.

Behrens, G. *Römische Gläser aus den Rheinlanden.* Berlin: Forschungen und Fortschritte, 1934.

Bichir, Gh. *The Archaeology and History of the Carpi from the Second to the Fourth Century* A.D. British Archaeological Reports Supplementary Series, 16. Oxford: British Archaeological Reports, 1976.

Bidwell, Paul T. *Hadrian's Wall Bridges.* London: Historic Buildings and Monuments Commission for England, 1989.

Birley, Anthony. *The People of Roman Britain.* Berkeley: University of California Press, 1980.

————. "The Economic Effects of Roman Frontier Policy." In *The Roman West in the Third Century,* edited by A. King and M. Henig, pp. 39–54. British Archaeological Reports, S–109. Oxford: 1981.

————. "Vindolanda: New Writing Tablets, 1986–89." In *Roman Frontier Studies 1989,* edited by V. A. Maxfield and M. J. Dobson, pp. 16–20. Exeter: Exeter University Press, 1991.

Birley, Eric. "The Hinterland of Hadrian's Wall." *Durham and Northumberland Transactions* 11 (1958):45–63.

————. *Research on Hadrian's Wall.* Kendall: Titus Wilson and Son, 1961.

————. "Religion of the Roman Army." In *Aufstieg und Niedergang der römischen Welt,* edited by Hildegard Temporini and Wolfgang Haase. 2:16.2. Berlin: Walter de Gruyter, 1975.

————. *The Roman Army: Papers 1929–1986.* Amsterdam: J. C. Gieben, 1988.

Birley, Robin. *Hadrian's Wall.* London: Allen Lane, 1976.

————. *Vindolanda: A Roman Frontier Post on Hadrian's Wall.* London: Thames and Hudson Ltd., 1977.

————. "The Distribution of Equipment in Forts of the First Century A.D." *Studien zur den Militargrenzen Roms 3.* Stuttgart: Kommissionsverlag, Konrad Pheiss Verlag, 1986.

————. *Roman Military Equipment.* N.P.: Princes Risborough, 1989.

————. "Soldiers and Military Equipment in the Towns of Roman Britain." In *Roman Frontier Studies 1989,* edited by V. A. Maxfield and M. J. Dobson, pp. 21–27. Exeter: Exeter University Press, 1991.

Bishop, M. C., ed. *The Production and Distribution of Roman Military Equipment: Proceedings of the Second Roman Military Equipment Research Seminar.* Oxford: British Archaeological Reports, 1985.

Blagg, T. F. C. "Roman Civil and Military Architecture in the Province of Britain: Aspects of Patronage, Influence and Craft Organization." *World Archaeology* 12.1 (1980): 27–42.

————, ed. *Military and Civilian in Roman Britain: Cultural Relationships in a*

Frontier Province. British Archaeological Reports British Series, 136. Oxford: British Archaeological Reports, 1984.

Blockley, Kevin. *Marshfield: Ironmongers Piece Excavations, 1982–3: An Iron Age and Romano-British Settlement in the South Cotswolds*. Oxford: British Archaeological Reports, 1985.

————. *Prestatyn, 1984–5: An Iron Age Farmstead and Romano-British Industrial Settlement in North Wales*. Oxford: British Archaeological Reports, 1989.

Bloemers, J. H. F. "Acculturation in the Rhine/Meuse Basin in the Roman Period: Some Demographical Considerations." In *Barbarians and Romans in North-West Europe*, edited by J. C. Barrett, A. P. Fitzpatrick, and L. Macinnes. Oxford: British Archaeological Reports S–471, 1989.

Boak, A. E. R. *Manpower Shortage and the Fall of the Roman Empire in the West*. Ann Arbor, Michigan: University of Michigan Press, 1955.

Bowen, H. C. "The Celtic Background." In *The Roman Villa in Britain*, edited by A. L. F. Rivet, pp. 1–48. London: Routledge and Kegan Paul, 1969.

Bowman, Alan K. *Vindolanda: The Latin Writing-Tablets*. London: Society for the Promotion of Roman Studies, 1984.

Bowman, Alan K., and Thomas, J. David. *Vindolanda: The Latin Writing-Tablets*. Britannia Monograph 4, 1983.

————. "Vindolanda 1985: The New Writing Tablets." *Journal of Roman Studies* 76 (1986):120–123.

————. "A Military Strength Report from Vindolanda." *Journal of Roman Studies* 31 (1991):62–73.

Bradley, K. R. *Slaves and Masters in the Roman Empire: A Study in Social Control*. Brussels: Latomus, 1984.

Brandt, Roel, and Slofstrar, Jan, eds. *Roman and Native in the Low Countries: Spheres of Interaction*. British Archaeological Reports International Series, 184. Oxford: British Archaeological Reports, 1983.

Branigan, Keith. *Gatcombe: The Excavation and Study of a Romano-British Villa Estate, 1967–1976*. British Archaeological Reports, 44. Oxford: British Archaeological Reports, 1977.

Branigan, K., and Miles, D., eds. *The Economy of Romano-British Villas*. Sheffield: University of Sheffield, 1989.

Braund, David. *Rome and the Friendly King: The Character of the Client Kingship*. New York: St. Martin's, 1984.

————. *The Administration of the Roman Empire: 241 B.C.–A.D. 193*. Exeter: Exeter University Press, 1988.

Breeze, David J. *Hadrian's Wall*. London: Allen Lane, 1976.

————. *The Northern Frontiers of Roman Britain*. London: Batsford Academic and Educational, 1982.

————. "Roman Forces and Native Populations." *Proceedings of the Society of Antiquaries of Scotland* 115 (1985):223–228.

————. "The Impact of the Roman Army in North Britain." In *Barbarians and Romans in North-West Europe*, edited by J. C. Barrett, A. P. Fitzpatrick, and L. Macinnes, pp. 227–234. Oxford: British Archaeological Reports S–471, 1989.

Breeze, David J., and Dobson, Brian. "Fort Types as a Guide to Garrisons: A Reconsideration." In *Roman Frontier Studies: 1969*, edited by Eric Birley, pp. 13–19. Cardiff: University of Wales Press, 1974.

————. "Roman Military Deployment in North England." *Britannia* 16 (1985): 1–19.

Breglia, Laura. *Roman Imperial Coins*. New York: Frederick A. Praeger, 1968.

British Archaeological Reports. *Armies and Frontiers in Roman and Byzantine Anatolia: Proceedings of a Colloquium Held at University College, Swansea, in April 1981*. British Archaeological Reports International Series, 156. Oxford: British Archaeological Reports, 1983.

Brodribb, Gerald. *Roman Brick and Tile*. Gloucester: Sutton, 1987.

Brogan, Olwen. "Trade between the Roman Empire and the Free Germans." *Journal of Roman Studies* 26 (1936):196–223.

Brunt, P. A. "Conscription and Volunteering in the Roman Imperial Army." *Scripta Classica Israelica* 1 (1974):110.

Buckland, William W. *The Roman Law of Slavery: The Condition of the Slave in Private Law from Augustus to Justinian*. New York: AMS Press, 1969.

Burke, John F. *Roman England*. New York: W. W. Norton, 1984.

Campbell, Brian. "The Marriage of Soldiers under the Empire." *Journal of Roman Studies* 68 (1978):153–166.

Campbell, J. B. "Roman Legionaries at Corbridge, Their Supply-Base, Temples, and Religious Cults." *Archaeological Aeliana* 21 (1943):127–223.

————. *Roman Britain*. London: Jonathan Cape, 1963.

————. "Roman Body Armour in the First Century A.D." In *Congress of Roman Frontier Studies:1969*, edited by Eric Birley. Cardiff: University of Wales Press, 1974.

————. *The Emperor and the Roman Army, 31 B.C.–A.D. 235*. Oxford: Clarendon Press, 1984.

Casson, Lionel. *Ancient Trade and Society*. Detroit: Wayne State University Press, 1984.

Cataniciu, I. B. *Evolution of the Defensive Works in Roman Dacia*. Oxford: British Archaeological Reports Supplementary Series 116, 1981.

Centre National de la Recherche Scientifique. *Armées et fiscalité dans le monde antique: Actes du Colloque National. Paris, 14–16 octobre 1976*. Paris: Editions du Centre National de la Recherche Scientifique, 1977.

————. *Mines et fonderies antiques de la Gaule: Université de Toulouse-Le Mirail, 21–22 novembre 1980: table ronde du CNRS*. Paris: Editions du CNRS, 1982.

Charlesworth, M. P. "The Provisioning of Roman Forts." *Cumberland and Westmorland Antiquarian and Archaeological Society* 20 (1920): 141.

————. *Trade-Routes and Commerce in the Roman Empire*. New York: Square Publishers, 1979.

Cheesman, George L. *The Auxilia of the Roman Imperial Army*. Rome: "L'Erma" di Bretschneider, 1968.

Chilver, Guy Edward Farquhar. *A Historical Commentary on Tacitus' Histories I and II*. New York: Oxford: University Press, 1979.

————. *A Historical Commentary on Tacitus' Histories IV and V*. New York: Oxford: University Press, 1985.

Cichorius, Conrad. *Trajan's Column: A New Edition of the Cichorius Plates*. Edited by Frank Lepper and Sheppard Frere. Gloucester: Alan Sutton, 1988.

Clack, P. A. G. "The Northern Frontier: Farmers in the Military Zone." In *The

Romano-British Countryside: Studies in Rural Settlement and Economy. Edited by D. Miles, pp. 377–402. Oxford: British Archaeological Report 103, 1982.

Collingwood, R. G., and Richmond, Ian A. *The Archaeology of Roman Britain.* London: Methuen, 1969.

Connolly, Peter. *Greece and Rome at War.* Englewood Cliffs, NJ: Prentice Hall, 1981.

Coulston, J. C. *Hadrian's Wall West of the North Tyne and Carlisle.* Oxford: Published for the British Academy by the Oxford University Press, c. 1988.

Cunliffe, Barry. *Greeks, Romans and Barbarians: Spheres of Interaction.* London: Batsford, 1988.

Daniels, C. M. "The Role of the Roman Army in the Spread and Practice of Mithraism." *Mithraic Studies: Proceedings of the First International Congress of Mithraic Studies.* Vol. 2. Manchester: Manchester University Press, 1975.

————. "The Flavian and Trajanic Northern Frontier." In *Research on Roman Britain 1960–89,* edited by M. Todd. Britannia Monograph 11, 1989.

D'Arms, John H. *Commerce and Social Standing in Ancient Rome.* Cambridge, MA: Harvard University Press, 1981.

D'Arms, John H., and Kopff, E. C., eds. *The Seaborne Commerce of Ancient Rome.* Rome: American Academy in Rome, 1980.

Darvil, T., and McWhirr, A. "Brick and Tile Production in Roman Britain." *World Archaeology* 15 (1984):239–261.

Dauge, Yves Albert. *Le Barbare: recherches sur la conception romaine de la barbarie et de la civilisation.* Brussels: Latomus, 1981.

Davies, Oliver. *Roman Mines in Europe.* Oxford: Clarendon Press, 1965.

Davies, Roy W. "Social and Economic Aspects." In *The Roman Villa in Britain.* Edited by A. L. F. Rivet, pp. 173–216. London: Routledge and Kegan Paul, 1969.

————. "The Supply of Animals to the Roman Army and the Remount System." *Latomus* 28 (1969):429–453.

————. *Service in the Roman Army.* Edinburgh: Edinburgh University Press with the Publications Board of the University of Durham, c. 1989.

Davison, David P. *The Barracks of the Roman Army from the 1st to 3rd Centuries A.D.: A Comparative Study of the Barracks from Fortresses, Forts, and Fortlets with an Analysis of Building Types and Construction, Stabling, and Garrisons.* Oxford: British Archaeological Reports, 1989.

Dickinson, B. M., and Hartley, K. F. "The Evidence of Potters' Stamps on Samian Ware and on the Mortaria for the Trading Connections of Roman York." In *Soldier and Civilian in Roman Yorkshire,* edited by R. M. Butler. Leicester: University Press, 1971.

Die Römer an Mosel und Saar: Zeugnisse der Römerzeit in Lothringen, in Luxemburg, im Raum Trier und im Saarland, edited by Heinz Cuppers. Mainz: P. von Zabern, c. 1983.

Divine, David. *Hadrian's Britain: A Study of the North-West Frontier of Rome.* Boston: Gambit, 1969.

Dobson, B. "The Function of Hadrian's Wall." *Archaeologia Aeliana.* 5th Series. 14 (1986):1–30.

Dornberg, John. "Battle of the Teutoberg Forest." *Archaeology* 45/5 (September/October 1992):26–32.

Drinkwater, J. F. "A Note on Local Careers in the Three Gauls under the Empire." *Britannia* 10 (1979):89–100.

———. *Roman Gaul: The Three Provinces, 58 B.C.–A.D. 260.* Ithaca, NY: Cornell University Press, 1983.

Duncan-Jones, Richard. *The Economy of the Roman Empire: Quantitative Studies.* 2d ed. Cambridge: Cambridge University Press, 1982.

Durant, G. M. *Britain, Rome's Most Northerly Province.* New York: St. Martin's, 1969.

Dusanic, S. "Aspects of Roman Mining in Noricum, Pannonia, Dalmatia and Moesia Superior." *Aufstieg und Niedergang der römischen Welt* 2.6 (1977).

Duval, Paul Marie. *La Vie quotidienne en Gaule pendant la paix romaine (Ier–IIe siècles après J.-C.).* Paris: Hachette, 1977.

Dyson, Stephen L. *The Creation of the Roman Frontier.* Princeton, NJ: Princeton University Press, 1985.

Ebel, Charles. *Transalpine Gaul: The Emergence of a Roman Province.* Leiden: E. J. Brill, 1976.

Eckoldt, M. "Navigation on Small Rivers in Central Europe in Roman and Medieval Times." *International Journal of Nautical Archaeology* 13 (1984):3–10.

Edmondson, J. C. *Two Industries in Roman Lusitania: Mining and Garum Production.* British Archaeological Reports International Series, 362. Oxford: British Archaeological Reports, 1987.

———. "Mining in the Later Roman Empire and Beyond: Continuity or Disruption?" *Journal of Roman Studies* 79 (1989):84–102.

Elbe, Joachim von. *Roman Germany: A Guide to Sites and Museums.* Mainz: P. von Zabern, 1977.

Elkington, H. D. H. "The Mendip Lead Industry." In *The Roman West Country*, edited by Keith Branigan and P. J. Fowler. London: David and Charles, 1976.

Evans, Robert F. *Soldiers of Rome: Praetorians and Legionaires.* Cabin John, MD: Seven Locks Press, 1986.

Fentress, Elizabeth W. B. *Numidia and the Roman Army: Social, Military and Economic Aspects of the Frontier Zone.* British Archaeological Reports International Series, 53. Oxford: British Archaeological Reports, 1979.

Ferrill, Arther. *The Fall of the Roman Empire: The Military Explanation.* London: Thames and Hudson, 1986.

Fink, Robert O.; Hoey, Allan S.; and Snyder, Walter F. "The Feriale Duranum." *Yale Classical Studies.* Vol. 7. New Haven: Yale University Press, 1940.

———. *The Climax of Rome.* New York: New American Library, 1968.

Finley, M. I. "Technical Innovation and Economic Progress in the Ancient World." *Economic History Review.* 2d Series. 8 (August 1965):37.

———. *The Ancient Economy.* 2d ed. London: Hogarth, 1985.

Fischer, Ulrich. "Frankfurt–Heddernheim: A Roman Frontier Town beyond the Rhine." *Archaeology* 14 (1961):36–44.

———. "Verulamium and the Towns of Britannia." In *Aufstieg und Niedergang der römischen Welt*, edited by Hildegard Temporini and Wolfgang Haase, 2.2:290–327. Berlin and New York: Walter de Gruyter, 1975.

Fishwick, Duncan. *The Imperial Cult in the Latin West: Studies in the Ruler Cult of the Western Provinces of the Roman Empire.* Leiden: E. J. Brill, 1987.

Fitz, Jeno. *Honorific Titles of Roman Military Units in the 3rd Century.* Trans.

Maria Baranyai. Budapest: Akademiai Kiado; Bonn: Habelt, 1983.

Forbes, R. J. *Studies in Ancient Technology.* 8 vols. Leiden: E. J. Brill, 1966.

Forde-Johnston, James L. *Hadrian's Wall.* London: Joseph, 1978.

Frank, Tenny. *An Economic History of Rome.* Baltimore, MD: John Hopkins Press, 1927.

Frayn, Joan M. *Sheep-rearing and the Wool Trade in Italy during the Roman Period.* Liverpool: F. Cairns, 1984.

Fremersdorf, Fritz. *Von Römischen Gläsern Kölns.* Berlin: J. Springer, 1942.

Frere, Sheppard Sunderland. *Britannia: A History of Roman Britain.* Cambridge, MA: Harvard University Press, 1967.

Fulford, Michael G. *New Forest Roman Pottery: Manufacture and Distribution, with a Corpus of the Pottery Types.* British Archaeological Reports, 17. Oxford: British Archaeological Reports, 1975.

Gàge, Jean. *Recherches sur les Jeux séculaires.* Paris, 1934.

Gaitzsch, Wolfgang. *Eiserne römische Werkzeuge: Studien zur römischen Werkzeugkunde in Italien und den nordlichen Provinzen des Imperium Romanum.* British Archaeological Reports International Series, 78. Oxford: British Archaeological Reports, 1980.

Garnsey, Peter. "Septimius Severus and the Marriage of Roman Soldiers." *California Studies in Classical Antiquity* 3 (1970): 45.

Genser, Kurt. *Der österreichische Donaulimes in der Römerzeit: ein Forschungsbericht.* Vienna: Verlag der Osterreichischen Akademie der Wissenschaften, 1986.

Gentry, Anne P. *Roman Military Stone-built Granaries in Britain.* British Archaeological Reports, 32. Oxford: British Archaeological Reports, 1976.

Gilliam, J. F. *Roman Army Papers.* Amsterdam: J. C. Gieben, 1986.

Glodariu, Ioan. *Dacian Trade with the Hellenistic and Roman World.* British Archaeological Reports Supplementary Series, 8. Oxford: British Archaeological Reports, 1976.

Gottlieb, Gunther. *Das römische Augsburg: historische und methodische Probleme einer Stadtgeschichte.* Munich: Vogel, 1981.

Grant, Michael. *The Roman Citizenship.* Oxford: Clarendon Press, 1939.

———. *The Army of the Caesars.* New York: Scribner, 1974.

Green, Miranda J. *The Wheel as a Cult-Symbol in the Romano-Celtic World: With Special Reference to Gaul and Britain.* Brussels: Latomus, 1984.

Green, Stanton W., and Perlman, Stephen M., eds. *The Archaeology of Frontiers and Boundaries.* Orlando, FL: Academic Press, 1985.

Greene, Kevin, "Perspectives on Roman Technology." Oxford: *Journal of Archaeology* 9.2 (1990):209–219.

Griffin, Miriam T. *Seneca: A Philosopher in Politics.* Oxford: Clarendon Press, 1975.

Grimal, Pierre. *Roman Cities.* Translated and edited by G. Michael Woloch. Madison: University of Wisconsin Press, 1983.

Hall, David. "Survey Results in the Cambridgeshire Fenlands." *Antiquity* 62 (June 1988): 311–314.

Hammond, Mason. "Composition of the Senate, A.D. 68–235." *Journal of Roman Studies* 47 (1957):74–81.

Hanson, W. S., and Keppie, L. J. F. *Roman Frontier Studies: 1979.* Oxford: British Archaeological Reports International Series, 71. Oxford: British Archaeological Reports, 1980.

Hanson, William, and Maxwell, Gordon. *Rome's Northwest Frontier: The Antonine Wall*. New York: Columbia University Press, 1983.

Harl, Ortolf. *Vindobona, das römische Wien*. Vienna: P. Zsolnay, 1979.

Harris, Eve. *The Oriental Cults in Roman Britain*. Leiden: E. J. Brill, 1965.

Harris, W. V. "Roman Terracotta Lamps: The Organization of an Industry." *Journal of Roman Studies* 70 (1980):126–145.

Hassall, M. "The Internal Planning of Roman Auxiliary Forts." In *Rome and Her Northern Provinces*, edited by B. R. Hartley and J. S. Wacher, p. 99. Gloucester: A. Sutton, 1983.

Haversath, Johann-Bernhard. *Die Agrarlandschaft im römischen Deutschland der Kaiserzeit (1.–4. Jh. n. Chr.)*. Passau: Passavia Universitätsverlag, 1984.

Hawkes, Charles F. *Greeks, Celts, and Romans: Studies in Venture and Resistance*. Edited by Christopher and Sonia Hawkes. London: Dent, 1973.

Healey, J. F. *Mining and Metallurgy in the Greek and Roman World*. London: Thames and Hudson, 1978.

Helgeland, John. "Roman Army Religion." In *Aufsteig und Niedergang der römischen Welt*, edited by Hildegard Temporini and Wolfgang Haase, 2.2:1477. Berlin and New York: Walter de Gruyter, 1975.

Henig, Martin. *Religion in Roman Britain*. New York: St. Martin's, 1984.

Henig, Martin, and King, Anthony, eds. *Pagan Gods and Shrines of the Roman Empire*. Oxford: University Committee for Archaeology, Institute of Archaeology, 1986.

Higham, N. J., and Jones, G. D. B. "Frontier, Forts, and Farmers." *Archaeological Journal* 132 (1975):16–28.

Hingley, Richard. *Rural Settlement in Roman Britain*. London: B. A. Seaby, 1989.

Hoddinott, Ralph F. *Bulgaria in Antiquity: An Archaeological Introduction*. New York: St. Martin's, 1975.

Hodge, Peter. *Roman Trade and Travel*. London: Longman, 1978.

Hoey, Allan S. "Official Policy towards Oriental Cults in the Roman Army." *Transactions of the American Philological Association* 70 (1939):456–481.

Holder, P. A. *Studies in the Auxilia of the Roman Army from Augustus to Trajan*. British Archaeological Reports International Series, 70. Oxford: British Archaeological Reports, 1980.

———. *The Roman Army in Britain*. London: B. T. Batsford, 1982.

Hopkins, Keith. "Roman Army and Roman Religion." *Bulletin of the John Rylands Library* 45 (September 1962):185–197.

———. "The Roman Fenland." In *The Fenland in Roman Times. Studies of a Major Area of Peasant Colonization*, edited by C. W. Phillips. London: Royal Geographical Society, 1970.

———. *Conquerors and Slaves*. Cambridge: Cambridge University Press, 1978.

———. "Economic Growth in Towns in Classical Antiquity." In *Towns in Societies*, edited by Philip Abrams and E. A. Wrigley. Cambridge and New York: Cambridge University Press, 1978.

———. "Taxes and Trade in the Roman Empire (200 B.C.–A.D. 400)." *Journal of Roman Studies* 70 (1980):101–125.

Humphrey, J. *Roman Circuses: Arenas for Chariot Racing*. London: Batsford, 1986.

Hurst, H. "Gloucester (Glevum): A Colonia in the West Country." In *The Roman*

West Country, edited by Keith Branigan and P. J. Fowler. London: David and Charles, 1976.

Hyland, Ann. *Equus: The Horse in the Roman World.* New Haven, CT: Yale University Press, 1990.

Isaac, Benjamin. "The Meaning of the Terms Limes and Limitanei." *Journal of Roman Studies* 78 (1988):125–147.

Jennison, George. *Animals for Show and Pleasure in Ancient Rome.* New York: Barnes and Noble, 1937.

Johnson, Anne. *Roman Forts of the First and Second Centuries* A.D. *in Britain and the German Provinces.* London: A. and C. Black, 1983.

Johnson, Stephen. *Later Roman Britain.* New York: Scribner, 1980.

Johnston, David E. *An Illustrated History of Roman Roads in Britain.* Bourne End: Spurbooks, 1979.

Jones, A. H. M. "The Cloth Industry under the Roman Empire." *Economic History Review* 13 (December 1960): 185.

Jones, G. D. B. "The Emergence of the Tyne–Solway Frontier." In *Roman Frontier Studies: 1989,* edited by V. A. Maxfield and M. J. Dobson, pp. 98–107. Exeter: Exeter University Press, 1991.

Jones, Michael J. *Roman Fort-Defences to* A.D. *117 with Special Reference to Britain.* British Archaeological Reports, 21. Oxford: British Archaeological Reports, 1975.

Kahrstadt, U. "The Roman Frontier on the Lower Rhine in the Early Imperial Period." In *Congress of Roman Frontier Studies. 1949,* edited by Eric Birley. Durham, NC: University of North Carolina Press, 1952.

Keppie, L. J. F. *The Making of the Roman Army: From Republic to Empire.* London: B. T. Batsford, 1984.

King, Anthony, and Henig, Martin, eds. *The Roman West in the Third Century: Contributions from Archaeology and History.* British Archaeological Reports International Series, 109. Oxford: British Archaeological Reports, 1981.

King, C. E., ed. *Imperial Revenue, Expenditure and Monetary Policy in the Fourth Century* A.D.*: The Fifth Oxford Symposium on Coinage and Monetary History.* British Archaeological Reports International Series, 76. Oxford: British Archaeological Reports, 1980.

Kirschenbaum, Aaron. *Sons, Slaves, and Freedmen in Roman Commerce.* Jerusalem: Magnes Press, Hebrew University, 1987.

Kornemann, E. "Concilium." *Pauly-Wissowa Real-Encyclopädie.* Vol. 14. Stuttgart: J. B. Metzlersche Buchdruckerei, 1930.

Kraskovska, L. *Roman Bronze Vessels from Slovakia.* British Archaeological Reports International Series, 44. Oxford: British Archaeological Reports, 1978.

Kunow, Jurgen. *Der römische Import in der Germania libera bis zu den Markomannenkriegen: Studien zu Bronze- und Glasgefassen.* Neumunster: K. Wachholtz, 1983.

Landels, J. G. *Engineering in the Ancient World.* Berkeley: University of California Press, 1981.

Lander, James. *Roman Stone Fortifications: Variation and Change from the First Century* A.D. *to the Fourth.* Oxford: British Archaeological Reports, 1984.

Lengyel, A., and Radan, G. T. B., eds. *The Archaeology of Roman Pannonia.*

Lexington: University Press of Kentucky, c. 1980; Budapest: Akademiai Kiado, c. 1980.

Le Roux, Patrick. *L'Armée romaine et l'organisation des provinces iberiques d'Auguste à l'invasion de 409*. Paris: Boccard, 1982.

Liebeschuetz, J. H. W. G. *Continuity and Change in Roman Religion*. Oxford: Oxford University Press, 1979.

Luttwak, Edward. *The Grand Strategy of the Roman Empire from the First Century A.D. to the Third*. Baltimore, MD: Johns Hopkins University Press, 1976.

MacAdam, Henry Innes. *Studies in the History of the Roman Province of Arabia: The Northern Sector*. British Archaeological Reports International Series, 295. Oxford: British Archaeological Reports, 1986.

Macinnes, L. "Baubles, Bangles and Beads: Trade and Exchange in Roman Scotland." In *Barbarians and Romans in North-West Europe*, edited by J. C. Barrett, A. P. Fitzpatrick, and L. Macinnes., pp. 108–116. Oxford: British Archaeological Reports S–471, 1989.

McIntyre, James, and Richmond, Ian A. "Tents of the Roman Army and Leather from Birdoswald." *Cumberland and Westmorland Antiquarian and Archaeological Society* 34 (1943):63.

Mackendrick, Paul. "Roman Town Planning." *Archaeology* 9 (1956):126–133.

MacMullen, Ramsay. *Enemies of the Roman Order: Treason, Unrest, and Alienation in the Empire*. Cambridge: Harvard University Press, 1967.

————. *Pagans in the Roman Empire*. New Haven, CT: Yale University Press, 1981.

————. *Roman Social Relations: 50 B.C. to A.D. 284*. New Haven, CT: Yale University Press, 1981.

————. "The Legion as a Society." *Historia* 33 (1984) 4:440–456.

McWhirr, Alan, ed. *Roman Brick and Tile: Studies in Manufacture, Distribution and Use in the Western Empire*. British Archaeological Reports International Series, 68. Oxford: British Archaeological Reports, 1979.

Maloney, John, and Hobley, Brian, eds. *Roman Urban Defences in the West: A Review of Current Research on Urban Defences in the Roman Empire with Special Reference to the Northern Provinces, Based on Papers Presented to the Conference on Roman Urban Defences Held at the Museum of London on 21–23 March 1980*. London: Council for British Archaeology, 1983.

Mann, J. C. "A Note on the Numeri." *Hermes* 82 (1954):501–504.

————. *Legionary Recruitment and Veteran Settlement during the Principate*. Edited by M. M. Roxan. London: Institute of Archaeology, 1983.

Marsden, Eric William. *Greek and Roman Artillery: Historical Development*. Oxford: Clarendon Press, 1971.

Marsden, Peter. *The Roman Forum Site in London: Discoveries before 1985*. London: HMSO for the British Museum of London, 1987.

Mason, D. J. P. "Chester: The Canabae Legionis." *Britannia* 18 (1987):143–168.

————. "The Roman Site at Heronbridge; near Chester, Cheshire; Aspects of Civilian Settlement in the Vicinity of Legionary Fortresses in Britain and Beyond." *Archaeological Journal* 145 (1988):123–157.

Mattingly, Harold. *Roman Coins from the Earliest Times to the Fall of the Western Empire*. London: Meuthen, 1967.

Maxfield, V. A. *The Military Decorations of the Roman Army*. Berkeley: University of California Press, 1981.

———. "Pre-Flavian Forts and Their Garrisons," *Britannia* 17 (1986):59–72.

Maxfield, V. A., and Dobson, M. J., eds. *Roman Frontier Studies: 1989*. Exeter: University Press, 1991.

Maxwell, G. S. *The Romans in Scotland*. Edinburgh: J. Thin, 1989.

Meiggs, Russell. *Trees and Timber in the Ancient Mediterranean World*. Oxford: Clarendon Press, 1982.

Merrifield, Ralph. *London: City of the Romans*. Berkeley: University of California Press, 1983.

Mertens, J. "The Military Origin of Some Roman Settlements in Belgium." In *Rome and Her Northern Provinces*, edited by Brian Hartley and John Wacher, pp. 40, 155–168. Gloucester: Alan Sutton, 1983.

Middleton, P. "Army Supply in Roman Gaul." In *Invasion and Response*, edited by B. L. Burnham and H. B. Johnson, pp. 81–98. Oxford: British Archaeological Reports, 1979.

———. "La Graufesenque: A Question of Marketing." *Athenaeum* 58 (1980): 186–191.

Mielsch, Harald. *Die römische Villa: Architektur und Lebensform*. Munich: C. H. Beck, c. 1987.

Miles, David. *The Romano British Countryside*. British Archaeological Reports, 102. Oxford: British Archaeological Reports, 1982.

Millar, Fergus. *The Roman Empire and its Neighbours*. 2d ed. London: Duckworth, 1981.

Miller, David Harry, et al., eds. *The Frontier: Comparative Studies*. Norman: University of Oklahoma Press, 1977–.

Millett, Martin, *The Romanization of Britain: An Essay in Archaeological Interpretation*. Cambridge and New York: Cambridge University Press, 1990.

Milne, Gustav. *The Port of Roman London*. London: B. T. Batsford, 1985.

Mócsy, Andrés. *Pannonia and Upper Moesia: A History of the Middle Danube Provinces of the Roman Empire*. London: Routledge and Kegan Paul, 1974.

Moeller, Walter O. *The Mithraic Origin and Meanings of the Rotas–Sator Square*. Leiden: E. J. Brill, 1973.

Mommsen, Theodor. *The Provinces of the Roman Empire*, edited by T. Robert and S. Broughton. Chicago: Unviersity of Chicago Press, 1968.

Morris, Pat. *Agricultural Buildings in Roman Britain*. Oxford: British Archaeological Reports, 1979.

Mosci Sassi, Maria Grazia. *Il sermo castrensis*. Bologna: Pàtron, 1983.

Najdenova, V. "Thracian Paganism and Roman Religion on the Lower Danubian Limes." In *Roman Frontier Studies: 1989*, edited by V. A. Maxfield and M. J. Dobson, pp. 291–294. Exeter: Exeter University Press, 1991.

Niblett, Rosalind. *Sheepen: An Early Roman Industrial Site at Camulodunum*. London: Council for British Archaeology, 1985.

Nock, Arthur D. "The Roman Army and the Religious Year." *Harvard Theological Review* 45 (October 1952):187–252.

Norling-Christensen, Hans. "Danish Imports of Roman and Roman Provincial Objects in Bronze and Glass." In *Congress of Roman Frontier Studies: 1949*, edited by Eric Birley. Durham: University of North Carolina Press, 1952.

Okun, Marcia L. "An Example of the Process of Acculturation in the Early Roman Frontier." *Journal of Archaeology* 8 (1989):41–54.

Oldenstein, J. "Manufacture and Supply of the Roman Army with Bronze Fittings." In *The Production and Distribution of Roman Military Equipment*, edited by M. C. Bishop, pp. 82–94. Oxford: British Archaeological Reports, S–275, 1985.

Painter, K. S. "Gold and Silver in the Roman World." In *Aspects of Early Metallurgy*, edited by W. A. Oddy, pp. 135–158. 2d ed. London: The Historical Metallurgy Society and British Museum Research Laboratory, 1980.

Parker, H. M. D. *The Roman Legions.* Cambridge: W. Heffer and Sons, 1958.

Parker, S. Thomas. *Romans and Saracens: A History of the Arabian Frontier.* Philadelphia: American Schools of Oriental Research; Winona Lake, IN: Distributed by Eisenbrauns, 1986.

Peacock, D. P. S. "Roman Shipping and Trade: Britain and the Rhine Provinces." In *The Council for British Archaeology Research Report* 24 (1978):49. Edited by J. du Plat Taylor and H. Cleere.

Percival, John. *The Roman Villa: An Historical Introduction.* London: B. T. Batsford, 1976.

Petit, Paul. *Pax Romana.* Berkeley: University of California Press, 1976.

Pflaum, Hans-Georg, comp. *Gaule et empire romain.* Paris: Editions l'Harmattan, 1981.

Phillips, Edward J. *Corbridge: Hadrian's Wall East of the North Tyne.* Oxford: Published for the British Academy by the Oxford University Press, 1977.

Pippidi, M., ed. *Assimilation et resistance à la culture greco-romaine dans le monde ancien: travaux du VI-e Congrès International d'Etudes Classiques (Madrid, septembre 1974).* Sixth International Congress of Classical Studies. Madrid, 1974. Bucharest: Editura Academiei; Paris: "Les Belles Lettres," 1976.

Pitts, Lynn F. "Relations between Rome and the Germanic 'Kings' on the Middle Danube in the First to Fourth Centuries A.D." *Journal of Roman Studies* 79 (1989): 45–58.

Popa, Alexaru. *Le Culte de Jupiter Dolichenus dans la Dacie romaine.* Leiden: E. J. Brill, 1978.

Potter, Timothy W. *Romans in North-West England: Excavations at the Roman Forts of Ravenglass, Watercrook and Bowness on Solway.* (sine loca.) Cumberland and Westmorland Antiquarian and Archaeological Society, c. 1979.

———. *Roman Britain.* Cambridge, MA: Harvard University Press, 1983.

Potter, T. W., and Jackson, R. P. J. "The Roman Site of Stonea, Cambridgeshire." *Antiquity* 56 (July 1982):111–120.

Preston, Richard Arthur. *Men in Arms: A History of Warfare and its Interrelationships with Western Society.* 4th ed. New York: Holt, Rinehart, and Winston, 1979.

Ramin, J. *La Technique miniere et metallurgique des anciens.* Brussels: Latomus, 1977.

Randsborg, Klaus, ed. *The Birth of Europe: Archaeology and Social Development in the First Millennium B.C.* Rome: "L'Erma" di Bretschneider for Accademia di Danimarca, 1989.

———. *The First Millennium A.D. in Europe and the Mediterranean: An*

Archaeological Essay. Cambridge and New York: Cambridge University Press, 1991.

Rees, Sian E. *Agricultural Implements in Prehistoric and Roman Britain.* British Archaeological Reports British Series, 69. Oxford: British Archaeological Reports, 1979.

Richardson, J. S. "Imperium Romanum: Empire and the Language of Power." *Journal of Roman Studies* 81 (1991):1–9.

Richmond, Ian A. "Hadrian's Wall, 1939–1949." *Journal of Roman Studies* 40 (1950):43–56.

———. *Roman Britain.* Baltimore, MD: Penguin, 1955.

———. *Trajan's Army on Trajan's Column.* London: British School at Rome, 1982.

Rickman, Geoffrey. *Roman Granaries and Store Buildings.* Cambridge: Cambridge University Press, 1971.

———. *The Corn Supply of Ancient Rome.* Oxford: Clarendon Press, 1980.

Ristow, Gunter. *Mithras im römischen Köln.* Leiden: E. J. Brill, 1974.

Rivet, A. L. F. "South Shields Roman Fort." *Archaeological Journal* 111 (1954): 209.

———. "The Rural Economy of Roman Britain." In *Aufsteig und Niedergang der römischen Welt,* edited by Hildegard Temporini and Wolfgang Haase, 2.3:328–363. Berlin and New York: Walter de Gruyter, 1975.

Robertson, Anne. "Bar Hill: A Roman Fort and Its Finds." *British Archaeological Report* 16 (1975):10.

———. "Race Relations in the Early Roman Empire." In *Aufsteig und Niedergang der römischen Welt,* edited by Hidegard Temporini and Wolfgang Haase, 2.3:112–137. Berlin and New York: Walter de Gruyter, 1975.

Robinson, H. Russell. *The Armour of Imperial Rome.* New York: Charles Scribner and Sons, 1975.

Roldán Hervas, José Manuel. *Hispania y el ejército Romano. Contribución a la historia social de la España antigua.* Salamanca: University of Salamanca, 1974.

Roman, Yves. *De Narbonne Bordeaux: un axe economique au Ier siècle avant J.-C.: (125 av. J.-C.–14 ap. J.-C.).* Lyon: Presses Universitaires de Lyon, 1983.

Röring, Christoph Wilhelm. *Untersuchungen zu römischen Reisewagen.* Koblenz: Numismatischer Verlag G.M. Forneck, 1983.

Rossi, Lino. *Trajan's Column and the Dacian Wars.* Trans. J. M. C. Toynbee. London: Thames and Hudson, 1971.

Rostovtzeff, M. *Social and Economic History of the Roman Empire.* 2d ed. 2 vols. Oxford: Clarendon Press, 1957. Vol. 1.

Rowell, H. T. "Numerus." *Pauly-Wissowa Real-Encyclopädie.* Vol. 17. Stuttgart: J. B. Metzlersche Buchdruckerei, 1930.

Roxan, M. M. *Roman Military Diplomas, 1978–84.* Occasional Pub. No. 9. London: Institute of Archaeology, 1985.

———. "Women on the Frontiers." In *Roman Frontier Studies: 1989,* edited by V. A. Maxfield and M. J. Dobson, pp. 462–467. Exeter: Exeter University Press, 1991.

Saddington, D. B. "The Development of the Roman Auxiliary Forces from Augustus to Trajan." In *Aufsteig und Niedergang der römischen Welt,* edited by

Hildegard Temporini and Wolfgang Haase, 2.3:176–201. Berlin and New York: Walter de Gruyter, 1975.

———. *The Development of the Roman Auxiliary Forces from Caesar to Vespasian (49 B.C.–A.D. 79)*. Harare: University of Zimbabwe, 1982.

———. "The Parameters of Romanization." In *Roman Frontier Studies: 1989*, edited by V. A. Maxfield and M. J. Dobson, pp. 413–418. Exeter: Exeter University Press, 1991.

Sakar, V. "Roman Imports in Bohemia." *Fontes Archaeologici Pragenses* 14 (1970).

Salmon, Pierre. *Population et depopulation dans l'Empire Romain*. Brussels: Latomus, 1974.

Salway, Peter. *The Frontier People of Roman Britain*. Cambridge: Cambridge University Press, 1965.

———. "The Roman Fenland." In *Roman Times: Studies of a Major Area of Peasant Colonization*, edited by C. W. Phillips. London: Royal Geographical Society, 1970.

———. *Roman Britain*. New York: Oxford: Oxford University Press, 1981.

Schlippschuh, Otto. *Die Händler im römischen Kaiserreich in Gallien, Germanien und den Donauprovinzen Ration, Noricum und Pannonien*. Amsterdam: Hakkert, 1974.

Schon, Franz. *Der Beginn der römischen Herrschaft in Ratien*. Sigmaringen: J. Thorbecke, 1986.

Schonberger, H. "The Roman Frontier in Germany: An Archaeological Survey." *Journal of Roman Studies* 59 (1969):149–170.

Schutz, Herbert. *The Romans in Central Europe*. New Haven, CT: Yale University Press, 1985.

Schwertheim, Elmar. *Die Denkmaler orientalischer Gottheiten in römischen Deutschland: mit Ausnahme der agyptischen Gottheiten*. Leiden: E. J. Brill, 1974.

Scorpan, Constantin. *Limes Scythiae: Topographical and Stratigraphical Research on the Late Roman Fortifications on the Lower Danube*. British Archaeological Reports International Series, 88. Oxford: British Archaeological Reports, 1980.

Scullard, H. H. *Roman Britain: Outpost of the Empire*. London: Thames and Hudson, 1979, 1986.

Sedgley, Jeffrey P. *The Roman Milestones of Britain: Their Petrography and Probable Origin*. British Archaeological Reports, 18. Oxford: British Archaeological Reports, 1975.

Sharpe, Margaret E. "Roman and Native: Vici on the North British Frontier." In *Roman Frontier Studies 1989*, edited by V. A. Maxfield and M. J. Dobson. Exeter: University Press, 1991.

Shchukin, Mark B. *Rome and the Barbarians in Central and Eastern Europe: First Century B.C.–First Century A.D.* Oxford: British Archaeological Reports International Series S–542, 1989.

Sherwin-White, A. N. *Racial Prejudice in Imperial Rome*. Cambridge: Cambridge University Press, 1967.

———. *The Roman Citizenship*. Oxford: Clarendon Press, 1973.

Simpson, Grace. *Britons and the Roman Army: A Study of Wales and the Southern Pennines in the 1st–3rd Centuries*. London: Gregg Press, 1964.

Smith, R. E. "The Army Reforms of Septimius Severus." *Historia* 21 (1972):481.

Sommer, C. Sebastian. *The Military Vici in Roman Britain: Aspects of Their Origins, Their Location and Layout, Administration, Function, and End.* British Archaeological Reports British Series, 129. Oxford: British Archaeological Reports, 1984.

Sordi, Marta, ed. *Conoscenze etniche e rapporti di convivenza nell'antichità.* Milano: Vita e pensiero, 1979.

Speidel, Michael P. *Guards of the Roman Armies: An Essay on the Singulares of the Provinces.* Bonn: Rudolf Habelt Verlag, 1978.

————. *The Religion of Jupiter Dolichenus in the Roman Army.* Leiden: E. J. Brill, 1978.

————. *Mithras-Orion. Greek Hero and Roman Army God.* Leiden: E. J. Brill, 1980.

————. *Roman Army Studies.* Amsterdam: J. C. Gieben, 1984.

Stambaugh, John E. *The Ancient Roman City.* Baltimore, MD: Johns Hopkins University Press, 1988.

Starr, Chester G. *The Roman Imperial Navy, 31 B.C.–A.D. 324.* 2d ed. Cambridge: Cambridge University Press, 1960.

Stead, Ian M. *Verulamium. The King Harry Lane Site.* London: English Heritage in Association with British Museum Publications, 1989.

Strobel, Karl. *Untersuchungen zu den Dakerkriegen Trajans: Studien zur Geschichte des mittleren und unteren Donauraumes in der Hohen Kaiserzeit.* Bonn: R. Habelt, 1984.

Studien zu den Militärgrenzen Roms. Vortrage des 6. Internationalen Limeskongresses in Suddeutschland. Koln: Bohlau Verlag, 1967.

Sutherland, C. H. V. *Coinage and Currency in Roman Britain.* London and Oxford: Oxford University Press, H. Milford, 1937.

Sutherland, C. H. V., and Carson, R. A. G. *Roman Imperial Coinage.* Vol. 1. London: Spink and Son, 1967.

Syme, Ronald. "The Northern Frontier under Augustus." In *Cambridge Ancient History*, General Editor J. B. Bury. Vol. 10. London: Cambridge University Press, 1939.

————. *Roman Papers III–V*, edited by Anthony Birley. Oxford: Clarendon Press; New York: Oxford University Press, 1984 (III), 1988 (IV–V).

Tapio, Helen. "Roman Attitudes to the Externae Gentes of the North." *Acta Classica* 4 (1961): 90–102.

————. *Organization of Roman Brick Production in the First and Second Centuries A.D.: An Interpretation of Roman Brick Stamps.* Helsinki: Suomalainen Tiedeakatemia, 1975.

Taylor, Lily Ross. *The Divinity of the Roman Emperor.* New York: Arno Press, 1975.

Teichert, M. "Size Variation in Cattle from Germania Romana and Germania Libra." In *Animals and Archaeology.* Vol. 4, *Husbandry in Europe*, edited by C. Grigson and J. Clutton-Brock, pp. 93–103. Oxford: British Archaeological Report S–227, 1984.

Tengstrom, Emin. *Bread for the People: Studies of the Corn-Supply of Rome during the Late Empire.* Stockholm: P. Astrom, 1975.

Thomas, Edith B. *Helme, Schilde, Dolche: Studien über römisch-pannonische Waffenfunde.* Amsterdam, A. M. Hakkert, 1971.

Toynbee, Jocelyn M.C. *Animals in Roman Life and Art*. London: Thames and Hudson, 1973.

Tudor, Dumitru. *Corpus monumentorum religionis equitum Danuvinorum (CMRED)*. Leiden: E. J. Brill, 1969–1976.

Turcan, Robert. *Les Religions de l'Asie dans la vallee du Rhone*. Leiden: E. J. Brill, 1972.

Veen, M. van der. "Native Communities in the Frontier Zone—Uniformity or Diversity?" In *Roman Frontier Studies: 1989*, edited by V. A. Maxfield and M. J. Dobson, pp. 446–450. Exeter: University Press, 1991.

Wacher, J. S. *The Towns of Roman Britain*. Berkeley: University of California Press, 1975.

———. *Roman Britain*. London: Dent, 1978.

———. *The Coming of Rome*. London: Routledge and Kegan Paul, 1979.

Walbank, F. W. *The Decline of the Roman Empire in the West*. London: Cobbett Press, 1946.

Walker, R. E. "Roman Cavalry Rations." *Veterinary History* 4 (1974–1975):16–19.

Wardsman, Alan. *Religion and Statecraft among the Romans*. London: Granada, 1982.

Watson, G. R. *The Roman Soldier*. Ithaca, NY: Cornell University Press, 1985.

Webster, Graham. *The Roman Imperial Army of the First and Second Centuries A.D.* 3d ed. London: A. and C. Black, 1985.

———, ed. *Fortress into City: The Consolidation of Roman Britain, First Century A.D.* London: Batsford, 1988.

Wells, Colin M. *The German Policy of Augustus*. Oxford: Clarendon Press, 1972.

Welsby, Derek A. *The Roman Military Defence of the British Provinces in its Later Phases*. Oxford: British Archaeological Reports, 1982.

West, Louis C. *Roman Gaul: The Objects of Trade*. Oxford: Blackwell, 1935.

———. "The Rise of Ethnic Units in the Roman Imperial Army." In *Aufsteig und Niedergang der römischen Welt*, edited by Hildegard Temporini and Wolfgang Haase, 2.3:202–231. Berlin and New York: Walter de Gruyter, 1975.

Wheeler, R. M. *Rome beyond the Imperial Frontiers*. London: G. Bell and Sons, 1935.

White, K. D. "Technology and Industry in the Roman Empire." *Acta Classica* 2 (1959):82.

———. *A Bibliography of Roman Agriculture*. Reading: University of Reading (Institute of Agricultural History), 1970.

———. *Roman Farming*. Ithaca, NY: Cornell University Press, 1970.

———. *Farm Equipment of the Roman World*. Cambridge: Cambridge University Press, 1975.

———. *Agricultural Implements of the Roman World*. London: Cambridge University Press, 1976.

———. *Greek and Roman Technology*. London: Thames and Hudson, 1984.

Whittaker, C. R. "Trade and Frontiers in the Roman Empire." In *Trade and Famine in Classical Antiquity*, edited by P. Garnsey and C. R. Whittaker, vol. 8, p. 118. Cambridge Philological Society, Supplement, 1983.

———, ed. *Pastoral Economies in Classical Antiquity*. Cambridge: Cambridge Philological Society, 1988.

Wiedemann, Thomas. *Greek and Roman Slavery*. Baltimore, MD: Johns Hopkins University Press, 1981.

Wierschowski, Lothar. *Heer und Wirtschaft: das römische Heer der Prinzipätszeit als Wirtschaftsfaktor*. Bonn: Habelt, 1984.

Wightman, Edith. *Trier and the Treveri*. London: Rupert Hart-Davis, 1970.

———. "The Pattern of Rural Settlement in Roman Gaul." In *Aufsteig und Niedergang der römischen Welt*, edited by Hildegard Temporini and Wolfgang Haase, 2.4:584–657. Berlin and New York: Walter de Gruyter, 1975.

———. "Cultural Factors within a Roman Province." *Comparative Frontier Studies* 10 (Spring 1978): 10.

———. *Gallia Belgica*. London: B. T. Batsford, Ltd., 1985.

Wikander, O. *Exploitation of Water-Power or Technological Stagnation? A Reappraisal of the Productive Forces in the Roman Empire*. Lund: C. W. K. Gleerup, 1984.

Wild, J. P. *Textile Manufacture in the Northern Roman Provinces*. Cambridge: Cambridge University Press, 1970.

Wilkes, J. J. "Romans, Dacians and Sarmatians." In *Rome and Her Northern Neighbors*, edited by Brian Hartley and John Wacher, pp. 255–289. Gloucester: Alan Sutton, 1983.

Wilson, David R. *Roman Frontiers of Britain*. London: Heinemann, 1967.

Woolf, G. "World-Systems Analysis and the Roman Empire." *Journal of Roman Archaeology* 3 (1990):44–58.

Zanker, Paul. *The Power of Images in the Age of Augustus*. Translated by Alan Shapiro. Ann Arbor: University of Michigan Press, c. 1988.

INDEX

Aachen, 27, 235
Aelius Gracilis, 108
Africa, 24
Agricola, 117, 135, 150*n.18*, 193*n.19*, 228
Agriculture
  British frontier, 55–58
  Celtic, 57, 58
  Danube frontier, 60–68
  demand and supply, 42–43
  and feeding of Roman army, 46, 52–53, 56, 59, 69
  vs. ranching, 96
  Roman, 10, 72*n.16*
  Roman frontier, 42–70
  Strabo on, 175–76
  surplus commodities, 43, 56
Alaric, 224, 235
Alexander Severus, 232
Allemanni, 12
Allobroges, 176
Alps, 61, 62
Amber, 101–2, 116
Amber Coast route, 101, 102, 235
Ambrosius Aurelianus, 60
American army, 7
American frontier, 3–6, 30, 33, 193*n.18*, 221–22
Amphora, 162, 236
Ampsivarii, 90, 96, 236
Animals and animal products, 77–84, 90–91, 94, 95, 115

Animals and animal products
  (continued) see also Leather and leather goods; Pack animals; specific animals
Antoninus Pius, 230
Archaeological research, 3, 38*n.30*
Aristides, 181–82
Arminius, 37*n.24*, 180, 225
Armor, 78, 97*nn.1, 3, 4, 5*, 110, 169*nn.3–4*
Army. *See* Roman army
Arthur (legendary leader), 60
Augustus Caesar, 6–8, 19–21, 24, 28, 35*n.5*, 37*nn.21, 24*, 60, 61, 78, 121, 212*n.1*, 225–26
Aurelian, 67, 233–34
Aurochs, 82
Auxiliary troops (*auxilia*), 15, 27, 28, 36*n.7*, 52, 96*n.1*, 177, 186–90, 192*n.15*, 194*n.39*, 217, 223, 228, 230, 236

Baltic Sea, 101, 105
Barley, 9, 84, 85
Barrels, 80, 171*n.28*
Basilica-type villas, 52, 236
Basra, 41*n.51*
Battle of Adrianople, 106
Battle of Teutoberg Forest, 37*n.24*, 225
Beards, 174–75
Belgae, 163, 236
Belgium, 163

ABOUT THE AUTHORS

Steven K. Drummond is a postdoctoral research associate at the University of Kansas. He specializes in Roman frontier studies and in comparative cultures. He has published several books on the interaction of diverse cultures.

Lynn H. Nelson has been professor of medieval history at the University of Kansas since 1973. He has published *The Human Perspective* (1987), *Global Perspectives* (1988), and works in medieval and Aragonese history, among other subjects. He has also been active in developing international telecommunications facilities for historians.